Learning Social Media Analytics with R

D1388285

Transform data from social media platforms into actionable insights

Raghav Bali

Dipanjan Sarkar

Tushar Sharma

BIRMINGHAM - MUMBAI

Learning Social Media Analytics with R

First published: May 2017

Production reference: 1220517

Published by Packt Publishing Ltd.
Livery Place
35 Livery Street
Birmingham B3 2PB, UK.

ISBN 978-1-78712-752-4

www.packtpub.com

Credits

Authors
Raghav Bali
Dipanjan Sarkar
Tushar Sharma

Reviewer
Karthik Ganapathy

Commissioning Editor
Amey Varangaonkar

Acquisition Editor
Tushar Gupta

Content Development Editor
Amrita Noronha

Technical Editor
Akash Patel

Copy Editors
Vikrant Phadkay
Safis Editing

Project Coordinator
Shweta H Birwatkar

Proofreader
Safis Editing

Indexer
Pratik Shirodkar

Graphics
Tania Dutta

Production Coordinator
Shantanu Zagade

Cover Work
Shantanu Zagade

About the Author

Raghav Bali has a master's degree (gold medalist) in information technology from International Institute of Information Technology, Bangalore. He is a data scientist at Intel, the world's largest silicon company, where he works on analytics, business intelligence, and application development to develop scalable machine learning-based solutions. He has worked as an analyst and developer in domains such as ERP, finance, and BI with some of the top companies of the world.

Raghav is a technology enthusiast who loves reading and playing around with new gadgets and technologies. He recently co-authored a book on machine learning titled *R Machine Learning by Example*, Packt Publishing. He is a shutterbug, capturing moments when he isn't busy solving problems.

I would like to express my gratitude to my family, teachers, friends, colleagues and mentors who have encouraged, supported and taught me over the years. I would also like to take this opportunity to thank my co-authors and good friends Dipanjan Sarkar and Tushar Sharma, who made this project a memorable and enjoyable one.

I would like to thank Tushar Gupta, Amrita Noronha, Akash Patel, and Packt for the opportunity and their support throughout this journey. Last but not least, thanks to the R community for the amazing stuff that they do!

Dipanjan Sarkar is a data scientist at Intel, the world's largest silicon company, on a mission to make the world more connected and productive. He primarily works on data science, analytics, business intelligence, application development, and building large-scale intelligent systems. He holds a master of technology degree in information technology with specializations in data science and software engineering from the International Institute of Information Technology, Bangalore.

Dipanjan has been an analytics practitioner for over 5 years now, specializing in statistical, predictive, and text analytics. He has also authored several books on machine learning and analytics including *R Machine Learning by Example* and What you need to know about R, Packt. Besides this, he occasionally spends time reviewing technical books and courses. Dipanjan's interests include learning about new technology, financial markets, disruptive start-ups and data science. In his spare time he loves reading, gaming, watching popular sitcoms and football.

I am indebted to my parents, partner, friends, and well-wishers for always standing by my side and supporting me in all my endeavors. Your support keeps me going day in and day out to take on new challenges! I would also like to thank my good friends and fellow colleagues, Raghav Bali and Tushar Sharma, for co-authoring and making the experience more enjoyable. Last but never the least, I would like to thank Tushar Gupta, Amrita Noronha, Akash Patel, and Packt for giving me this wonderful opportunity to share my knowledge and experiences with analytics and R enthusiasts out there who are doing truly amazing things every day. And a big thumbs up to the R community for building an excellent analytics ecosystem.

Tushar Sharma has a master's degree specializing in data science from the International Institute of Information Technology, Bangalore. He works as a data scientist with Intel. In his previous job he used to work as a research engineer for a financial consultancy firm. His work involves handling big data at scale generated by the massive infrastructure at Intel. He engineers and delivers end to end solutions on this data using the latest machine learning tools and frameworks. He is proficient in R, Python, Spark, and mathematical aspects of machine learning among other things.

Tushar has a keen interest in everything related to technology. He likes to read a wide array of books ranging from history to philosophy and beyond. He is a running enthusiast and likes to play badminton and tennis.

I would like to express my gratitude to my family, teachers and friends who have encouraged, supported and taught me over the years. Special thanks to my classmates, friends, and colleagues, Dipanjan Sarkar and Raghav Bali for co-authoring and making this journey wonderful through their input and eye for detail.

I would like to thank Tushar Gupta, Amrita Noronha, and Packt for the opportunity and their support throughout the journey.

About the Reviewer

Karthik Ganapathy is an analytics professional with over 12 years of professional experience in analytics, predictive modeling, and project management. He has worked with several Fortune 500 clients and helped them derive business value using data.

I would like to thank my wife Sudharsana and my daughter Amrita for being a great support during the period I was reviewing the content.

www.PacktPub.com

eBooks, discount offers, and more

For support files and downloads related to your book, please visit www.PacktPub.com.

Did you know that Packt offers eBook versions of every book published, with PDF and ePub files available? You can upgrade to the eBook version at www.PacktPub.com and as a print book customer, you are entitled to a discount on the eBook copy. Get in touch with us at customercare@packtpub.com for more details.

At www.PacktPub.com, you can also read a collection of free technical articles, sign up for a range of free newsletters and receive exclusive discounts and offers on Packt books and eBooks.

https://www.packtpub.com/mapt

Get the most in-demand software skills with Mapt. Mapt gives you full access to all Packt books and video courses, as well as industry-leading tools to help you plan your personal development and advance your career.

Why subscribe?

- Fully searchable across every book published by Packt
- Copy and paste, print, and bookmark content
- On demand and accessible via a web browser

Customer Feedback

Thanks for purchasing this Packt book. At Packt, quality is at the heart of our editorial process. To help us improve, please leave us an honest review on this book's Amazon page at https://www.amazon.com/dp/1787127524. If you'd like to join our team of regular reviewers, you can e-mail us at customerreviews@packtpub.com. We award our regular reviewers with free eBooks and videos in exchange for their valuable feedback. Help us be relentless in improving our products!

Table of Contents

Preface

The Internet has truly grown to be humongous, especially in the last decade, with the rise of various forms of social media that give users a platform to express themselves and also communicate and collaborate with each other. The current social media landscape is a complex mesh of social network platforms and applications, catering to specific audiences with unique as well as overlapping features. Each of these social networks are potential gold mines of data which are being (and can be) used to study, leverage and improve our understanding of demographics, behaviors, collaboration, user engagement, branding and so on across different domains and spheres of our lives.

This book will help the reader to understand the current social media landscape and help in understanding how analytics and machine learning can be leveraged to derive insights from social media data. It will enable readers to utilize R and its ecosystem to visualize and analyze data from different social networks. This book will also leverage machine learning, data science and other advanced concepts and techniques to solve real-world use cases spread across diverse social network domains including Twitter, Facebook, GitHub, FourSquare, StackExchange, Flickr, and more.

What this book covers

Chapter 1, *Getting Started with R and Social Media Analytics*, builds on foundations related to social media platforms and analyzing data relevant to social media. A concise introduction to R is given, including coverage of R syntax, data constructs, and functions. Basic concepts from machine learning, data analytics, and text analytics are also covered, setting the tone for the content in subsequent chapters.

Chapter 2, Twitter – What's Happening with 140 Characters, sets the theme for social media analytics with a focus on Twitter. It leverages R packages to extract and analyze Twitter data to uncover interesting insights through multiple use-cases, involving machine learning techniques such as trend analysis, sentiment analysis, clustering, and social graph analysis.

Chapter 3, Analyzing Social Networks and Brand Engagements with Facebook, focuses on analyzing data from perhaps the most popular social network in the world — Facebook! Readers will learn how to use the Graph API to retrieve data as well as use frameworks such as Netvizz to extract brand page data. Techniques to analyze personal social networks will be covered in detail. Besides this, readers will gain conceptual knowledge about social network analysis and graph theory. This knowledge will be used in action by analyzing a huge network of football brand pages to understand relationships, page engagement, and popularity.

Chapter 4, Foursquare – Are You Checked in Yet?, targets the popular social media channel Foursquare. Readers will learn how to collect this data using the Foursquare APIs. Steps for visualizing and analyzing this data will be depicted to uncover insights into user behavior. This data will be used to define and solve some analytics use-cases, which include sentiment analysis, graph analytics, and much more.

Chapter 5, Analyzing Software Collaboration Trends I – Social Coding with GitHub, introduces the popular social coding and collaboration platform GitHub for analyzing software collaboration trends. Readers will gain insights into using the GitHub API from R to extract useful data pertaining to users and repositories. Detailed analyzes of repository activity, repository trends, language trends, and user trends will be presented with real-world examples.

Chapter 6, Analyzing Software Collaboration Trends II – Answering Your Questions with StackExchange, introduces the StackExchange platform through its data organization and access methods. Readers learn and uncover interesting collaboration, demographic, and other patterns through use cases which leverage visualizations and different analysis techniques learned in previous chapters.

Chapter 7, Believe What You See – Flickr Data Analysis, presents Flickr through its APIs and uses some amazing packages such as piper, dplyr, and so on to extract data and insights from some complex data formats. The chapter also leverages machine learning concepts like clustering and classification to better understand Flickr.

Chapter 8, News – The Collective Social Media!, deals with analysis of free and unstructured text. Readers will learn how to collect news data from web sources using methodologies like scraping. The basic analysis on the textual data will consist of various statistical measures. Readers will also gain hands-on knowledge on advanced analysis like sentiment analysis, topic modeling, and text summarization on news data based on some interesting use cases.

What you need for this book

Chapter number	Software required (with version)	Hardware specifications	OS required
1-8	R 3.3.x (or higher) RStudio Desktop 1.0.x	• At least 1 GB of RAM, a mouse, and enough disk space for recovered files, image files, and so on • A network connection for installing packages, connecting to social networks, and downloading datasets	An Intel/AMD-compatible platform running Windows 2000/XP/2003/Vista/7/8/2012 Server/8.1/10 or any Unix-based OS

Who this book is for

This book is for IT professionals, data scientists, analysts, developers, machine learning enthusiasts, social media marketers, and anyone with a keen interest in data, analytics, and generating insights from social data. Some background experience in R would be helpful but is not necessary. The book has been written keeping in mind the varying levels of expertise of its readers. It also includes links, pointers, and exercises for intermediate to advanced readers to explore further.

Conventions

In this book, you will find a number of styles of text that distinguish between different kinds of information. Here are some examples of these styles, and an explanation of their meaning.

Code words in text, database table names, folder names, filenames, file extensions, pathnames, dummy URLs, user input, and Twitter handles are shown as follows: "We can include other contexts through the use of the `include` directive."

A block of code is set as follows:

```
# create data frame
df <- data.frame(
  name = c("Wade", "Steve", "Slade", "Bruce"),
  age = c(28, 85, 55, 45),
  job = c("IT", "HR", "HR", "CS")
)
```

New terms and **important words** are shown in bold. Words that you see on the screen, in menus or dialog boxes for example, appear in the text like this: "selecting them from the **Add filters...** option box".

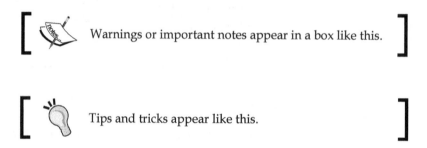

Warnings or important notes appear in a box like this.

Tips and tricks appear like this.

Reader feedback

Feedback from our readers is always welcome. Let us know what you think about this book—what you liked or may have disliked. Reader feedback is important for us to develop titles that you really get the most out of.

To send us general feedback, simply send an e-mail to feedback@packtpub.com, and mention the book title via the subject of your message.

If there is a topic that you have expertise in and you are interested in either writing or contributing to a book, see our author guide on www.packtpub.com/authors.

Customer support

Now that you are the proud owner of a Packt book, we have a number of things to help you to get the most from your purchase.

Downloading the example code

You can download the example code files for this book from your account at
`http://www.packtpub.com`. If you purchased this book elsewhere, you can visit
`http://www.packtpub.com/support` and register to have the files e-mailed directly
to you.

You can download the code files by following these steps:

1. You can download the code files by following these steps:
2. Log in or register to our website using your e-mail address and password.
3. Hover the mouse pointer on the **SUPPORT** tab at the top.
4. Click on **Code Downloads & Errata**.
5. Enter the name of the book in the **Search** box.
6. Select the book for which you're looking to download the code files.
7. Choose from the drop-down menu where you purchased this book from.
8. Click on **Code Download**.

Once the file is downloaded, please make sure that you unzip or extract the folder
using the latest version of:

- WinRAR / 7-Zip for Windows
- Zipeg / iZip / UnRarX for Mac
- 7-Zip / PeaZip for Linux

The code bundle for the book is also hosted on GitHub at `https://github.com/PacktPublishing/Learning-Social-Media-Analytics-with-R`. We also have
other code bundles from our rich catalog of books and videos available at `https://github.com/PacktPublishing/`. Check them out!

Downloading the color images of this book

We also provide you with a PDF file that has color images of the screenshots/
diagrams used in this book. The color images will help you better understand the
changes in the output. You can download this file from `https://www.packtpub.com/sites/default/files/downloads/LearningSocialMediaAnalyticswithR_ColorImages.pdf`.

Errata

Although we have taken every care to ensure the accuracy of our content, mistakes do happen. If you find a mistake in one of our books-maybe a mistake in the text or the code-we would be grateful if you could report this to us. By doing so, you can save other readers from frustration and help us improve subsequent versions of this book. If you find any errata, please report them by visiting http://www.packtpub. com/submit-errata, selecting your book, clicking on the **Errata Submission Form** link, and entering the details of your errata. Once your errata are verified, your submission will be accepted and the errata will be uploaded to our website or added to any list of existing errata under the Errata section of that title.

To view the previously submitted errata, go to https://www.packtpub.com/books/ content/support and enter the name of the book in the search field. The required information will appear under the Errata section.

Piracy

Piracy of copyright material on the Internet is an ongoing problem across all media. At Packt, we take the protection of our copyright and licenses very seriously. If you come across any illegal copies of our works, in any form, on the Internet, please provide us with the location address or website name immediately so that we can pursue a remedy.

Please contact us at copyright@packtpub.com with a link to the suspected pirated material.

We appreciate your help in protecting our authors, and our ability to bring you valuable content.

Questions

You can contact us at questions@packtpub.com if you are having a problem with any aspect of the book, and we will do our best to address it.

1
Getting Started with R and Social Media Analytics

The invention of computers, digital electronics, social media, and the Internet have truly ushered us from the industrial age into the information age. The Internet, and more specifically the invention of World Wide Web in the early 1990s, helped people to build an inter-connected universal platform where information can be stored, shared and consumed by anyone with an electronic device capable of connecting to the Web. This has led to the creation of vast amounts of information, ideas and opinions which people, brands, organizations and businesses want to share with everyone around the world. So, social media was born which provides interactive platforms to post content, share ideas, messages and opinions about everything under the sun.

This book will take you on a journey to understand various popular social media, analyzing rich data generated by these media and gaining valuable insights. We will focus on social media which cater to audiences in different forms, like micro-blogging, social networking, software collaboration, news and media sharing platforms. The main objective is to use standardized data access and retrieval techniques using social media **application programming interfaces** (**APIs**) to gather data from these websites and apply different data mining, statistical and machine learning, and natural language processing techniques on the data by leveraging the R programming language. This book will provide you with the tools, techniques, and approaches which would help you achieve the same. This introductory chapter will cover several important concepts which would help you get a jumpstart on social media analytics. They are mentioned as follows:

- Social media – significance and pitfalls
- Social media analytics – opportunities and challenges
- Getting started with R

- Data analytics
- Machine learning
- Text analytics

We will look at social media, the various forms of social media which exist today, and how it has impacted our society. This will help us understand the entire scope pertaining to social media analytics and the opportunity presented by it which would be valuable for consumers as well as businesses and brands. Concepts related to analytics, machine learning and text analytics coupled with hands on examples depicting the various features of the R programming language will help you get a grip on essential things which are necessary for the rest of this book. Without further delay, let's get started!

Understanding social media

The Internet and the information age have been responsible for revolutionizing the way we humans interact with each other in the 21st Century. Almost everyone uses some form of electronic communication, be it a laptop, tablet, smartphone or a personal computer. Social media is built upon the concept of platforms where people use **computer-mediated communication** (CMC) methods to communicate with others. This can range from instant messaging, emails, and chat rooms to social forums and social networking. To understand social media, you need to understand the origins of legacy or traditional media which gradually evolved into social media. Entities like the popular television, newspapers, radio, movies, books and magazines are various ways of sharing and consuming information, ideas and opinions. It's important to remember that social media has not replaced the older legacy based media; they co-exist peacefully together as we use and consume them both in our day-to-day lives.

Legacy media typically follow a one-way communication system. For instance, I can always read a magazine or watch a show on the television or get updated about the news from newspapers, but I cannot voice my opinions or share my ideas using the same media instantly. The communication mechanism in the various forms of social media is a two-way street, where audiences can share information and ideas and others can consume them and voice their own ideas, opinions and feedback on the same, and even share their own content based on what they see. Legacy based media, like radio or television, now use social media to provide a two-way communication mechanism to support their communications, but it's much more seamless in social media where anyone and everyone can share content, communicate with others, freely voice their ideas and opinions on a huge scale.

We can now formally define social media as interactive applications or platforms based on the principles of Web 2.0 and computer-mediated communication, which enable users to be publishers as well as consumers, to create and share ideas, opinions, information, emotions and expressions in various forms. While different and diverse forms of social media exist, they have several key features in common which are mentioned briefly as follows:

- Web 2.0 Internet based applications or platforms
- Content is created as well as consumed by users
- Profiles give users have their own distinct and unique identity
- Social networks help connect different users, similarly to communities

Indeed social media give users their own unique identity and the freedom to express themselves in their own user profiles. These profiles are maintained as accounts by social media companies. Features like **what you see is what you get (WYSIWYG)** editors, emoticons, photos and videos help users in creating and sharing rich content. Social networking capabilities enables users to add other users to their own friend or contact lists and create groups and forums where they can share and talk about like-minded interests. The following figure shows us some of the popular social media used today across the globe:

I am sure you recognize several of these popular social media from their logos, which you must have seen on your own smartphone or on the web. Social media is used in various ways and media can be grouped into distinct buckets by the nature of its usage and its features. We mention several popular social media in the following points, some of which we will be analyzing in the future chapters:

- Micro-blogging platforms, like Twitter and Tumblr
- Blogging platforms, like WordPress, Blogger and Medium
- Instant messaging application, like WhatsApp and Hangouts

- Networking platforms, like Facebook and LinkedIn
- Software collaboration platforms, like GitHub and StackOverflow
- Audio collaboration platforms, like SoundCloud
- Photo sharing platforms, like Instagram and Flickr
- Video sharing platforms, like YouTube and Vimeo

This list is not an exhaustive list of social media because there are so many applications and platforms out there. We apologize in advance if we missed out mentioning your favorite social media! The list should clarify the different forms of communication and content sharing mechanisms that are available for users, and that they can leverage any of these social media to share content and connect with other users. We will now discuss some of the key advantages and significance which social media has to offer.

Advantages and significance

Social media has gained immense popularity and importance so that today almost everyone can't stay away from it. Not only is social media a medium for people to express their views, but also a very powerful tool which can be used by businesses to target new and existing customers and increase revenue. We will discuss some of the main advantages of social media as follows:

- **Cost savings**: One of the main challenges for businesses is to reach out to their customers or clients through advertising on traditional and legacy based media, which can be expensive. However, social media allows businesses to have branded pages and to post sponsored content and advertisements for a fraction of the cost, thus helping them save costs in the process of increasing visibility.

- **Networking**: With social media, you can build your social as well as professional network with people across the globe. This has opened up a myriad of possibilities where people from different continents and countries work together on cutting-edge innovations, share news, talk about their personal experiences, offer advice and share interesting opportunities, which can help develop personalities, careers, and skills.

- **Ease of use**: It is quite easy to get started with social media. All you need is to create an account by registering your details in the application or website and within minutes you are ready to go! Besides this, it is quite easy to navigate through any social media website or application without any sophisticated technical skills. You just need an Internet connection and an electronic device, like a smartphone or a computer. Perhaps this could be the reason that a lot of parents and grandparents are now taking to social media to share their moments and connect with their long lost friends.

- **Global audience**: With social media, you can also make your content reach out to a global audience across the world. The reason is quite simple: because social media applications are available openly on the web, users all across the world use it. Businesses that engage with customers in different parts of the world have a key advantage to push their promotions and new products and services.

- **Prompt feedback**: Businesses and organizations can get prompt feedback on their new product launches and services being used directly from the users. There is much less calling up people asking them about their satisfaction levels. Tweets, posts, videos, comments and many more features exist to give instant feedback to organizations by posting generally, or conversing with them directly on their official social media channels.

- **Grievance redressal**: One of the great advantages of social media is that users can now express any sort of grievances or inconveniences, like electricity, water supply or security issues. Most governments and organizations, including law enforcement have public social media channels which can be used for instant notification of grievances.

- **Entertainment**: This is perhaps the most popular advantage used to the maximum by most users. Social media provides an unlimited source of entertainment where you can spend your time playing interactive games, watching videos, and participating in competitions with users across the world. Indeed the possibilities of entertainment from social media are endless.

- **Visibility**: Anyone can leverage their social media profile to gain visibility in the world. Professional networking platforms like LinkedIn are an excellent way for people to get noticed by recruiters and also for companies to recruit great talent. Even small startups or individuals can develop inventions, build products, or announce discoveries and leverage social media to *go viral* and gain the necessary visibility which can propel them to the next level.

The significance and importance of social media is quite evident from the preceding points. In today's interconnected world, social media has almost become indispensable and although it might have a lot of disadvantages, including distractions, if we use it for the right reasons, it can indeed be a very important tool or medium to help us achieve great things.

Disadvantages and pitfalls

Even though we have been blowing the trumpet about social media and its significance, I'm sure you are already thinking about pitfalls and disadvantages, which are directly or indirectly caused from social media. We want to cover all aspects of social media including the good and the bad, so let's look at some negative aspects:

- **Privacy concerns**: Perhaps one of the biggest concerns with regards to using social media is the lack of privacy. All our personal data, even though often guaranteed to be secure by the social media organizations that host it, have a risk of being illegally accessed. Further, many social media platforms have been accused, time and again, of selling or using users' personal data without their consent.

- **Security issues**: Often users enter personal information on their social media profiles which can be used by hackers and other harmful entities to gain insights into their personal lives and use it for their own personal gain. You will have heard, several times in the past, that social media websites have been hacked and personal information from user accounts has been leaked. There are other issues also like users' bank accounts being compromised, and even theft and other harmful actions happening as a result of sensitive information obtained from social media.

- **Addiction**: This is relevant to a large percentage of people using social media. Social media addiction is indeed real and a serious concern, especially among the millennials. There are so many forms of social media and you can really get engrossed in playing games, trying to keep up with what everyone is doing, or just sharing moments from your life every other minute. A lot of us tend to check social media websites every now and then, which can be a distraction, especially if you are trying to meet deadlines. There are even a few stories of people accessing social media whilst driving, with fatal results.

- **Negativity**: Social media allows you to express yourself freely and this is often misused by people, terrorist, and other extremist groups to spread hateful propaganda and negativity. People often post sarcastic and negative reactions based on their opinions and feelings, which can lead to trolling and racism. Even though there are ways to report such behavior, it is often not enough because it is impossible to monitor a vast social network all the time.

- **Risks**: There are several potential risks of leveraging social media for your personal use or business promotions and campaigns. One wrong post can potentially prove to be very costly. Besides this, there is the constant risk of hackers, fraud, security attacks and unwanted spam. Continuous usage of social media and addiction to it also poses a potential health risk. Organizations should have proper social media use policies to ensure that their employees do not end up being unproductive by wasting too much time on social media, and do not leak trade secrets or confidential information on social media.

We have discussed several pitfalls attached to using social media and some of them are very serious concerns. Proper social media usage guidelines and policies should be borne in mind by everyone because social media is like a magnifying glass: anything you post can be used against you or can potentially prove harmful later. Be it extremely sensitive personal information, or confidential information, like design plans for your next product launch, always think carefully before sharing anything with the rest of the world.

However, if you know what you are doing, social media can definitely be used as a proper tool for your personal as well as professional gain.

Social media analytics

We now have a detailed overview of social media, its significance, pitfalls, and various facets. We will now discuss social media analytics and the benefits it offers for data analysts, scientists and businesses in general looking to gather useful insights from social media. Social media analytics, also known as social media mining or social media intelligence, can be defined as the process of gathering data (usually unstructured) from social media platforms and analyzing the data using diverse analytical techniques to extract vital insights, which can be used to make data-driven business decisions. There are lots of opportunities and challenges involved in social media analytics, which we will be discussing in further detail in later sections. An important thing to remember is that the processes involved in social media analytics are usually domain-agnostic and you can apply them on data belonging to any organization or business in any domain.

The most important step in going forward with any social media analytics based workflow or process is to determine the business goals or objectives and the insights that we want to gather from our analyzes. These goals are usually in the form of **key performance indicators (KPIs)**. For instance, the total number of followers, number of likes and shares can be KPIs to measure brand engagement with customers using social media. Sometimes data is not structured and the end objectives are not very concrete. Techniques like natural language processing and text analytics can be leveraged in such cases to extract insights from noisy unstructured text data like understanding the sentiment or mood of customers for a particular service or product and trying to understand the key trends and themes based on customer tweets or posts at any point in time.

A typical social media analytics workflow

We will be analyzing data from diverse social media applications and platforms throughout the course of this book. However, it is essential to have a good grasp of the essential concepts behind any typical analytics process or workflow. While we will be expanding more on data analytics and mining processes later, let us look at a typical social media analytics workflow in the following figure:

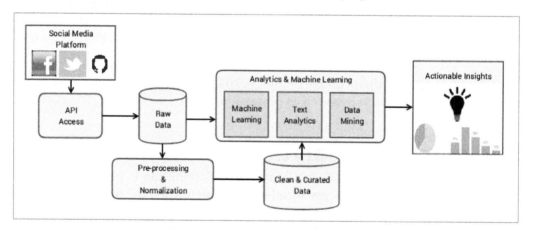

From the preceding diagram, we can broadly classify the main steps involved in the analytics workflow as follows:

- Data access
- Data processing and normalization
- Data analysis
- Insights

We will now briefly expand upon each of these four processes since we will be using them extensively in future chapters.

Data access

For access to social media data, you can usually do it using standard data retrieval methods in two ways.

The first technique is to use official APIs provided by the social media platform or organization itself.

The second technique is to use unofficial mechanisms, like web crawling and scraping. An important point to remember is that crawling and scraping social media websites and using that data for commercial purposes, like selling the data to other organizations, is usually against their terms of service. We will therefore not be using such methods in our book. Besides this, we will be following the necessary politeness policies while accessing social media data using their APIs, so that we do not overload them with too many requests. The data we'll obtain is the raw data which can be further processed and normalized as needed.

Data processing and normalization

The raw data obtained from data retrieval using social media APIs may not be structured and clean. In fact most of the data obtained from social media is noisy, unstructured and often contains unnecessary tokens such as **Hyper Text Markup Language** (HTML) tags and other metadata. Usually, data streams from social media APIs have **JavaScript Object Notation** (**JSON**) response objects, which consist of key value pairs just like the example shown in the following snippet:

```
{
"user": {
                "profile_sidebar_fill_color": "DDFFCC",
                "profile_sidebar_border_color": "BDDCAD",
                "profile_background_tile": true,
                "name": "J'onn J'onzz",
                "profile_image_url": "http://test.com/img/prof.
jpg",
                "created_at": "Tue Apr 07 19:05:07 +0000 2009",
                "location": "Ox City, UK",
                "follow_request_sent": null,
                "profile_link_color": "0084B4",
                "is_translator": false,
                "id_str": "2921138"
        },
```

```
"followers_count": 2452,
"statuses_count": 7311,
"friends_count": 427
}
```

The preceding JSON object consists of a typical response from the Twitter API showing details of a user profile. Some APIs might return data in other formats, such as **Extensible Markup Language (XML)** or **Comma Separated Values (CSV)**, and each format needs to be handled properly.

Often social media data contains unstructured textual data which needs additional text pre-processing and normalization before it can be fed into any standard data mining or machine learning algorithm. Text normalization is usually done using several techniques to clean and standardize the text. Some of them are:

- Text tokenization
- Removing special characters and symbols
- Spelling corrections
- Contraction expansions
- Stemming
- Lemmatization

More advanced processing can insert additional metadata to describe the text better, such as adding **parts of speech (POS)** tags, phrase tags, named entity tags, and so on.

Data analysis

This is the core of the whole workflow, where we apply various techniques to analyze the data: this could be the raw native data itself, or the processed and curated data. Usually the techniques used in analysis can be broadly classified into three areas:

- Data mining or analytics
- Machine learning
- Natural language processing and text analytics

Data mining and machine learning have several overlapping concepts, including the fact that both use statistical techniques and try to find patterns from underlying data. Data mining is more about finding key patterns or insights from data; and machine learning is more about using mathematics, statistics, and even some of these data mining algorithms, to build models to predict or forecast outcomes. While both of these techniques need structured and numeric data to work with, more complex analyzes with unstructured textual data is usually handled in the separate realm of text analytics by leveraging natural language processing which enables us to use several tools, techniques and algorithms to analyze free-flowing unstructured text. We will be using techniques, from these three areas to analyze data from various social media platforms throughout this book. We will cover important concepts from data analytics and text analytics briefly towards the end of this chapter.

Insights

The end results from our workflow are the actual insights which act as facts or concrete data points to achieve the objective of the analysis. This can be anything from a business intelligence report to visualizations such as bar graphs, histograms, or even word or phrase clouds. Insights should be crisp, clear, and actionable so that it can be easy for businesses to take valuable decisions in time by leveraging them.

Opportunities

Based on the advantages of social media, we can derive plentiful opportunities which lie within the scope of social media analytics. You can save a lot of cost involved in targeted advertising and promotions by analyzing your social media traffic patterns. You can see how users engage with your brand or business using social media, for instance, when it is the perfect time to share something interesting, such as a new service, product, or even an interesting anecdote about your company. Based on traffic from different geographies, you can analyze and understand the preferences of users from different parts of the world. Users love it if you publish promotions in their local language, and businesses are already leveraging such capabilities from social media platforms such as Facebook to target users in specific countries based on localized content.

The social media analytics landscape is still young and emerging and has a lot of untapped potential.

Let us understand the potential of social media analytics better by taking a real-world example.

Consider you are running a profitable business with active engagement on various social media channels. How can you use the data generated from social media to know how you are doing and how your competitors are doing? Live data streams from Twitter could be continuously analyzed to get real-time mood, sentiment, emotion, and reactions of people to your products and services. You could even analyze the same for your rival competitors to see when they are launching their commodities and how users are reacting to them. With Facebook, you can do the same and even push localized promotions and advertisements to see if they help in generating better revenue. News portals would give you live feeds of trending news articles and insights into the current state of the economy and current events and help you decide if these are favorable times for a thriving business or should you be preparing for some hard times. Sentiment analysis, concept mining, topic models, clustering, and inference are just a few examples of using analytics on social media. The opportunities are huge—you just need to have a clear objective in mind so that you can use analytics effectively to solve that objective.

Challenges

Before we delve into the challenges associated with social media analytics let us look at the following interesting facts:

- There are over 300 million active Twitter users
- Facebook has over 1.8 billion active users
- Facebook generates 600-700+ terabytes of data daily (and it could be more now)
- Twitter generates 8-10+ terabytes of data daily
- Facebook generates over 4 to 5 million posts per minute
- Instagram generates over 2 million likes per minute

These statistics give you a rough idea about the massive scale of data being generated and consumed in these social media platforms. This leads to some challenges:

- **Big data**: Due to the massive amount of data produced by social media platforms, it is sometimes difficult to analyze the complete dataset using traditional analytical methods since the complete data would never fit in memory. Other approaches and tools, such as Hadoop and Spark, need to be leveraged.

- **Accessibility issues**: Social media platforms generate a lot of data but getting access to them directly is not always easy. There are rate limits for their official APIs and it's rare to be able to access and store complete datasets. Besides this, each platform has its own terms and conditions, which should be adhered to when accessing their data.

- **Unstructured and noisy data**: Most of the data from social media APIs are unstructured, noisy, and have a lot of junk in them. Dealing with data cleaning and processing becomes really cumbersome and often analysts and data scientists end up spending 70% of their time and effort in trying to clean and curate the data for analysis.

These are perhaps the most prevalent challenges when analyzing social media data, amongst many other challenges, that you might face in your social media analytics journey. Let's now get acquainted with the R programming language, which will be useful to us when we are performing our analyzes.

Getting started with R

This section will help you get started with setting up your analysis and development environment and also acquaint you with the syntax, data structures, constructs, and other important concepts related to the R programming language. Feel free to skim through this section if you consider yourself to be a master of R! We will be mainly focusing our attention on the following topics:

- Environment setup
- Data types
- Data structures
- Functions
- Controlling code flow
- Advanced operations
- Visualizing data
- Next steps

We will be explaining each construct or concept with hands-on examples and code so that it is easier to understand and you can also learn by doing. Before we dive into further details, let us briefly get to know more about R. R is actually a scripting language but is used extensively for statistical modeling and analysis. The roots of R lie in the S language which was a statistical programming language developed by AT&T. R is a community-driven language and has grown by leaps and bounds over the years. It now has a vast arsenal of tools, frameworks, and packages for processing, analyzing, and visualizing any type of data. Because it's open source, the community posts constant improvements to the base R language, and it introduces extremely powerful R packages capable of performing complex analyzes and visualizations.

R and Python are perhaps the two most popular languages to be used for statistical analysis; and R is often preferred by statisticians, mathematicians, and data scientists because it has more capabilities related to statistical modeling, learning, and algorithms. R is maintained by the **Comprehensive R Archival Network (CRAN)** and includes all the latest and past versions, binaries, and source code for R, and its packages for different operating systems. Capabilities also exist to connect and interface R with other frameworks including big data frameworks such as Hadoop and Spark, computing platforms, and languages such as Python, Matlab, SPSS, and data interfaces to any possible source such as social media platforms, news portals, the Internet of Things based device data, web traffic data, and so on.

Environment setup

We will be discussing the necessary steps for setting up a proper analysis environment by installing the necessary dependencies around the R ecosystem and also the necessary code snippets, functions, and modules which we will be using across all the chapters. You can refer to any code snippet being used across any chapter from the code files which will be provided for each chapter along with this book. Besides that, you can also access our GitHub repository `https://github.com/dipanjanS/learning-social-media-analytics-with-r` for necessary code modules, snippets and functions which will be used in the book and adopt them for your own analyzes!

The R language is free and open-source as we mentioned earlier, and is available for all major operating systems. At the time of writing this book, the latest version of R is **3.3.1** (code named `Bug in Your Hair`) and is available for downloading at `https://www.r-project.org/`. This link includes detailed steps, but the direct download page can be accessed at `https://cloud.r-project.org/` if you are interested. Download the necessary binary distribution based on your operating system of choice and run the executable setup following the necessary instructions for the Windows platform. If you are using Unix or any *nix like environment, you can install it directly from the terminal too if needed.

Once R is installed, you can fire up the R interpreter directly. This has a **graphical user interface (GUI)** containing an editor where you can write your code and then execute it. We recommend using an **Integrated Development Environment (IDE)** instead which eases development and helps maintain code in a more structured way. Besides this you can also use it for other capabilities like generating R markdown documents, R notebooks and Shiny Web Applications. We recommend using RStudio which provides a user-friendly interface for working with R. You can download and install it from `https://www.rstudio.com/products/rstudio/download3/` which contains installers for various operating systems.

Once installed, you can start RStudio and use R directly from the IDE itself. It usually contains a code editor window at the top and the R interactive interpreter in the bottom. The interactive interpreter is often called a **Read-Evaluate-Print-Loop (REPL)**. The interpreter asks for input, evaluates and instantly returns the output if any in the interpreter window itself. The interface usually shows the > symbol when waiting for any input and often shows the + symbol in the prompt when you enter code which spans multiple lines. Anything in R is usually a vector and outputs are usually returned with square brackets preceding it, like [1] indicating the output is a vector of size one. Comments are used to describe functions or sections of code. We can specify comments by using the # symbol followed by text. A sample execution in the R interpreter is shown in the following code for convenience:

```
> 10 + 5
[1] 15
> c(1,2,3,4)
[1] 1 2 3 4
> 5 == 5
[1] TRUE
> fruit = 'apple'
> if (fruit == 'apple'){
+     print('Apple')
+ }else{
+     print('Orange')
+ }
[1] "Apple"
```

You can see various operations being performed in the R interpreter in the preceding code snippet, including some conditional evaluations and basic arithmetic. We will now delve deeper into the various constructs of R.

Data types

There are several basic data types in R for handling different types of data and values:

- `numeric`: The `numeric` data type is used to store real or decimal vectors and is identical to the `double` data type.
- `double`: This data type can store and represent double precision vectors.
- `integer`: This data type is used for representing 32-bit integer vectors.
- `character`: This data type is used to represent character vectors, where each element can be a string of type character
- `logical`: The reserved words `TRUE` and `FALSE` are logical constants in the R language and `T` and `F` are global variables. All these four are logical type vectors.
- `complex`: This data type is used to store and represent complex numbers
- `factor`: This type is used to represent nominal or categorical variables by storing the nominal values in a vector of integers ranging from ($1…n$) such that n is the number of distinct values for the variable. A vector of character strings for the actual variable values is then mapped to this vector of integers
- Miscellaneous: There are several other types including `NA` to denote missing values in data, `NaN` which *denotes not a number*, and *ordered* is used for factoring ordinal variables

Common functions for each data type include `as` and `is`, which are used for converting data types (typecasting) and checking the data type respectively.

For example, `as.numeric(...)` would typecast the data or vector indicated by the ellipses into numeric type and `is.numeric(...)` would check if the data is of numeric type.

Let us look at a few more examples for the various data types in the following code snippet to understand them better:

```
# typecasting and checking data types
> n <- c(3.5, 0.0, 1.7, 0.0)
> typeof(n)
```

```
[1]  "double"
> is.numeric(n)
[1]  TRUE
> is.double(n)
[1]  TRUE
> is.integer(n)
[1]  FALSE
> as.integer(n)
[1]  3  0  1  0
> as.logical(n)
[1]    TRUE FALSE   TRUE FALSE

# complex numbers
> comp <- 3 + 4i
> typeof(comp)
[1]  "complex"

# factoring nominal variables
> size <- c(rep('large', 5), rep('small', 5), rep('medium', 3))
> size
 [1] "large"  "large"  "large"  "large"  "large"  "small"  "small"
"small"  "small"  "small"
[11] "medium" "medium" "medium"
> size <- factor(size)
> size
 [1] large  large  large  large  large  small  small  small  small
small  medium medium medium
Levels: large medium small
> summary(size)
 large medium  small
     5      3      5
```

The preceding examples should make the concepts clearer. Notice that non-zero numeric values are logically TRUE always, and zero values are FALSE, as we can see from typecasting our numeric vector to logical. We will now dive into the various data structures in R.

Data structures

The base R system has several important core data structures which are extensively used in handling, processing, manipulating, and analyzing data. We will be talking about five important data structures, which can be classified according to the type of data which can be stored and its dimensionality. The classification is depicted in the following table:

Content type	Dimensionality	Data structure
Homogeneous	One-dimensional	Vector
Homogeneous	N-dimensional	Array
Homogeneous	Two-dimensional	Matrix
Heterogeneous	One-dimensional	List
Heterogeneous	N-dimensional	DataFrame

The content type in the table depicts whether the data stored in the structure belongs to the same data type (homogeneous) or can contain data of different data types, (heterogeneous). The dimensionality of the data structure is pretty straightforward and is self-explanatory. We will now examine each data structure in further detail.

Vectors

The vector is the most basic data structure in R and here vectors indicate atomic vectors. They can be used to represent any data in R including input and output data. Vectors are usually created using the c (...) function, which is short for combine. Vectors can also be created in other ways such as using the : operator or the seq (...) family of functions. Vectors are homogeneous, all elements always belong to a single data type, and the vector by itself is a one-dimensional structure. The following snippet shows some vector representations:

```
> 1:5
[1] 1 2 3 4 5
> c(1,2,3,4,5)
[1] 1 2 3 4 5
> seq(1,5)
[1] 1 2 3 4 5
> seq_len(5)
[1] 1 2 3 4 5
```

You can also assign vectors to variables and perform different operations on them, including data manipulation, mathematical operations, transformations, and so on. We depict a few such examples in the following snippet:

```
# assigning two vectors to variables
> x <- 1:5
> y <- c(6,7,8,9,10)
> x
[1] 1 2 3 4 5
> y
[1]  6  7  8  9 10

# operating on vectors
> x + y
[1]  7  9 11 13 15
> sum(x)
[1] 15
> mean(x)
[1] 3
> x * y
[1]  6 14 24 36 50
> sqrt(x)
[1] 1.000000 1.414214 1.732051 2.000000 2.236068

# indexing and slicing
> y[2:4]
[1] 7 8 9
> y[c(2,3,4)]
[1] 7 8 9

# naming vector elements
> names(x) <- c("one", "two", "three", "four", "five")
> x
  one   two three  four  five
    1     2     3     4     5
```

The preceding snippet should give you a good flavor of what we can do with vectors. Try playing around with vectors and transforming and manipulating data with them!

Arrays

From the table of data structures we mentioned earlier, arrays can store homogeneous data and are N-dimensional data structures unlike vectors. Matrices are a special case of arrays with two dimensions, but more on that later. Considering arrays, it is difficult to represent data higher than two dimensions on the screen, but R can still handle it in a special way. The following example creates a three-dimensional array of *2x2x3*:

```
# create a three-dimensional array
three.dim.array <- array(
    1:12,      # input data
    dim = c(2, 2, 3),    # dimensions
    dimnames = list(     # names of dimensions
        c("row1", "row2"),
        c("col1", "col2"),
        c("first.set", "second.set", "third.set")
    )
)

# view the array
> three.dim.array
, , first.set

     col1 col2
row1    1    3
row2    2    4

, , second.set

     col1 col2
row1    5    7
row2    6    8

, , third.set

     col1 col2
row1    9   11
row2   10   12
```

From the preceding output, you can see that R filled the data in the column-first order in the three-dimensional array. We will now look at matrices in the following section.

Matrices

We've briefly mentioned that matrices are a special case of arrays with two dimensions. These two dimensions are represented by properties in rows and columns. Just like we used the array(...) function in the previous section to create an array, we will be using the matrix(...) function to create matrices.

The following snippet creates a *4x3* matrix:

```
# create a matrix
mat <- matrix(
    1:12,    # data
    nrow = 4,   # num of rows
    ncol = 3,   # num of columns
    byrow = TRUE  # fill the elements row-wise
)


# view the matrix
> mat
     [,1] [,2] [,3]
[1,]    1    2    3
[2,]    4    5    6
[3,]    7    8    9
[4,]   10   11   12
```

Thus you can see from the preceding output that we have a *4x3* matrix with 4 rows and 3 columns and we filled in the data in row-wise fashion by using the by row parameter in the matrix(...) function.

The following snippet shows some mathematical operations with matrices which you should be familiar with:

```
# initialize matrices
m1 <- matrix(
    1:9,    # data
    nrow = 3,   # num of rows
    ncol = 3,   # num of columns
    byrow = TRUE  # fill the elements row-wise
)
m2 <- matrix(
    10:18,    # data
    nrow = 3,   # num of rows
    ncol = 3,   # num of columns
    byrow = TRUE  # fill the elements row-wise
)
```

```
# matrix addition
> m1 + m2
     [,1] [,2] [,3]
[1,]   11   13   15
[2,]   17   19   21
[3,]   23   25   27

# matrix transpose
> t(m1)
     [,1] [,2] [,3]
[1,]    1    4    7
[2,]    2    5    8
[3,]    3    6    9

# matrix product
> m1 %*% m2
     [,1] [,2] [,3]
[1,]   84   90   96
[2,]  201  216  231
[3,]  318  342  366
```

We encourage you to try out more complex operations using matrices. See if you can find the inverse of a matrix.

Lists

Lists are a special type of vector besides the atomic vector which we discussed earlier. The difference with atomic vectors is that lists are heterogeneous and can hold different types of data such that each element of a list can itself be a list, an atomic vector, an array, matrix, or even a function. The following snippet shows us how to create lists:

```
# create sample list
list.sample <- list(
    nums = seq.int(1,5),
    languages = c("R", "Python", "Julia", "Java"),
    sin.func = sin
)

# view the list
> list.sample
$nums
[1] 1 2 3 4 5
```

```
$languages
[1] "R"       "Python" "Julia"  "Java"

$sin.func
function (x)  .Primitive("sin")

# accessing individual list elements
> list.sample$languages
[1] "R"       "Python" "Julia"  "Java"
> list.sample$sin.func(1.5708)
[1] 1
```

You can see from the preceding snippet that lists can hold different types of elements and accessing them is really easy.

Let us look at a few more operations with lists in the following snippet:

```
# initializing two lists
l1 <- list(nums = 1:5)
l2 <- list(
    languages = c("R", "Python", "Julia"),
    months = c("Jan", "Feb", "Mar")
)

# check lists and their type
> l1
$nums
[1] 1 2 3 4 5

> typeof(l1)
[1] "list"
> l2
$languages
[1] "R"       "Python" "Julia"

$months
[1] "Jan" "Feb" "Mar"

> typeof(l2)
[1] "list"

# concatenating lists
> l3 <- c(l1, l2)
> l3
```

```
$nums
[1] 1 2 3 4 5

$languages
[1] "R"       "Python" "Julia"

$months
[1] "Jan" "Feb" "Mar"

# converting list back to a vector
> v1 <- unlist(l1)
> v1
nums1 nums2 nums3 nums4 nums5
    1     2     3     4     5
> typeof(v1)
[1] "integer"
```

Now that we know how lists work, we will be moving on to the last and perhaps most widely used data structure in data processing and analysis, the DataFrame.

DataFrames

The DataFrame is a special data structure which is used to handle heterogeneous data with N-dimensions. This structure is used to handle data tables or tabular data having several observations, samples or data points which are represented by rows, and attributes for each sample, which are represented by columns. Each column can be thought of as a dimension to the dataset or a vector. It is very popular since it can easily work with tabular data, notably spreadsheets.

The following snippet shows us how we can create DataFrames and examine their properties:

```
# create data frame
df <- data.frame(
  name =  c("Wade", "Steve", "Slade", "Bruce"),
  age = c(28, 85, 55, 45),
  job = c("IT", "HR", "HR", "CS")
)

# view the data frame
> df
  name age job
1  Wade  28  IT
2 Steve  85  HR
3 Slade  55  HR
```

```
4 Bruce   45   CS

# examine data frame properties
> class(df)
[1] "data.frame"
> str(df)
'data.frame':      4 obs. of  3 variables:
 $ name: Factor w/ 4 levels "Bruce","Slade",..: 4 3 2 1
 $ age : num  28 85 55 45
 $ job : Factor w/ 3 levels "CS","HR","IT": 3 2 2 1
> rownames(df)
[1] "1" "2" "3" "4"
> colnames(df)
[1] "name" "age" "job"
> dim(df)
[1] 4 3
```

You can see from the preceding snippet how DataFrames can represent tabular data where each attribute is a dimension or column. You can also perform multiple operations on DataFrames such as merging, concatenating, binding, sub-setting, and so on. We will depict some of these operations in the following snippet:

```
# initialize two data frames
emp.details <- data.frame(
    empid = c('e001', 'e002', 'e003', 'e004'),
    name = c("Wade", "Steve", "Slade", "Bruce"),
    age = c(28, 85, 55, 45)
)
job.details <- data.frame(
    empid = c('e001', 'e002', 'e003', 'e004'),
    job = c("IT", "HR", "HR", "CS")
)

# view data frames
> emp.details
  empid  name age
1  e001  Wade   28
2  e002 Steve   85
3  e003 Slade   55
4  e004 Bruce   45
> job.details
  empid job
1  e001  IT
2  e002  HR
3  e003  HR
```

```
4   e004   CS

# binding and merging data frames
> cbind(emp.details, job.details)
  empid  name age empid job
1  e001  Wade  28  e001   IT
2  e002 Steve  85  e002   HR
3  e003 Slade  55  e003   HR
4  e004 Bruce  45  e004   CS
> merge(emp.details, job.details, by='empid')
  empid  name age job
1  e001  Wade  28  IT
2  e002 Steve  85  HR
3  e003 Slade  55  HR
4  e004 Bruce  45  CS

# subsetting data frame
> subset(emp.details, age > 50)
  empid  name age
2  e002 Steve  85
3  e003 Slade  55
```

Now that we have a good grasp of data structures, we will look at concepts related to functions in R in the next section.

Functions

So far we have dealt with various variables and data types and structures for storing data. Functions are just another data type or object in R, albeit a special one which allows us to operate on data and perform actions on data. Functions are useful for modularizing code and separating concerns where needed by dedicating specific actions and operations to different functions and implementing the logic needed for any action inside the function. We will be talking about two types of functions in this section: the built-in functions and the user-defined functions.

Built-in functions

There are several functions which come with the base installation of R and its core packages. You can access these built-in functions directly using the function name and you can get more functions as you install newer packages. We depict operations using a few built-in functions in the following snippet:

```
> sqrt(7)
[1] 2.645751
```

```
> mean(1:5)
[1]  3
> sum(1:5)
[1]  15
> sqrt(1:5)
[1]  1.000000 1.414214 1.732051 2.000000 2.236068
> runif(5)
[1]  0.8880760 0.2925848 0.9240165 0.6535002 0.1891892
> rnorm(5)
[1]   1.90901035 -1.55611066 -0.40784306 -1.88185230  0.02035915
```

You can see from the previous examples that functions such as sqrt (...), mean (...), and sum (...) are built-in and pre-implemented. They can be used anytime in R without the need to define these functions explicitly or load other packages.

User-defined functions

While built-in functions are good, often you need to incorporate your own algorithms, logic, and processes for solving a problem. That is where you need to build you own functions. Typically, there are three main components in the function. They are mentioned as follows:

- The environment (...) which contains the location map of the defined function and its variables

- The formals (...) which depict the list of arguments which are used to call the function

- The body (...) which is used to depict the code inside the function which contains the core logic of the function

Some depictions of user-defined functions are shown in the following code snippet:

```
# define the function
square <- function(data){
  return (data^2)
}

# inspect function components
> environment(square)
<environment: R_GlobalEnv>

> formals(square)
$data
```

```
> body(square)
{
    return(data^2)
}

# execute the function on data
> square(1:5)
[1]   1   4   9  16  25
> square(12)
[1]  144
```

We can see how user-defined functions can be defined using `function(...)` and we can also examine the various components of the function, as we discussed earlier, and also use them to operate on data.

Controlling code flow

When writing complete applications and scripts using R, the flow and execution of code is very important. The flow of code is based on statements, functions, variables, and data structures used in the code and it is all based on the algorithms, business logic, and other rules for solving the problem at hand. There are several constructs which can be used to control the flow of code and we will be discussing primarily the following two constructs:

- Looping constructs
- Conditional constructs

We will start with looking at various looping constructs for executing the same sections of code multiple times.

Looping constructs

Looping constructs basically involve using loops which are used to execute code blocks or sections repeatedly as needed. Usually the loop keeps executing the code block in its scope until some specific condition is met or some other conditional statements are used. There are three main types of loops in R:

- `for`
- `while`
- `repeat`

We will explore all the three constructs with examples in the following code snippet:

```
# for loop
> for (i in 1:5) {
+       cat(paste(i," "))
+ }
1  2  3  4  5


> sum <- 0
> for (i in 1:10){
+       sum <- sum + i
+ }

> sum
[1] 55

# while loop
> n <- 1
> while (n <= 5){
+       cat(paste(n, " "))
+       n <- n + 1
+ }
1  2  3  4  5

# repeat loop
> i <- 1
> repeat{
+       cat(paste(i, " "))
+       if (i >= 5){
+            break  # break out of the infinite loop
+       }
+       i <- i + 1
+ }
1  2  3  4  5
```

An important point to remember here is that, with larger amounts of data, vectorization-based constructs are more optimized than loops and we will cover some of them in the *Advanced operations* section later.

Conditional constructs

There are several conditional constructs which help us in executing and controlling the flow of code conditionally based on user-defined rules and conditions. This is very useful when we do not want to execute all possible code blocks in a script sequentially but we want to execute specific code blocks if and only if they meet or do not meet specific conditions.

There are mainly four constructs which are used frequently in R:

- `if` or `if...else`
- `if...else if...else`
- `ifelse(...)`
- `switch(...)`

The bottom two are functions compared to the other statements, which use the `if`, `if...else`, and `if...else if...else` syntax. We will look at them in the following code snippet with examples:

```
# using if
> num = 10
> if (num == 10){
+     cat('The number was 10')
+ }
The number was 10

# using if-else
> num = 5
> if (num == 10){
+     cat('The number was 10')
+ } else{
+     cat('The number was not 10')
+ }
The number was not 10

# using if-else if-else
> if (num == 10){
+     cat('The number was 10')
+ } else if (num == 5){
+     cat('The number was 5')
+ } else{
+     cat('No match found')
+ }
The number was 5

# using ifelse(...) function
> ifelse(num == 10, "Number was 10", "Number was not 10")
[1] "Number was not 10"

# using switch(...) function
> for (num in c("5","10","15")){
+     cat(
```

```
+          switch(num,
+               "5" = "five",
+               "7" = "seven",
+               "10" = "ten",
+               "No match found"
+          ), "\n")
+ }
five
ten
No match found
```

From the preceding snippet, we can see that switch(...) has a default option which can return a user-defined value when no match is found when evaluating the condition.

Advanced operations

We can perform several advanced vectorized operations in R, which is useful when dealing with large amounts of data and improves code performance with regards to time taken in executing code. Some advanced constructs in the apply family of functions will be covered in this section, as follows:

- apply: Evaluates a function on the boundaries or margins of an array
- lapply: Loops over a list and evaluates a function on each element
- sapply: A more simplified version of the lapply(...) function
- tapply: Evaluates a function over subsets of a vector
- mapply: A multivariate version of the lapply(...) function

Let's look at how each of these functions work in further detail.

apply

As we mentioned earlier, the apply(...) function is used mainly to evaluate any defined function over the margins or boundaries of any array or matrix.

An important point to note here is that there are dedicated aggregation functions rowSums(...), rowMeans(...), colSums(...) and colMeans(...) which actually use apply internally but are more optimized and useful compared to other functions when operating on large arrays.

The following snippet depicts some aggregation functions being applied to a matrix:

```
# creating a 4x4 matrix
> mat <- matrix(1:16, nrow=4, ncol=4)

# view the matrix
> mat
     [,1] [,2] [,3] [,4]
[1,]    1    5    9   13
[2,]    2    6   10   14
[3,]    3    7   11   15
[4,]    4    8   12   16

# row sums
> apply(mat, 1, sum)
[1] 28 32 36 40
> rowSums(mat)
[1] 28 32 36 40

# row means
> apply(mat, 1, mean)
[1]  7  8  9 10
> rowMeans(mat)
[1]  7  8  9 10

# col sums
> apply(mat, 2, sum)
[1] 10 26 42 58
> colSums(mat)
[1] 10 26 42 58

# col means
> apply(mat, 2, mean)
[1]  2.5  6.5 10.5 14.5
> colMeans(mat)
[1]  2.5  6.5 10.5 14.5

# row quantiles
> apply(mat, 1, quantile, probs=c(0.25, 0.5, 0.75))
     [,1] [,2] [,3] [,4]
25%     4    5    6    7
50%     7    8    9   10
75%    10   11   12   13
```

You can see aggregations taking place without the need of extra looping constructs.

lapply

The lapply(...) function takes a list and a function as input parameters. Then it evaluates that function over each element of the list. If the input list is not a list, it is coerced to a list using the as.list(...) function before the final output is returned. All operations are vectorized and we will see an example in the following snippet:

```
# create and view a list of elements
> l <- list(nums=1:10, even=seq(2,10,2), odd=seq(1,10,2))
> l
$nums
 [1]  1  2  3  4  5  6  7  8  9 10

$even
[1]  2  4  6  8 10

$odd
[1] 1 3 5 7 9

# use lapply on the list
> lapply(l, sum)
$nums
[1] 55

$even
[1] 30

$odd
[1] 25
```

sapply

The sapply(...) function is quite similar to the lapply(...) function, the only exception is that it will always try to simplify the final results of the computation. Suppose the final result is such that every element is of length 1, then sapply(...) would return a vector. If the length of every element in the result is greater than 1, then a matrix would be returned. If it is not able to simplify the results, then we end up getting the same result as lapply(...). The following example will make things clearer:

```
# create and view a sample list
> l <- list(nums=1:10, even=seq(2,10,2), odd=seq(1,10,2))
> l
$nums
```

```
[1]  1  2  3  4  5  6  7  8  9 10

$even
[1]  2  4  6  8 10

$odd
[1] 1 3 5 7 9

# observe differences between lapply and sapply
> lapply(l, mean)
$nums
[1] 5.5

$even
[1] 6

$odd
[1] 5
> typeof(lapply(l, mean))
[1] "list"

> sapply(l, mean)
nums even   odd
 5.5  6.0   5.0
> typeof(sapply(l, mean))
[1] "double"
```

tapply

The `tapply(...)` function is used to evaluate a function over specific subsets of input vectors. These subsets can be defined by the users.

The following example depicts the same:

```
> data <- 1:30
> data
 [1]  1  2  3  4  5  6  7  8  9 10 11 12 13 14 15 16 17 18 19 20 21 22
23 24 25 26 27 28 29 30
> groups <- gl(3, 10)
> groups
 [1] 1 1 1 1 1 1 1 1 1 1 2 2 2 2 2 2 2 2 2 2 3 3 3 3 3 3 3 3 3 3
Levels: 1 2 3
> tapply(data, groups, sum)
  1   2   3
 55 155 255
```

```
> tapply(data, groups, sum, simplify = FALSE)
$'1'
[1] 55

$'2'
[1] 155

$'3'
[1] 255
```

mapply

The mapply (...) function is used to evaluate a function in parallel over sets of arguments. This is basically a multi-variate version of the lapply (...) function.

The following example shows how we can build a list of vectors easily with mapply (...) as compared to using the rep (...) function multiple times otherwise:

```
> list(rep(1,4), rep(2,3), rep(3,2), rep(4,1))
[[1]]
[1] 1 1 1 1

[[2]]
[1] 2 2 2

[[3]]
[1] 3 3

[[4]]
[1] 4

> mapply(rep, 1:4, 4:1)
[[1]]
[1] 1 1 1 1

[[2]]
[1] 2 2 2

[[3]]
[1] 3 3

[[4]]
[1] 4
```

Visualizing data

One of the most important aspects of data analytics is to depict meaningful insights with crisp and concise visualizations. Data visualization is one of the most important aspects of exploratory data analysis, as well as an important medium to present results from any analyzes. There are three main popular plotting systems in R:

- The base plotting system which comes with the basic installation of R
- The lattice plotting system which produces better looking plots than the base plotting system
- The ggplot2 package which is based on the grammar of graphics and produces beautiful, publication quality visualizations

The following snippet depicts visualizations using all three plotting systems on the popular iris dataset:

```
# load the data
> data(iris)

# base plotting system
> boxplot(Sepal.Length~Species,data=iris,
+          xlab="Species", ylab="Sepal Length", main="Iris Boxplot")
```

This gives us a set of boxplots using the base plotting system as depicted in the following plot:

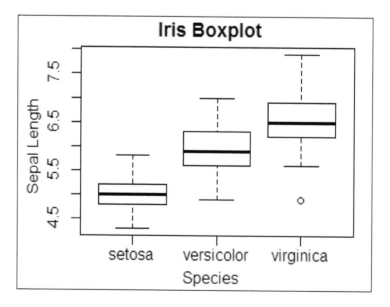

```
# lattice plotting system
> bwplot(Sepal.Length~Species,data=iris, xlab="Species", ylab="Sepal
Length", main="Iris Boxplot")
```

This snippet helps us in creating a set of boxplots for the various species using the lattice plotting system:

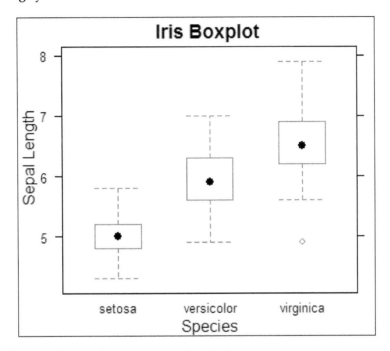

```
# ggplot2 plotting system
> ggplot(data=iris, aes(x=Species, y=Sepal.Length)) + geom_
boxplot(aes(fill=Species)) +
+       ylab("Sepal Length") + ggtitle("Iris Boxplot") +
+       stat_summary(fun.y=mean, geom="point", shape=5, size=4) + theme_
bw()
```

This code snippet gives us the following boxplots using the `ggplot2` plotting system:

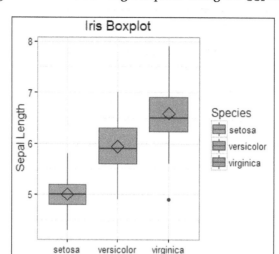

You can see from the preceding visualizations how each plotting system works and compare the plots across each system. Feel free to experiment with each system and visualize your own data!

Next steps

This quick refresher in getting started with R should gear you up for the upcoming chapters and also make you more comfortable with the R eco-system, its syntax and features. It's important to remember that you can always get help with any aspect of R in a variety of ways. Besides that, packages in R are perhaps going to be the most important tool in your arsenal for analyzing data. We will briefly list some important commands for each of these two aspects which may come in handy in the future.

Getting help

R has thousands of packages, functions, constructs and structures! Hence it is impossible for anyone to keep track and remember of them all. Luckily, help in R is readily available and you can always get detailed information and documentation with regard to R, its utilities, features and packages using the following commands:

- `help(<any_R_object>)` or `?<any_R_object>`: This provides help on any R object including functions, packages, data types, and so on

- `example(<function_name>)`: This provides a quick example for the mentioned function
- `apropos(<any_string>)`: This lists all functions containing the `any_string` term

Managing packages

R, being open-source and a community-driven language, has tons of packages for helping you with your analyzes which are free to download, install and use.

In the R community, the term library is often used interchangeably with the term package.

R provides the following utilities to manage packages:

- `install.packages(...)`: This installs a package from **Comprehensive R Archive Network (CRAN)**. CRAN helps maintain and distribute the various versions and documentation of R
- `libPaths(...)`: This adds this library path to R
- `installed.packages(lib.loc=)`: This lists installed packages
- `update.packages(lib.loc=)`: This updates a package
- `remove.packages(...)`: This removes a package
- `path.package(...)`: This is the package loaded for the session
- `library(...)`: This loads a package in a script to use its functions or utilities
- `library(help=)`: This lists the functions in a package

This brings us to the end of our section on getting started with R and we will now look at some aspects of analytics, machine learning and text analytics.

Data analytics

Data analytics is basically a structured process of using statistical modeling, machine learning, knowledge discovery, predictive modeling and data mining to discover and interpret meaningful patterns in the data, and to communicate them effectively as actionable insights which help in driving business decisions. Data analytics, data mining and machine learning are often said to be covering similar concepts and methodologies. While machine learning, being a branch or subset of artificial intelligence, is more focused on model building, evaluation and learning patterns, the end goal of all three processes is the same: to generate meaningful insights from the data. In the next section, we will briefly discuss the industry standard process followed in analytics which is rigorously followed by organizations.

Analytics workflow

Analyzing data is a science and an art. Any analytics process usually has a defined set of steps, which are generally executed in sequence. More than often, analytics being an iterative process, it leads to several of these steps being repeated many times over if necessary. There is an industry standard that is widely followed for data analysis, known as **CRISP-DM**, which stands for **Cross Industry Standard Process for Data Mining**. This is a standard data analysis and mining process workflow that describes how to break up any particular data analysis problem into six major stages.

The main stages in the CRISP-DM model are as follows:

- **Business understanding**: This is the initial stage that focuses on the business context of the problem, objective or goal which we are trying to solve. Domain and business knowledge are essential here along with valuable insights from subject matter experts in the business for planning out the key objectives and end results that are intended from the data analysis workflow.

- **Data acquisition and understanding**: This stage's main focus is to acquire data of interest and understand the meaning and semantics of the various data points and attributes that are present in the data. Some initial exploration of the data may also be done at this stage using various exploratory data analysis techniques.

- **Data preparation**: This stage usually involves data munging, cleaning, and transformation. **Extract-Transform-Load (ETL)** processes of ten come in handy at this stage. Data quality issues are also dealt with in this stage. The final dataset is usually used for analysis and modeling.

- **Modeling and analysis**: This stage mainly focuses on analyzing the data and building models using specific techniques from data mining and machine learning. Often, we need to apply further data transformations that are based on different modeling algorithms.

- **Evaluation**: This is perhaps one of the most crucial stages. Building models is an iterative process. In this stage, we evaluate the results that are obtained from multiple iterations of various models and techniques, and then we select the best possible method or analysis, which gives us the insights that we need based on our business requirements. Often, this stage involves reiterating through the previous two steps to reach a final agreement based on the results.

- **Deployment**: This is the final stage, where decision systems that are based on analysis are deployed so that end users can start consuming the results and utilizing them. This deployed system can be as complex as a real-time prediction system or as simple as an ad-hoc report.

The following figure shows the complete flow with the various stages in the CRISP-DM model:

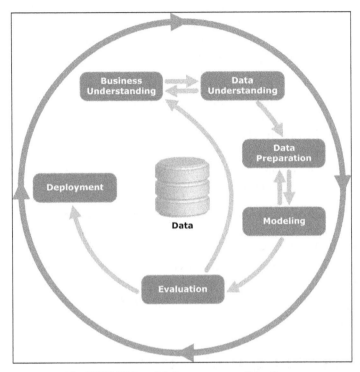

The CRISP-DM model. Source: www.wikipedia.org

In principle, the CRISP-DM model is very clear and concise with straightforward requirements at each step. As a result, this workflow has been widely adopted across the industry and has become an industry standard.

Machine learning

Machine learning is one of the trending buzzwords in the technology domain today, along with *big data*. Although a lot of it is over-hyped, **machine learning** (**ML**) has proved to be really effective in solving tough problems and has been significant in propelling the rise of **artificial intelligence** (**AI**). Machine learning is basically an intersection of elements from the fields of computer science, statistics, and mathematics. This includes a combination of concepts from knowledge mining and discovery, artificial intelligence, pattern detection, optimization, and learning theory to develop algorithms and techniques which can learn from and make predictions on data without being explicitly programmed.

The learning here refers to the ability to make computers or machines intelligent, based on the data and algorithms which we provide to them, also known as training the model, so that they start detecting patterns and insights from new data. This can be better understood from the definition of machine learning by the well-known professor *Tom Mitchell* who said, "*A computer program is said to learn from experience E with respect to some task T and some performance measure P, if its performance on T, as measured by P, improves with experience E.*"

Let's consider the task (T) of the system is to predict the sales of an organization for the next year. To perform such a task, it needs to rely upon historical sales information. We shall call this experience (E). Its performance (P) is measured on how well it predicts the sales in any given year. Thus, we can generalize that a system has successfully learned how to predict the sales (or task T) if it gets better at predicting it (or improves its performance P), utilizing the past information (or experience E).

Machine learning techniques

Machine-learning techniques are basically algorithms which can work on data and extract insights from it, which can include discovering, forecasting, or predicting trends and patterns. The idea is to build a model using a combination of data and algorithms which can then be used to work on new, previously unseen data and derive actionable insights.

Each and every technique depends on what type of data it can work on and the objective of the problem we are trying to solve. People often get tempted to learn a couple of algorithms and then try to apply them to every problem. An important point to remember here is that there is no universal machine-learning algorithm which fits all problems. The main inputs to machine-learning algorithms are features which are extracted from data using a process known as feature extraction, which is often coupled with another process called feature engineering (or building new features from existing features). Each feature can be described as an attribute of the dataset, such as your location, age, number of posts, shares and so on, if we were dealing with data related to social media user profiles. Machine-learning techniques can be classified into two major types namely supervised learning and unsupervised learning.

Supervised learning

Supervised learning techniques are a subset of the family of machine -learning algorithms which are mainly used in predictive modeling and forecasting. A predictive model is basically a model which can be constructed using a supervised learning algorithm on features or attributes from training data (available data used to train or build the model) such that we can predict using this model on newer, previously unseen data points. Supervised learning algorithms try to model relationships and dependencies between the target prediction output and the input features such that we can predict the output values for new data based on those relationships which it learned from the dataset used during model training or building.

There are two main types of supervised learning techniques

- **Classification**: These algorithms build predictive models from training data where the response variable to be predicted is categorical. These predictive models use the features learnt from training data on new, previously unseen data to predict their class or category labels. The output classes belong to discrete categories. Types of classification algorithms include decision trees, support vector machines, random forests and many more.

- **Regression**: These algorithms are used to build predictive models on data such that the response variable to be predicted is numerical. The algorithm builds a model based on input features and output response values of the training data and this model is used to predict values for new data. The output values in this case are continuous numeric values and not discrete categories. Types of regression algorithms include linear regression, multiple regression, ridge regression and lasso regression, among many others.

Unsupervised learning

Unsupervised learning techniques are a subset of the family of machine-learning algorithms which are mainly used in pattern detection, dimension reduction and descriptive modeling. A descriptive model is basically a model constructed from an unsupervised machine learning algorithm and features from input data similar to the supervised learning process. However, the output response variables are not present in this case. These algorithms try to use techniques on the input data to mine for rules, detect patterns, and summarize and group the data points which help in deriving meaningful insights and describe the data better to the users. There is no specific concept of training or testing data here since we do not have any specific relationship mapping between input features and output response variables (which do not exist in this case). There are three main types of unsupervised learning techniques:

- **Clustering**: The main objective of clustering algorithms is to cluster or group input data points into different classes or categories using features derived from the input data alone and no other external information. Unlike classification, the output response labels are not known beforehand in clustering. There are different approaches to build clustering models, such as by using centroid based approaches, hierarchical approaches, and many more. Some popular clustering algorithms include k-means, k-medoids, and hierarchical clustering.

- **Association rule mining**: These algorithms are used to mine and extract rules and patterns of significance from data. These rules explain relationships between different variables and attributes, and also depict frequent item sets and patterns which occur in the data.

- **Dimensionality reduction**: These algorithms help in the process of reducing the number of features or variables in the dataset by computing a set of principal representative variables. These algorithms are mainly used for feature selection.

Text analytics

Text analytics is also often called text mining. This is basically the process of extracting and deriving meaningful patterns from textual data which can in turn be translated into actionable knowledge and insights. Text analytics consist of a collection of machine learning, natural language processing, linguistic, and statistical methods that can be leveraged to analyze text data. Machine-learning algorithms are built to work on numeric data in general, so extra processing and feature extraction and engineering is needed for text analytics to make regular machine learning and statistical methods work on unstructured data.

Natural language processing, popularly known as NLP, aids in doing this. NLP is defined as a specialized field in computer science and engineering and artificial intelligence which has its roots and origins in computational linguistics. Concepts and techniques from NLP are extremely useful and help in building applications and systems that enable interaction between machines and humans with the aid of natural language which is indeed a daunting task. Some of the main applications of NLP are:

- Question-answering systems
- Speech recognition
- Machine translation
- Text categorization and classification
- Text summarization

We will be using several concepts from these when we analyze unstructured textual data from social media in the upcoming chapters.

Summary

We've covered a lot in this chapter so I would like to commend your efforts for staying with us till the very end! We kicked off this chapter with a detailed look into social media, its scope, variants, significance and pitfalls. We also covered the basics of social media analytics, as well as the opportunities and challenges involved, to whet your appetite for social media analytics and to get us geared up for the journey we'll be taking throughout the course of this book. A complete refresher of the R programming language was also covered in detail, especially with regard to setting up a proper analytics environment, core structures, constructs and features of R. Finally, we took a quick glance at the basic concepts of data analytics, the industry standard process for analytics, and covered the core essentials of machine learning, text analytics and natural language processing.

We will be looking at analyzing data from various popular social media platforms in future chapters so get ready to do some serious analysis on social media!

2
Twitter – What's Happening with 140 Characters

An article in Forbes in 2012 outlined research undertaken by a Paris-based analytics firm. The research had found Jakarta to be the world's most active Twitter city (source: `http://www.forbes.com/sites/victorlipman/2012/12/30/the-worlds-most-active-twitter-city-you-wont-guess-it/#3b3f7d16343b`). This may be a surprise, given the population count and other dynamics of the city, but such insights aren't jaw-dropping any more. The world is now a place where every other person has a virtual identity on numerous social networking platforms. The previous chapter gave you a quick glimpse into what a social network is (in case you didn't already know it) and this chapter will build on those concepts and set the tone for the rest of the book.

Twitter, as we all know, is a chirpy social network that's meant for sharing information at break-neck speeds. Technically, it is a microblogging platform which helps its users share information in small 140 character units called Tweets! In the Twitter-verse there's no concept of a *friend*. Here people follow other people/accounts (aka `@handles`) that they are interested in. A handle may follow and be followed back to share tweets. Twitter is an active social network widely used across the world to not just share viral content, celebrity gossip, and funny images, but it is also widely used for rapidly sharing news, disaster notifications, and so on.

In this chapter, we will cover a lot of ground both in terms of utilizing Twitter and its data along with understanding analytical concepts to draw insights from it. We will be covering the following topics in this chapter:

- Understanding Twitter data, APIs, and a typical analysis workflow
- Uncovering trends in tweets
- Performing sentiment analysis
- Follower graph analysis
- Challenges associated with Twitter data

In this chapter, we will learn to deal with actual Twitter data and utilize different R packages to draw insights. We will also look at different visualizations (wherever necessary) to better understand the data.

Understanding Twitter

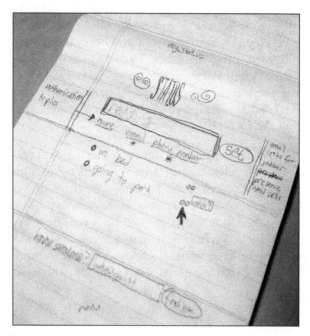

Twitter's initial design. Image source: https://www.flickr.com/photos/jackdorsey/182613360/

Born in 2006, Twitter is a social networking cum online news service which enables its users to share content in bursts of 140 characters. Over the years, it has evolved like any other successful thing on the Internet and added and/or removed features. Our aim in this chapter is to understand different aspects of this service and use them to draw different insights or solve business problems.

 Twitter was the brainchild of *Jack Dorsey*, *Noah Glass*, *Biz Stone* and *Evan Williams*. It started as the SMS of the Internet with very simple ideas. You can read the interesting story of its inception here: `http://latimesblogs.latimes.com/technology/2009/02/twitter-creator.html`

As discussed in the previous chapter, social networks are far reaching and dynamic. Twitter allows users to share information using text, images, videos, GIFs, links, hash tags, handles and so on from a variety of sources such as the Web, apps, SMS, and more. Thus a tweet may be a combination of any of the previously mentioned types originating from any one of the aforementioned sources.

A tweet though is far more than just the message. A tweet contains a lot under the hood which makes the game even more interesting. Each tweet contains a lot of metadata. Metadata, in simple words, is the data about the data. Metadata is what helps us in understanding or attaching meaning to each data point. In case of a tweet, its date-time, its source and the number of retweets is what makes up the metadata. This additional information about each tweet helps us draw various insights (which we will see in upcoming sections).

Tweets are at the core of twitter-verse and apart from the tweeted message itself, contain information related to the creation timestamp, like count, retweet count and 30 more such attributes (these may change as the service evolves, and not all attributes are available for every tweet).

APIs

Twitter's **Application Programming Interfaces** (**APIs**) are the gateway to the immense data of Twitter. These provide us with some very useful utilities for interacting with Twitter in a programmatic way. APIs may be used to develop third party apps along with a way to extract data for analysis/research purposes.

Twitter's APIs have been its strong point ever since. This, along with its unique mix of follower relationships and velocity, has always intrigued researchers. There have been numerous studies based on Twitter. In this section, we will look at various aspects of its APIs and objects and then use them for our analysis.

The following are the core four different objects of the Twitter API family:

- **Tweets**: The central entity of the twitter-verse. It contains the message along with the metadata attributes briefly discussed previously.

- **Users**: A Twitter user can be anybody or anything. Unlike other social networks which try to map virtual and physical entities, Twitter does not enforce any such restriction. Anybody or anything which can tweet, follow or perform any of the Twitter's actions is a user. Very commonly, business entities and governments have their own Twitter handles.

- **Entities**: These objects mostly help us work with the metadata attributes. These may include information on URLs, hashtags, user mentions, and so on. These objects enable quicker processing without parsing the tweet text.

- **Places**: Apart from other metadata attributes, the location of a tweet is handled as a separate object. This is due to privacy and other design considerations. This information has multiple uses; for instance for displaying *Trending Topics Near You* or targeted marketing.

For more information on these and other aspects, checkout the documentation at `https://dev.twitter.com/`. We urge our readers to go through it to understand the objects and APIs for an in-depth understanding.

To enable faster development and hassle free access, Twitter has libraries available in all major programming languages. For R we would be making use of the `twitteR` package. This package provides us ways to connect and extract information from Twitter very easily. It also provides some nice utilities to make our lives easier.

 Twitter has a set of best practices and a list of *don'ts* specified clearly on its developer site at `https://dev.twitter.com/`. Twitter tracks the use of its APIs and there is a defined rate limit on the number of times their APIs can be queried. Kindly go through the best practices and #playSafe!

Registering an application

Now that we have a fair idea about Twitter's objects and a quick overview of its APIs, we can get started with our interaction with Twitter. The first and foremost step is to register as a user and then create an app. Twitter requires users to create an app to use its APIs. It uses **Open Authentication** or **OAuth** to grant access to its APIs and data under certain terms and conditions. An app can be easily created by following these steps:

1. Log in to the app management console at `http://apps.twitter.com`.

2. Once logged in, click on the **Create New App** button. Fill up the required fields, you may provide the callback URL as `http://127.0.0.1:1410`. The callback URL is the address that Twitter's API replies to with a response to the queries. Since we'll be using our system for this chapter, the preceding URL works (you may choose to change it to your server's IP and port as well).

3. Click on **Create Your Twitter Application** to complete the process. Once done, you'll be redirected to the app details page which will contain the required details for connecting to it.

4. The following image shows a sample Twitter app details page:

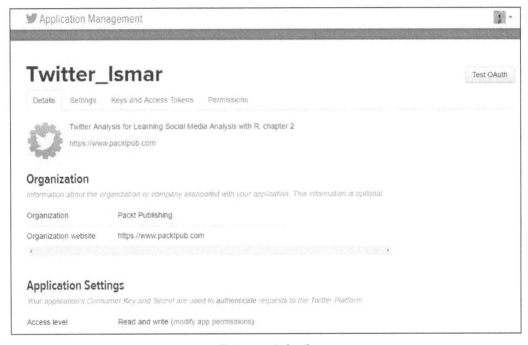

Twitter app's details

Just three simple steps and our Twitter application is ready to use. The app creation process provides us with OAuth parameters such as the API Key, API Token, Access Token, and Access Token Secret. Together, these four parameters help us tap into Twitter's APIs for our use cases.

To get these details, simply go to the **Keys and Access Tokens** tab and make a note of these parameters. We will be using this app in the upcoming sections for different use cases. The following image shows a sample **Keys and Access Tokens** tab for an app:

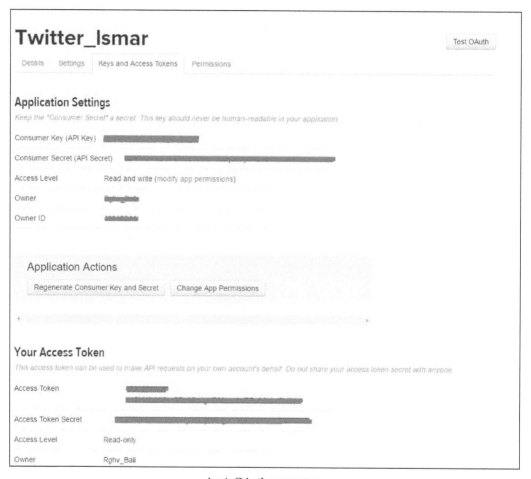

App's OAuth parameters

The OAuth parameters (API Key, API Token, Access Token and Access Token Secret) should be kept safe and secure. These are like your username and password. Exposing them or losing them may allow unwanted users to misuse the APIs under your credentials. In case of doubt, you can easily regenerate this from the **Application Management** console at https://apps.twitter.com/

Connecting to Twitter using R

In the previous section, we created a new Twitter app from the Application Management console to get required credentials for using its APIs. In this section, we will make use of the app (more so its OAuth credentials) to connect to Twitter using R.

Connecting to Twitter APIs using R is the first and foremost step before we can start working on some interesting use cases. To connect to the APIs we will make use of `twitteR`.

`twitteR` is an R package which helps us connect and extract data along with certain utilities to make our Twitter interaction easy.

To install R packages:

```
install.packages('twitteR')
```

Using the following code snippet, we will now load the `twitteR` package and use it to connect to our APP using its OAuth credentials:

```
# load the package
library(twitteR)

# set the credentials
CONSUMER_SECRET <- "XXXXXXXX"
CONSUMER_KEY <- "XXXXXX"

# connect to twitter app
setup_twitter_oauth(consumer_key = CONSUMER_KEY,
            consumer_secret = CONSUMER_SECRET)
```

Make use of your app credentials (Consumer key and Secret) before executing the preceding snippet. Upon execution of the function, `setup_twitter_oauth()`, we are prompted to either cache the credentials locally or not. For the time being, let's say no and proceed. The following is the prompt message:

```
> setup_twitter_oauth(consumer_key = CONSUMER_KEY,consumer_secret = CONSUMER_SECRET)
[1] "Using browser based authentication"
Use a local file ('.httr-oauth'), to cache OAuth access credentials between R sessions?

1: Yes
2: No

Selection: 2
```

Set up Twitter OAuth using R

Upon selecting option 2, the browser is loaded with Twitter's login page. Provide your details to confirm your identity and authorize the app. The following screenshot displays the app authorization page:

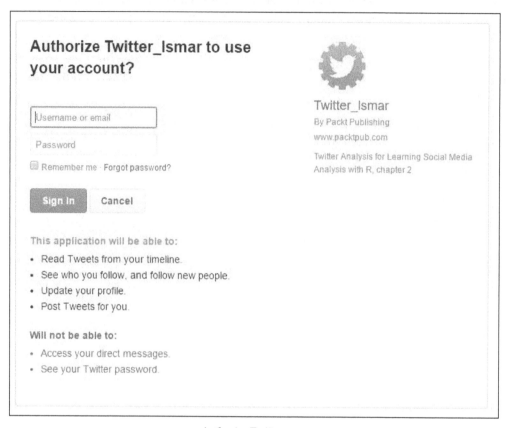

Authorize Twitter app

Once authorized, the app will redirect the browser to its callback URL (remember we had set the callback URL while setting up the app itself?). It will display the following standard message if authorization is successful:

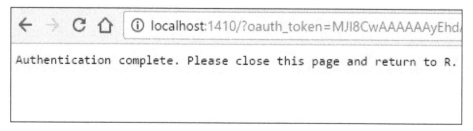

Authentication completed

This final step completes the simple process of connecting to Twitter using R. The app's credentials and the function `setup_twitter_oauth()` was all that was needed.

Extracting sample Tweets

Now that we are connected to Twitter using R, the logical next step is to start using the APIs. In this section we will try to extract some sample tweets for any user. We will also see what attributes a tweet contains.

The following snippet helps us extract information related to a particular user's timeline. As always, R has some cool utilities to make this look very simple:

```
# set twitter user
twitterUser <- getUser("jack")
# extract a few sample tweets from this user's timeline
tweets <- userTimeline(twitterUser, n = 10)
```

The preceding snippet collects 10 tweets from the said user's timeline. The following are the contents of the variable `tweets`:

```
> tweets
[[1]]
[1] "jack: @iSocialFanz @twitter @ciszek not sure what you mean"

[[2]]
[1] "jack: @Snowden reasonable and something we'll think about"

[[3]]
[1] "jack: And these 5 (Alyssa, Francoise, Sarah, Jackie, and Hillary) own and drive the majority of our revenue https://t.co/
rs2OH9gVq1"

[[4]]
[1] "jack: \"we have to exercise and spread the idea that critical thinking matters now more than ever...\" #PardonSnowden"

[[5]]
[1] "jack: #PardonSnowden (and watch this) https://t.co/LI1e3gfCNw"
```

Sample tweets

To view all the attributes and methods available for each tweet in the list of tweets, we use the function `getClass()`. Each tweet object has multiple attributes, one of them being the `favoriteCount`. The following snippet illustrates the same:

```
tweets[[1]]$getClass()
tweets[[1]]$favoriteCount
```

Similarly we can use other attributes/methods exposed by the tweet object to work around / build a dataset for our use cases. In the upcoming sections we will make use of this understanding and build different use cases on real Twitter data. #StayTuned!

Revisiting analytics workflow

As discussed in detail in *Chapter 1, Getting Started with R and Social Media Analytics* (see *A typical social media analytics workflow*), we defined some key steps involved in the analysis of data from different social networks. Continuing with the same theme for Twitter, the different use cases we will work on in the next sections can also be broken down into the following key steps:

- Data access
- Data processing and normalization
- Data analysis
- Insights

The data access step involves understanding the APIs and their corresponding R packages to tap into the social network. We've already talked about creating a Twitter app and did a quick connect and extraction of tweets using R. Each of the following sections will make use of the same initial step for data access and then build upon them based on the requirements. We will discuss and provide details for each of the other steps in this workflow as we progress with the use cases. Stay tuned.

Trend analysis

Twitter is a speedy medium. Information (along with rumors and nonsense) travels at breakneck speeds across the social network/world. It has now become a norm for an event or news to break first on Twitter and then on any other source of information. It is commonly observed that TV news channels usually play catchup with Twitter during any news breaks. Such a quick spread of information has its own pros and cons, but a discussion of these are out of the scope of this book.

It would be safe to say that if there's anything trending in the connected world, it will be on Twitter first. From brand promotions, sports events, government decisions, election results to news about terror attacks, natural disasters and the notorious fake celebrity death news, Twitter has it all.

Twitter uses search terms, what are called hashtags in Twitter-verse. Any word which begins with a # is termed as a hashtag and instantly becomes searchable on the platform. This not only helps users search for relevant topics, it also allows different users talking about the same event to tag their tweets for better reach. Hashtags which attract a lot of tweets are usually termed as **trends**. Trends are determined by Twitter's algorithm for the same which may look at various aspects to decide what a trend is.

Twitter has a lot of users generating a lot of content every second. Its algorithms make use of this immense data to come up with worldwide, localized, as well as personalized trends. More details on this are available at: `https://support.twitter.com/articles/101125`

Trends can be used for various different scenarios which can help us understand the dynamics of our society and world in general. Twitter data has been a source of curiosity for researchers across the world. Now let us also dive into this ocean of data to extract some insights of our own.

As mentioned earlier, Twitter helps share and spread information in superfast mode. This makes it a very good tool for spreading information about natural disasters, such as, for example, earthquakes. Earthquakes as we all know are devastating and happen without much of a warning. Every year there are many earthquakes across the planet. Let's see if Twitter can help us track them down.

The first and foremost step is to load the required packages for analysis. We will make use of packages such as `tm`, `ggplot2`, `worldcloud`, `lubridate` and so on apart from the `twitteR` package. Packages such as `tm` provide us with tools for text mining (such as stemming, stop word removal and so on) while `ggplot` and `wordcloud` help us in visualizing the data. You are encouraged to find and learn more about these packages as we go on.

The following snippet loads the required packages and connects to Twitter using our app credentials:

```
library(tm)
library(ggmap)
library(ggplot2)
library(twitteR)
library(stringr)
library(wordcloud)
library(lubridate)
library(data.table)


CONSUMER_SECRET = "XXXXXXXXXXXXXXXXXXXXX"
CONSUMER_KEY = "XXXXXXXXXXXXXXXXXXX"

# connect to twitter app
setup_twitter_oauth(consumer_key = CONSUMER_KEY,
          consumer_secret = CONSUMER_SECRET)
```

Once connected, our next step is to extract relevant tweets using a search term. Since we are trying to track down earthquakes, the search term #earthquake seems good enough. The following snippet makes use of the function `searchTwitter()` from the `twitteR` package itself to help us extract relevant tweets. Remember, Twitter has a rate limit on its APIs, and so we'll limit our search to just `1000` tweets:

```
# extract tweets based on a search term
searchTerm <- "#earthquake"
trendingTweets = searchTwitter(searchTerm,n=1000)
```

As an additional step, readers may choose to combine data extracted using different search terms for more comprehensive analysis of this trend.

The next step is to clean the extracted set of tweets and transform them into a data structure which would be easier for analysis. We begin by first converting the extracted set of tweets to a DataFrame (see *Chapter 1, Getting Started with R and Social Media Analytics* for more details on DataFrames) and then transforming the tweet text and dates to relevant formats. We make use of the package `lubridate` which makes playing with date fields a breeze. The following snippet illustrates the preceding discussion:

```
# perform a quick cleanup/transformation
trendingTweets.df = twListToDF(trendingTweets)

trendingTweets.df$text <- sapply(trendingTweets.df$text,
                function(x) iconv(x,to='UTF-8'))
trendingTweets.df$created <- ymd_hms(trendingTweets.df$created)
```

Once converted to a DataFrame along with a couple of transformations, the `trendingTweets` dataset takes shape of a tabular format with multiple attributes listed as columns and each row depicting one tweet. The following is a sample DataFrame:

	text	favorited	favoriteCount	replyToSN	created	truncated	replyToSID	id
1	#SISMO M 4.5, Fiji Islands Region https://t.co/x52iT6yhD...	FALSE	0	NA	2016-12-06 09:30:17	FALSE	NA	806068233535000576
2	#SISMO M 4.8, Mariana Islands https://t.co/IgVKrZiOh2 ...	FALSE	0	NA	2016-12-06 09:30:16	FALSE	NA	806068228237627392
3	#SISMO M 4.3, Eastern Honshu, Japan https://t.co/6LSul...	FALSE	0	NA	2016-12-06 09:30:14	FALSE	NA	806068222625619968
4	#SISMO M 4.7, Off East Coast of Honshu, Japan https://t...	FALSE	0	NA	2016-12-06 09:30:13	FALSE	NA	806068216447410176
5	#SISMO M 4.7, Mindanao, Philippines https://t.co/iR1AiY...	FALSE	0	NA	2016-12-06 09:30:11	FALSE	NA	806068208956356656
6	â€#USGS #Breakingâ€ #earthquakeâ€€M 1,1 - 4km S of ...	FALSE	0	NA	2016-12-06 09:30:04	FALSE	NA	806068177188720640
7	â€°€€/...â ± [é€±°â€] ⃑â⃑â`—â⃑è¿ æµ· [æ...	FALSE	0	NA	2016-12-06 09:29:53	FALSE	NA	806068134721355776
8	[Epicenter] Kagoshima Tokara Islands Offshore [Max Shin...	FALSE	0	NA	2016-12-06 09:29:34	FALSE	NA	806068052697546752

Trending tweets as a Dataframe

Now that we have the data in the desired format, let us visualize and understand different aspects of this dataset.

With this dataset, we ask a few questions and see what insights can be drawn from the same. The questions with respect to earthquakes could be:

- When was the earthquake reported?
- Where were some of the most recent earthquakes?
- What devices/services were used to report earthquake related tweets?
- Which agencies/accounts are to be trusted?

These are a few straightforward questions which we will try to find answers for. These questions can be used as a starting point of any analysis post which we can proceed to complex questions about correlating events and so on. This is by no means an exhaustive list of questions and is being used for illustrative purposes.

 Twitter is very dynamic in nature and in this chapter we are dealing with actual real-time Twitter data. This may lead to different results for readers depending upon when and what information they extract using the APIs.

To answer the question regarding when an earthquake was reported, let us first plot tweet counts by time and see if we can find something interesting about it.

The following snippet makes use of ggplot2 to plot a histogram of tweet counts with time on x-axis. The bars are color coded, with blue pointing towards low counts and green towards high:

```
# plot on tweets by time
ggplot(data = trendingTweets.df, aes(x = created)) +
  geom_histogram(aes(fill = ..count..)) +
  theme(legend.position = "none") +
  xlab("Time") + ylab("Number of tweets") +
  scale_fill_gradient(low = "midnightblue", high = "aquamarine4")
```

The output plot shows high activity around 3:00 am UTC which slowly tapers off towards 9:00 am. If one tries to narrow down to the time period between 2:00 am and 4:00 am, we can easily identify that maximum tremors were reported from New Zealand (we'll leave this activity for users to explore further):

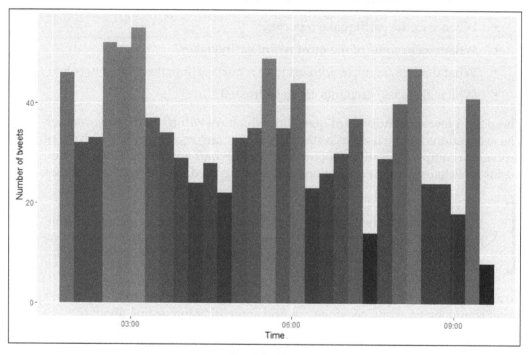

Tweets by time

Let us now try and identify which countries/places have reported most earthquake related tweets. To answer this question we first need to associate each tweet with a corresponding country. Upon inspecting the dataset, we found that there are two attributes which could be helpful, that is, $latitude and $longitude. These attributes should help us narrow it down to exact locations. However, before we use these attributes, we need to ascertain how many tweets have these attributes populated (not all attributes are available for all tweets; see the API documentation).

A quick check using the following snippet reveals that out of 1,000 tweets extracted, about 90% do not have these attributes populated. #OutOfLuck it seems!

```
> sapply(trendingTweets.df, function(x) sum(is.na(x)))
        text      favorited favoriteCount       replyToSN       created     truncated     replyToSID            id
           0              0             0             991             0             0            994             0
   replyToUID    statusSource    screenName    retweetCount     isRetweet     retweeted      longitude      latitude
          991              0             0               0             0             0            926           926
 quakeCountry     tweetSource
            0              0
```

Tweet attributes and their missing counts

Data science is an art, and with art comes creativity. Since the location related attributes did not turn out to be helpful, let us try something else. We analyzed the tweets themselves and found that most of the tweets contain the location of the earthquake in the text itself. For example:

4.9 magnitude #earthquake. 95km WNW of L'Esperance Rock, New Zealand earthquaketrack.com/quakes/2016-12 ...

Sample earthquake tweet

To utilize this information from tweet text itself, we write a simple utility function called `mapCountry()` and apply the same on our dataset using `sapply()` on the `$text` attribute of the dataset. We assign the extracted countries from each of the tweets to a new attribute of the dataset called as `$quakeCountry`. The following snippet assigns values to `$quakeCountry`:

```
# identify earthquake affected countries
trendingTweets.df$quakeCountry <- sapply(trendingTweets.df$text,
                      mapCountry)
```

Our simple utility maps a few countries known to have earthquakes fairly commonly and maps the rest of them as `rest_of_the_world`. We can tweak this function to include more countries or follow an even more sophisticated approach to identify countries using advanced text analytics concepts, but for now let us see what results we have from this mapping itself.

The following snippet again makes use of `ggplot2` to plot tweet counts by country:

```
# plot tweets by counts
ggplot(subset(trendingTweets.df,quakeCountry != 'rest_of_the_world'),
aes(quakeCountry)) +
  geom_bar(fill = "aquamarine4") +
  theme(legend.position="none", axis.title.x = element_blank()) +
  ylab("Number of tweets") +
  ggtitle("Tweets by Country")
```

The output of the preceding snippet is as follows:

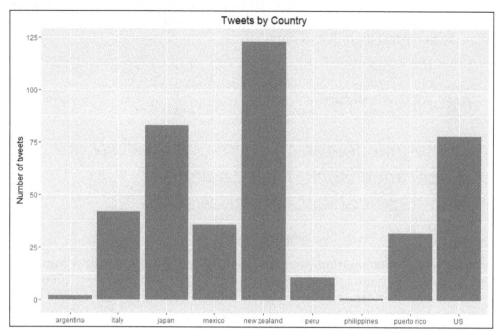

Tweet counts by country

The preceding plot clearly shows that New Zealand had that maximum number of tweets related to earthquakes, followed by Japan and United States. This falls in line with the devastating earthquake which New Zealand faced in November 2016, and there have been a series of tremors ever since. Japan, on the other hand, is a regular on the list of earthquake affected countries.

Note that we have removed the tweets marked as `rest_of_the_world` from this plot for better understanding. We can analyze left out population for improving our utility function along with some more interesting analysis like identifying the most unlikely countries to be affected by earthquakes.

Data analysis and visualization go hand in hand. It is commonly seen that with better visualizations, our understanding of data improves. This can in turn lead to uncovering more insights from the data.

To take a better view of the earthquake and tweet relationship, let us plot the same on a world map. In the following snippet, we make use of `ggplot2` and `ggmap` for plotting the world map and identifying the latitude and longitude of each country respectively. The `geocode` utility from `ggmap` makes use of Google's location APIs from its data science toolkit. The snippet first geocodes the countries and then plots it on the world map as follows:

```
# geocode tweets->map to earthquake locations
quakeAffectedCountries <- subset(trendingTweets.df,
              quakeCountry != 'rest_of_the_world')
              $quakeCountry
unqiueCountries <- unique(sort(quakeAffectedCountries))
geoCodedCountries <- geocode(unqiueCountries)
country.x <- geoCodedCountries$lon
country.y <- geoCodedCountries$lat

mp <- NULL

# create a layer of borders
mapWorld <- borders("world", colour="gray50", fill="gray50")
mp <- ggplot() +   mapWorld

#Now Layer the cities on top
mp <- mp+ geom_point(aes(x=country.x, y=country.y) ,color="orange", si
ze=sqrt(table(sort(quakeAffectedCountries))))
```

A world map with earthquake-related tweets plotted over it looks like (the size of each point corresponds to the number of tweets, that is. the larger the point, the greater the number of tweets):

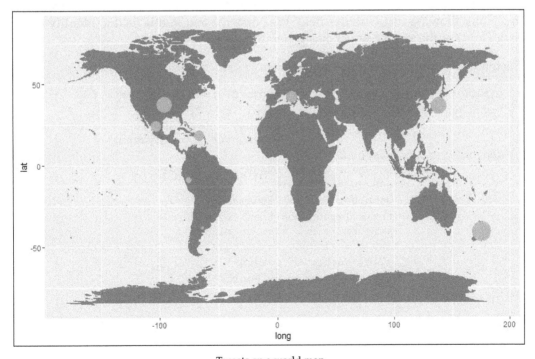

Tweets on a world map

We just saw that, with a few lines of code, we could mark out earthquake affected places on the planet. If we look carefully, the preceding plot roughly marks out the *ring of fire*, that is, the most vulnerable countries along the Pacific Ocean which are most likely to be affected by earthquakes.

As we know, Twitter as a social network is quite different from others like Facebook or Tumblr because it does not enforce the concept of a user being human. A Twitter handle could belong to an organization or a website. With the proliferation of Internet and Internet-enabled services, it has become very easy for organizations to spread information/awareness. There are multiple services on the Internet which link various systems (both online and offline) to send automated alerts/tweets. Similarly, there are multiple earthquake alert generating services, apart from a few like IFTTT and `https://dlvrit.com/`, which enable users to setup personal alerts which can tweet on their behalf.

In such a landscape, it would be interesting to find an answer to the question: *Which sources are generating the tweets in my dataset?* The answer to this question could be in the form of humans versus non-humans/services or by devices. Let us view a combined picture and see which devices and services contribute the most to earthquake related tweets.

We do this by creating another simple utility which makes use of the field `$statusSource`. As we discovered earlier, this field contains data for all tweets we have, thus allowing us to use this field. We parse the text in this field to identify the device and/or the service which has generated the tweet.

The following snippet generates a histogram of source versus tweet count:

```
# plot tweets by source system (android, iphone, web, etc)
trendingTweets.df$tweetSource = sapply(trendingTweets.df
                       $statusSource, function(sourceSystem)
                       enodeSource(sourceSystem))
ggplot(trendingTweets.df[
        trendingTweets.df$tweetSource != 'others',],
            aes(tweetSource)) +
            geom_bar(fill = "aquamarine4") +
            theme(legend.position="none",
            axis.title.x = element_blank(),
        axis.text.x = element_text(angle = 45, hjust = 1)) +
            ylab("Number of tweets") +
            ggtitle("Tweets by Source")
```

The output histogram is as follows:

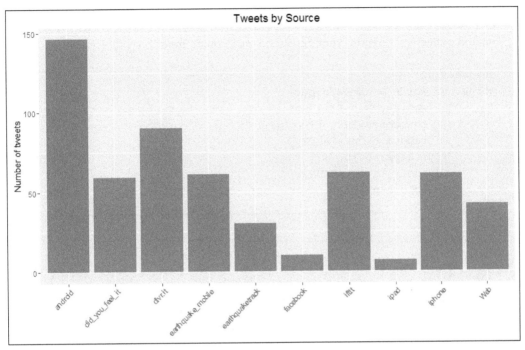

Tweet Counts by services

As expected, there are many services, such as did_you_feel_it, earthquake_mobile, and so on, which generate tweets automatically based on information from different sources. Yet the highest count comes from humans, as shown by the bar denoting Android!

The final question we need to answer before we conclude this use case is that of the Twitter handles behind these tweets. With the Internet in everybody's hands (thanks to smart phones), it is very important to identify the source of information. Twitter is known to be used for spreading both correct and false information. To remove noise from the actual information, let us try and identify the handles which generate these earthquake related tweets. This analysis will not only help us narrow down our dataset but also enable us to verify if the information related to earthquakes is valid or not. A similar analysis can be used in other scenarios with a bit of tweaking.

We will make use of tools from `stringr` and `tm` packages to accomplish this task. We will also use the `wordcloud` package to finally visualize our findings. We encourage readers to dive a little deeper into the `tm` package (we will be using more of it in the coming sections as well as chapters).

The following snippet helps us extract Twitter handles and prepare a `tm` corpus object. This object is then used by the `wordcloud` function to plot one:

```
quakeAccounts <- str_extract_all(trendingTweets.df$text, "@\\w+")
namesCorpus <- Corpus(VectorSource(quakeAccounts))

set.seed(42)
wordcloud(words = namesCorpus,
          scale=c(3,0.5),
          max.words=100,
          random.order=FALSE,
          rot.per=0.10,
          use.r.layout=TRUE,
          colors=pal)
```

Twitter user's wordcloud

The wordcloud shows that maximum tweets are coming from `@quakestoday` followed by `@wikisismos`. Upon inspection of these handles on `https://twitter.com/`, we found these to be reliable sources of information with `@quakestoday` sourcing its data from **US Geological Survey (USGS)** itself. `#connectedWorld`!

As we saw, it is simple to utilize Twitter and its APIs to find answers to some really interesting issues which affect us as humans. By following a proper analytics workflow along with a few questions to start with, we can go a long way.

Sentiment analysis

Twitter timelines are the new battlegrounds for brands, fans and organizations to fight it out and present a winner. Twitter is also a place where users usually rant about their disappointments or share their happiness. The dynamics of human interaction and our urge to share opinionated views on wide ranging topics, from cat pictures to wars and everything in between, have reached an altogether different level.

With its 300 million plus users and counting, Twitter is a virtual country in itself! Its huge user base which generates tweets (or opinions) by the count of millions every minute present a unique opportunity to study and utilize human sentiment and/or opinions. This study of our sentiments and emotion carries a lot more value than just pure academic research (which is, of course, still required by any standards). It carries a lot of business value for companies, governments and celebrities alike.

Before we dive into implementation details and a particular use case, let us first have a quick introduction to sentiment analysis. Since sentiment analysis is a complete research area on its own, we will be briefly touching upon the key concepts only. Detailed discussion on the topic is beyond the scope of this book.

Key concepts of sentiment analysis

The following are the key concepts/terms in context of sentiment analysis.

Subjectivity

The dictionary meaning of the word opinion is a *view or a judgement formed about something, not necessarily based on facts*. In simpler words, an opinion is a reflection of our beliefs irrespective of what the facts are. Therefore, subjectivity is an expression of our sentiments/opinions about things, people and so on. Subjectivity is the reason why some people like a particular product while others do not.

Subjectivity or subjective texts are a core concept behind sentiment analysis. Subjective texts are of importance to the field of sentiment analysis for the reasons stated preceding. Subjective sentences/texts of the form *I love reading books* express positive sentiment as opposed to objective sentences like *Twitter is a social network* which simply states a fact.

Sentiment analysis is broadly an analysis of subjective texts to understand the overall emotions expressed.

Sentiment polarity

For analytical purposes we usually assign a score or a label to the entity of interest. In the case of sentiment analysis, we usually assign a score to each of our subjective texts or words on a continuous or discrete scale (say between -5 and +5) to mark the degree of sentiment. Usually, negative scores denote negative sentiments with extreme negative values denoting very negative sentiments, and the opposite for the positive side of the scale. A score of 0 denotes neutral sentiment. Sentiment polarity may also work based on class labels like *liked* versus *disliked* (say a movie review system). The use of polarity scores or labels depends on the use case at hand usually.

Opinion summarization

Once a sentiment score/label is assigned to each of the texts in the corpus, the next step is usually summarization of opinions for deriving insights. It is important to aggregate and summarize the overall sentiments to draw conclusions and insights on the topic of interest, say if we are trying to determine if a movie was well received by the audience or not. Summarization is usually coupled with visualization for better understanding of data.

Features

In the analytics space, particularly machine learning and/or text analytics, a feature is one of the central entities upon which an algorithm works. A feature is simply a measureable entity being observed for the current problem at hand.

For example, while performing stock price prediction measures, like the current stock price, time, rate of change of stock price, and so on, are features utilized by different algorithms for generating outputs.

In most use cases, it is common to start with a basic set of features, analyze them and then gradually move towards feature generation and feature extraction/selection. While feature generation is a process of deriving new or additional features from data and existing feature set, feature extraction/selection in general refers to the process of fine tuning and/or reducing the feature set to the best possible subset which can describe a dataset.

The following are a few features commonly utilized in the context of text analytics:

- **Term Frequency – Inverse Document Frequency (TF-IDF)**: It has its roots in information retrieval. In the context of TF-IDF, a piece of text is broken (tokenized) into its constituents in the form of a vector. It is a numerical measure of how important a word/term is to a document in context to the whole corpus (set of documents).

- **Parts of Speech (POS)**: Text is generated using the rules of the grammar of a particular language. Analysis of textual data from a **Natural Language Processing (NLP)** point of view makes use of the underlying language semantics (structure and rules of the language). **Parts of Speech (POS)** analysis tries to map each word/token to different parts of speech like verbs, adjectives, nouns and so on. The following is a sample breakdown of a sentence into its parts of speech. The POS labels are assigned using `nltk` library (see `http://www.nltk.org`)

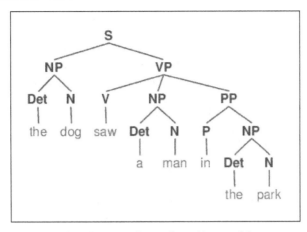

Sample PoS tagging Source: http://www.nltk.org

- **N-grams**: In computational linguistics, text is a continuous sequence of terms. In context of n-grams, the likelihood of the next token (character, word, and so on) depends upon n previous terms. For different values of n, a feature vector may be termed as unigram (n=1), bigram (n=2) and so on.

 Checkout analysis using N-grams from Google: `https://research.googleblog.com/2006/08/all-our-n-gram-are-belong-to-you.html`

The previous mentioned list of features are just the tip of the iceberg. As data scientists, we need to get creative and derive features based on the dataset at hand, given we have explored the standard plethora of existing features.

 Even though languages across the world follow rules of grammar, it is still a difficult task to understand this process of generating content. Though research into the field has made big leaps, concepts like sarcasm still confuse our algorithms. Some recent interesting papers on the topic: `http://cs229.stanford.edu/proj2015/044_report.pdf`, `https://www.aclweb.org/anthology/W/W10/W10-2914.pdf`

Sentiment analysis in R

Now that we have a sound understanding of sentiment analysis and its key concepts, let us get our hands dirty with an actual use case.

Twitter is a recent favorite amongst celebrities, politicians and leaders to get in touch with their respective audience. Making the best possible use of its follower relationship graph, Twitter enables them to get in touch and stay updated. Our next use case revolves around such Twitter handles itself. With this use case we intend to understand the personality behind one such Twitter handle and analyze:

- What kind of tweets they tweet? Basically, the sentiment behind their tweets

- What are the major topics they tweet about?

- Can we identify certain themes from their tweets?

For this use case, let us tap into the timeline of the most powerful and watched man on the planet, The President of United States of America. The official Twitter handle for **POTUS** (acronym for **President of the United States**) is @POTUS.

We will follow the usual analytical workflow again and try to answer the aforementioned questions regarding tweets from @POTUS.

We assume the required libraries such as twitteR, ggplot2, tm and so on are loaded and we have an active connection to our Twitter app using R. For this particular use case, we will load one additional package called the syuzhet.

syuzhet is an R package specially designed for sentiment analysis. It is based on the concepts of fabula (chronological order of narratives) and syuzhet (technique of the narrative). This package also packs in research and collaborative lexicons from other researchers as well. More details on this can be found at: https://github.com/mjockers/syuzhet

In the following snippet we connect to Twitter and extract 1500 tweets for the handle @POTUS. We have written a simple utility called extractTimelineTweets(), which extracts tweets, converts the text to UTF-8 format and returns as DataFrame:

```
# connect to twitter app
setup_twitter_oauth(consumer_key = CONSUMER_KEY,
                    consumer_secret = CONSUMER_SECRET)

tweetsDF <- extractTimelineTweets("POTUS",1500)
```

First let us begin with the topics Mr. President is talking about. A word cloud is usually a quick way to visualize such an analysis. Before we build one, we need to perform some text processing to clean up and transform the tweets. In our previous use case we were mostly concerned about handles generating the tweet for building the word cloud. In this case we are interested in the actual tweet text and hence the additional care.

We'll make use of the package tm's tools like `Corpus` and `VectorSource` to vectorize our tweets corpus and then use `tm_map` to apply transformations like `stopword` removal (a list of words like a, an, the and so on, which occur frequently in text but do not carry much factual information), whitespace removal and so on.

The following snippet prepares our data to be used for `wordcloud` generation:

```
nohandles <- str_replace_all(tweetsDF$text, "@\\w+", "")
wordCorpus <- Corpus(VectorSource(nohandles))
wordCorpus <- tm_map(wordCorpus, removePunctuation)
wordCorpus <- tm_map(wordCorpus, content_transformer(tolower))
wordCorpus <- tm_map(wordCorpus, removeWords, stopwords("english"))
wordCorpus <- tm_map(wordCorpus, removeWords, c("amp"))
wordCorpus <- tm_map(wordCorpus, stripWhitespace)

# prepare wordcloud
wordcloud(words = wordCorpus,
          scale=c(5,0.1),
          max.words=1000,
          random.order=FALSE,
          rot.per=0.35,
          use.r.layout=FALSE,
          colors=pal)
```

The following `wordcloud` marks out the common topics which interest the @POTUS, for example climate, world, health, women, gun, congress and so on. Of course, the word American comes out as the most used word in the center of the `wordcloud` as shown in the following figure:

Tweet text wordcloud from @POTUS

Next, let us now try to understand the sentiments expressed by this user. World leaders play an important role in the dynamics of the world and understanding their sentiments can help us understand them better.

In this case, we will perform sentiment analysis using polarity analysis. Polarity analysis is the process of scoring and aggregating sentiment of the corpus for deriving insights. Such an analysis utilizes a pre-compiled list of words which denotes positive, negative and neutral sentiments. We then parse each tweet/document against this list of polar words and assign a sentiment score based on a certain agreed upon equation.

For example, a simple way of assigning a score to each tweet could be:

Sentiment Score = Sum (positive words) – Sum (negative words)

We can build a sophisticated formula/equation based on our requirement and use case. For example, we may try to include neutral words as well, or we may normalize the whole score to get the final value in a pre-defined range.

We will make use of the `syuzhet` package to score our tweets. The function `get_sentiment()` works upon a corpus of text and returns a vector of scores for each text. The scores are on a real scale with negative values referring to negative polarity and vice-versa.

The following snippet performs sentiment scoring and then plots these scores on a histogram for better understanding:

```
tweetSentiments <- get_sentiment (tweetsDF$text,method = "syuzhet")
tweets <- cbind(tweetsDF, tweetSentiments)
tweets$sentiment <- sapply(tweets$tweetSentiments,encodeSentiment)

qplot(tweets$tweetSentiments) +
      theme(legend.position="none")+
      xlab("Sentiment Score") +
      ylab("Number of tweets") +
      ggtitle("Tweets by Sentiment Score")
```

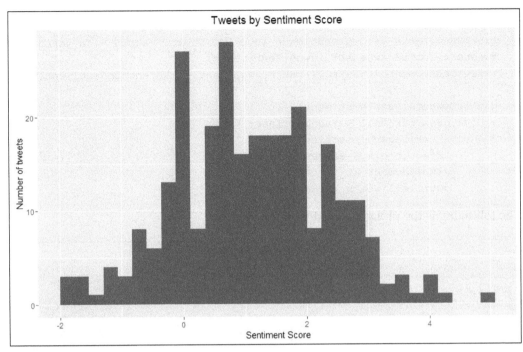

Polarity analysis of tweets from @POTUS

The plot is slightly skewed towards the right of 0, thus showing that most of the tweets are positive, but there are some tweets with negative sentiments. Users may subset and explore the occasions when @POTUS wasn't all that cheery.

Readers can perform a similar polarity analysis by writing a simple utility function of their own and checking tweets against a self-generated list of polar words and then comparing the results we got from the `syuzhet` package.

To start with, a list of polar words can be obtained from: `https://www.cs.uic.edu/~liub/FBS/sentiment-analysis.html`

It can be a little difficult to gauge different sentiment aspects from the previous plot. We can view the same from a different perspective by binning sentiments into categories such as positive, very positive, negative, very negative, and neutral. These categories could be based on a range of polarity scores, say from 0 to 0.5 could be marked positive and greater than 0.5 as very positive and similarly for negative polarity.

Let us see which class most sentiments belong to:

```
tweetSentiments <- get_sentiment (tweetsDF$text, method = "syuzhet")
tweets <- cbind(tweetsDF, tweetSentiments)
tweets$sentiment <- sapply(tweets$tweetSentiments,encodeSentiment)

ggplot(tweets, aes(sentiment)) +
        geom_bar(fill = "aquamarine4") +
        theme(legend.position="none",
        axis.title.x = element_blank()) +
        ylab("Number of tweets") +
        ggtitle("Tweets by Sentiment")
```

The following is the plot generated by using `ggplot`:

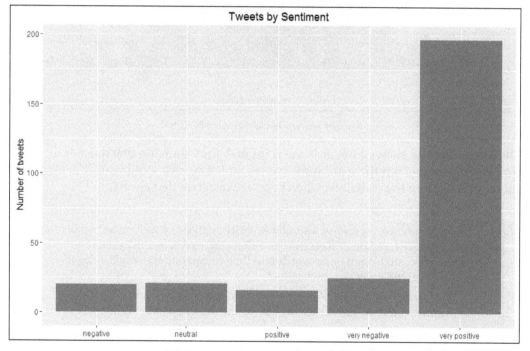

Polarity categories of tweets from @POTUS

The preceding plot shows that a very high percentage of tweets come under the very positive category while the other categories are all comparatively low. #phew!

Not just positive, negative, and neutral sentiments

As humans we express far more emotions than just positive, negative and neutral: we express anger, joy, fear, surprise, and so on. Significant research into the field of sentiment analysis has made it possible to generate lexicons and corpora which can help us better label sentiments. One such research by *Dr. Saif Mohammad* and *Peter Turney* is also exposed through the same `syuzhet` package. Readers are encouraged to explore this further. The previous polarity analysis using NRC lexicon (`http://saifmohammad.com/WebPages/NRC-Emotion-Lexicon.htm`) generates the following output: #amazing!

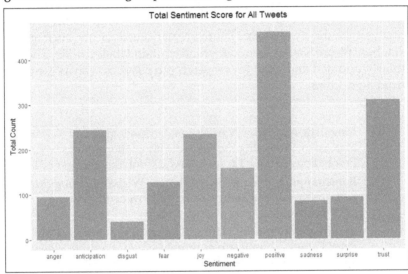

As discussed, polarity analysis utilizes a dictionary or list of polar words which are then used to score the text in our corpora. Yet, this is not the only way to perform sentiment analysis. If we look carefully, in the process of sentiment analysis we are basically trying to classify our tweets (or text in general) into positive, negative and neutral classes. In formal terms, this is what we term as a classical classification problem.

In machine learning, classification is a supervised learning problem. In this, we learn about the class labels from a training set which is usually labeled/scored manually or through some measurements.

For example, in the case of sentiment analysis, the training set will constitute a list of documents which would be manually labeled by a team as positive, negative or neutral based on certain pre-agreed rules. Once we have a labeled training set, an algorithm such as **Support Vector Machines (SVM)** would learn based on the training dataset and then utilize this information to assign labels to our new tweets or unlabeled documents. Such a process requires human supervision and is time-consuming. Yet it has the benefit of learning the underlying process of assigning sentiments to a certain document, which is generally not possible with the polarity based analysis we did previously. There are various datasets, such as **WordNet, SentiNet, SentiWordNet**, and so, on which contain labeled texts. These datasets are regularly updated and used for research purposes as well as for training supervised algorithms.

Linguistic heuristics: Vasileios Hatzivassiloglou and Kathleen McKeown. Predicting the semantic orientation of adjectives. In Proceedings of the Joint ACL/EACL Conference, pages 174–181, 1997.

Bootstrapping: Ellen Riloff and Janyce Wiebe. Learning extraction patterns for subjective expressions. In Proceedings of the Conference on

Empirical Methods in Natural Language Processing (EMNLP), 2003: Peter Turney. Thumbs up or thumbs down? Semantic orientation applied to unsupervised classification of reviews. In Proceedings of the Association for Computational Linguistics (ACL), pages 417–424, 2002.

Before we finish this use case, let us also touch upon an unsupervised approach for analysis of textual data or tweets in this case. Using a word cloud, we have already identified the various topics @POTUS tweets about. Let us now try and see if we can derive some common themes out of these tweets.

Hierarchical clustering is one such unsupervised learning algorithm widely used to generate hierarchical grouping of textual information. Like any clustering algorithm, hierarchical clustering helps us group similar entities together for better analysis. Hierarchical clustering can be understood in the form of the following three steps:

1. **Initialization**: This is the first step. For a corpus of n elements, each one is assigned to a unique cluster of its own, that is, for a dataset of n elements, this step generates n different clusters.

2. **Merge**: In this step, based on a pre-determined distance metric, the closest clusters are identified and merged into a single cluster. This step reduces the total number of clusters available as compared to the number before this step was executed.

3. **Compute**: After each step, the distance/similarity measures are calculated/recalculated for each of the existing clusters.

The merge and compute steps are repeated until we obtain a single cluster containing all the elements of the dataset. As the name suggests, the output of this algorithm is a hierarchical structure which is similar to an inverted tree, also called a dendrogram. The root of the tree represents the most general theme and it goes granular as we go deeper into the tree.

Let us now apply the algorithm on our dataset and analyze the results. We will begin by creating a Term-Document Matrix from our tweets DataFrame using the `tm` package. We then compute a distance matrix using the `dist()` function. For this use case, we utilize the Euclidian distance (readers may experiment with other measures as well). Once computed, we use the `hclust()` function to perform the hierarchical clustering and generate a dendrogram for our dataset.

A Term-Document Matrix is simply a data structure in which all the words (terms in general) of our dataset represent the rows while the documents are represented as columns. If a term exists in a particular document, that row-column intersection is marked as 1 (0 otherwise). The Term-Document Matrix may also utilize frequency of a term instead of 0-1 encoding depending upon the use case.

The following snippet illustrates this point:

```
# computer term-document matrix
twtrTermDocMatrix <- TermDocumentMatrix(wordCorpus)

twtrTermDocMatrix2 <- removeSparseTerms(twtrTermDocMatrix,
                                        sparse = 0.97)


tweet_matrix <- as.matrix(twtrTermDocMatrix2)

# prepare distance matrix
distMatrix <- dist(scale(tweet_matrix))
# perform hierarchical clustering
fit <- hclust(distMatrix,method="single")
# plot the dendrogram
plot(fit)
```

The output of this process clearly groups similar terms and can help us derive insights from such tweets by analyzing the grouped tweets together rather than in isolation:

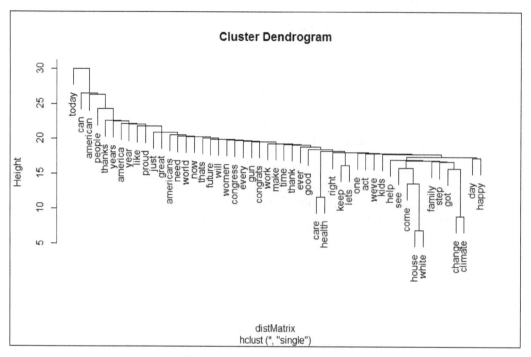

Cluster dendrogram of tweet corpus

With the help of this use case, we used real data from Twitter to analyze sentiments portrayed by tweeple (@POTUS in particular). We touched upon concepts of sentiment analysis and utilized powerful R packages like `tm`, `stringr` and `syuzhet` for the task at hand. Visualizations helped us better understand our data along with the ability to better express our results and insights. Sentiment analysis is utilized under various scenarios, and, most prominently, by brands and organizations. Techniques like sentiment analysis assist marketers to judge their audience/ customer perception/ feedback of a product and update their strategies accordingly. These, along with many more scenarios, showcase how important a technique like sentiment analysis could be in this data driven world!

Follower graph analysis

So far, we have analyzed Twitter and tweets to uncover some interesting insights using techniques and concepts of trend analysis and sentiment analysis. We've utilized different attributes of tweets, like creation time, location and even the text itself, to answer certain questions. In this section, we will touch upon Twitter's network aspects. #BraceYourSelves

A social network is a network or a graph at its core. In formal words, a social network is generally a graph representing its users as nodes (or vertices) linked to each other based on certain relationships called edges. Each social network has its own definition of these relationships. For this section, we will focus on Twitter's relationships and network in general.

In Twitter-verse as we all know, there are no friends! A *friend* relationship is usually a bidirectional relationship, that is, if A is a friend of B, then it is safe to say that B is also a friend of A (well, usually; see Facebook friends). Twitter has tweaked this concept of friendship and allows its users to form unidirectional relationships or follower relationships. On this platform, a user may choose to follow any number of users, based upon their interests. The person being followed though has no such obligation to return the favor, that is, if A is following B, then it is not necessary for B to follow A.

 B may block A from following him/her but we can skip such details for this discussion.

At first this sounds a bit awkward but it is rather an interesting and a very human concept. In our social setting we come across many people about whom we are interested, say celebrities or leaders. In general, we are curious and intrigued by such personalities and love to know more about them. The follower relationship model allows Twitter users to follow such personalities (aka handles) without the personality following the user back. Nothing stops people being followed to follow back, but imagine a Twitter where @KatyPerry would have to follow back all of her 94 million followers!

 Please note that the follower relationships work in general, but we chose to explain it using celebrities for ease of understanding.

Very much like other things associated with Twitter (like sentiments, trends, velocity and so on), these follower relationships have also intrigued researchers. As part of this section, let us touch upon the concept of follower graphs and see what magic unfolds.

> Though follower graphs are basically graphs themselves, in this section we will only use the very basic concepts related to graphs such as vertices, edges, weights and so on. We will provide brief details wherever necessary. Readers are encouraged to read more about graph theory and try to apply those concepts to Twitter data for some advanced analysis.

We use a social network like Twitter to share information about a number of topics and we all want our story to reach as many people as possible. With Twitter, it's the follower count that's most coveted. Popular accounts, such as those of Katy Perry, Barak Obama, Mars Rover and so on, have millions of followers. With this use case let us plot and analyze a given user's follower graph.

> For illustration purposes, we are utilizing one of our own Twitter handles and have renamed our followers for privacy concerns. Also, please note that Twitter rate limits the use of its APIs, hence build your follower graph with care and don't get blocked. #playSafe.

To begin with this use case, let us perform our ritual initialization steps of loading required packages and connecting to Twitter using the `twitteR` package. We use the `getUser()` function to extract a given user's details and then use the function `getFollowers()` to extract handles of his/her followers. The following snippet does the same:

```
setup_twitter_oauth(consumer_key = CONSUMER_KEY,
                    consumer_secret = CONSUMER_SECRET)

# Begin with a certain username
coreUserName <- "jack"
twitterUser <- getUser(coreUserName)

# Extract Followers for the core user
twitterUser_follower_IDs <- twitterUser$getFollowers(
                              retryOnRateLimit=10)
# Typecast as a dataframe
twitterUser_followers_df = rbindlist(
                lapply(
twitterUser_follower_IDs,
                    as.data.frame
                        ))
```

Once we have this data, we can proceed towards building a graph. But what fun would it be to have just you at the center of this graph and your followers listed out visually. We make this interesting by going one level deeper, that is, for each of our followers, we extract their list of followers as well.

For building a graph or network, R has another powerful package called igraph. The igraph package provides multiple ways of generating a graph. We prepare a data frame with two columns, that is, from and to. Each row of the data frame represent an edge from one user to another.

In the following snippet, we first filter our followers DataFrame(filtered_df) by removing dead and dummy accounts (you may choose to follow some other criteria or not do any clean-up at all). Then we iterate over each of our given user's followers, extract their followers and append that list to our DataFrame representing the edges:

```
# extract @ twitter handles of followers of given user
filtered_follower_IDs <- filtered_df$screenName

# prepare initial edge data frame
edge_df<-data.frame(from=filtered_follower_IDs,
                    to=rep('rghv_bali',
                           length(filtered_follower_IDs)),
                    stringsAsFactors=FALSE)


# Iterate and extract list of followers of followers

counter = 1
for(follower in filtered_follower_IDs){
  # fetch follower list for current user
  followerScreenNameList <- get_follower_list(follower)

  print(paste("Processing completed for:",
          follower,
          "(",counter,"/",
          length(filtered_follower_IDs),")"
          ))
  # append to edge list
  edge_df <- append_to_df(edge_df,
                    list(from=followerScreenNameList,
                  to=rep(follower,
                        length(followerScreenNameList)))))
    counter <- counter + 1
}
```

The edge data frame generated using the preceding snippet has each row representing a follower relationship as follows:

	from	to
1	user_2	core_user
2	user_4	core_user
3	user_6	core_user
4	user_12	core_user
5	user_10	core_user
6	user_9	core_user
7	user_13	core_user
8	user_1	core_user
9	user_7	core_user
10	user_14	core_user

Follower/Edge DataFrame

Now that we have our edge data frame ready, we'll prepare an `igraph` data frame object based on this. After that, we utilize a couple of `igraph` utility methods to remove loops and multiple edges (if any) using `simplify()` and make some aesthetic changes to node sizes for clearly marking out our core user. Check out the following snippet:

```
# prepare network object
net <- graph.data.frame(edge_df2, directed=T)

# simplify network
net <- simplify(net, remove.multiple = F, remove.loops = T)

# adjust the size of nodes based on in and out degrees
deg <- degree(net, mode="all")
V(net)$size <- deg*0.05 + 1
V(net)[name == "core_user"]$size <- 15

# node coloring
pal3 <- brewer.pal(10, "Set3")

# overall follower graph
plot(net,
     edge.arrow.size=0.01,
```

```
vertex.label = ifelse(V(net)$size >= 15,
V(net)$name, NA),
vertex.color = pal3)
```

The preceding snippet generates the following follower graph:

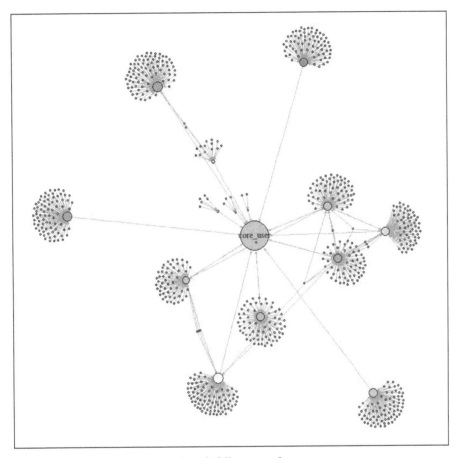

Sample follower graph

If we analyze the preceding graph carefully, we can see that there are quite a few users/nodes who have edges (that is, follower relationships) amongst themselves! Also, the size of each of the nodes (barring the core user's) is a representation of its follower count. To be precise, we adjusted node sizes to account for the number of incoming and outgoing connections (the in-degree and out-degree of each node). This helps us identify which of our followers are more popular than others.

Even though Twitter uses follower-based relationships, it doesn't stop users from following back. A follower who follows back sounds much like a friend relationship. It would be interesting to identify who our `core_user` follows back. For a real use case, it might be interesting to identify, for instance, which world leaders follows back who, and derive political insights of sorts from it.

Our graphing package, `igraph`'s utilities simply make our lives easy. It exposes a set of iterators for both edges and vertices along with a utility function called `ends()`. This function helps us identify whom does the `core_user` follow back from his list of followers!

In a very basic sense, an iterator is an object which helps us traverse a container, for instance a list. Iterators are not unique to R and are available in most modern programming languages. igraph also provides iterators for vertices and edges for ease of traversal, extraction, updation and so on.

The following snippet achieves the task of identifying friend nodes:

```
# identify friend vertices
friendVertices <- ends(net, es=E(net)[from('core_user')])[,2]
```

Now that we have our list of friend vertices, let us make some visual changes to our follower network visualization to clearly identify the friends amongst followers. The following snippet marks edges amongst friend nodes as red and enable vertex labels for the same:

```
# Generate edge color variable:
ecol <- rep("grey80", ecount(net))
ecol[which (V(net)$name %in% friendVertices)] <- 'red'

# Generate node color variable:
vcol <- rep("gray80", vcount(net))
vcol[which (V(net)$name %in% friendVertices)] <- "gold"

plot(net,
      vertex.color=vcol,
      edge.color=ecol,
      edge.width=ew,
      edge.arrow.mode=0,
      vertex.label = ifelse(V(net)$name %in% friendVertices,
             V(net)$name, NA),
    vertex.label.color="black",
     vertex.label.font=2,
     edge.curved=0.1
     )
```

The output plot shows the #friendsAmongstFollowers:

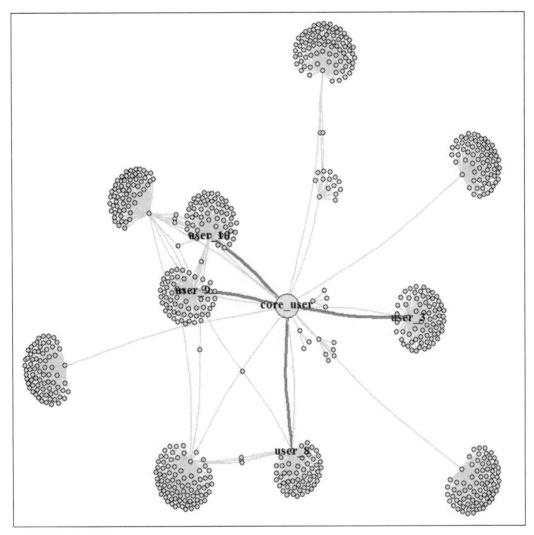

Friends in follower graph

The preceding follower graph analysis helps us understand a social network like Twitter from a network perspective. It also shows how different questions could be answered with such analysis and as always, R and its packages help us quickly get to the answers once we have an approach in our minds.

Please note that the preceding graph might look slightly different than the one we generated initially. This is due to the fact that `igraph` is generating a random layout at every execution. Readers may read more about `igraph` here: `http://igraph.org/r/doc/`

Challenges

Chapter 1, Getting Started with R and Social Media Analytics introduced certain challenges related to the analysis of social networks and their data. The challenges mentioned were related to the volume and velocity of data (big data), accessibility and data quality.

In this chapter, though we faced challenges already discussed in the previous chapter, there are a couple of points we should keep in mind:

- **Accessibility**: Twitter is an ever growing social network which supports millions of users and thousands of third party integrations. The rate limits and other governance criteria have become stringent over the years. Readers are requested to keep the rules of the game in mind and not try to exploit the APIs.

- **Privacy**: Though social networks provide users with privacy controls, scope for improvement remains. APIs keep policy rules enforced, yet as we perform analysis of real data, we should keep in mind the results we publish and insights we share.

- **API changes**: Twitter has a robust set of APIs which allows us to tap into Twitter-verse. Correspondingly R's `twitteR` package helps us connect and use these APIs seamlessly. However, over the years these APIs will be changed and it may be that packages are not able to keep up the pace. In such scenarios, we need to keep a check and update our code base as and when required.

- **Data**: Tweets have evolved from simply 140 characters to containers of rich media comprised of hyperlinks, images, emoticons, videos, and so on. In this chapter we analyzed textual, temporal and location-based attributes of tweets. Analysis of other contents would require more creativity and deeper understanding.

These were some of the challenges we faced and will face when dealing with Twitter (or any other social network) analysis. Even though each of the use cases we solved in this chapter followed a similar workflow, each required a different set of clean-up and transformation steps to extract insights and to answer questions. Twitter analysis is full of challenges, but they are often worth the results we get from such exercises.

Summary

A tweet is far more than just 140 characters, and Twitter offers quite a lot to play with for a social network. We covered a lot of ground in this chapter by looking at many concepts and solving use cases based on real Twitter data. We learned about different Twitter objects and its APIs. We created an app of our own and utilized R's `twitteR` package to connect and tap into its APIs. We performed trend analysis to understand how a hashtag is used by tweeple and its temporal affects. We also solved a use case involving sentiment analysis. Through this use case, we first understood the key concepts related to sentiment analysis and then employed them to understand what emotions `@POTUS` conveys through his tweets. We also performed hierarchical clustering of tweets to visualize common themes using a dendrogram. The final use case analyzed Twitter from a network/graph analysis stand point. We utilized R's different libraries to prepare a network map of followers and perform analysis over it. We closed the chapter by reiterating the challenges related to social media analysis in general and Twitter in particular. With this chapter, we have set the tone and pace for the upcoming ones.

The next set of chapters will be building upon these concepts and workflows and will help us analyze other interesting social networks! `#LetTheGamesBegin`!

3
Analyzing Social Networks and Brand Engagements with Facebook

In the last chapter, we got a flavor of the various aspects related to the most popular social micro-blogging platform, Twitter. In this chapter, we will look more closely at the most popular social networking platform, Facebook. With more than 1.8 billion monthly active users, over $18 billion annual revenue, and record breaking acquisitions for popular products including Oculus, WhatsApp and Instagram, Facebook is the core of the social media network today.

Before we put Facebook data under the microscope, let us briefly look at Facebook's origins. Like many popular products, businesses and organizations, Facebook had humble beginnings. In 2004, Mark Zuckerberg's brainchild was initially known as *Thefacebook* located at thefacebook.com, which was branded as an online social network, connecting university and college students. While this social network was initially only open to Harvard students, within a month it had expanded to include students from other popular universities. In 2005, the domain facebook.com was finally purchased and Facebook extended its membership to employees of companies and organizations. In 2006, Facebook was finally opened to everyone over 13 years of age with a valid email address.

The following snapshot shows us how the look and feel of the Facebook platform has evolved over the years:

Facebook's evolving look over time

While Facebook has a primary website, also known as a web application, it has also launched mobile applications for the major operating systems on handheld devices. In short, Facebook is not just a social network website but an entire platform including a huge social network of connected people and organizations through friends, followers and pages.

We will leverage Facebook's social *Graph API* to access actual Facebook data to perform various analyzes. Users, brands, businesses, news channels, media houses, retail stores and many more are using Facebook actively on a daily basis for producing and consuming content. This generates vast amounts of data, and a substantial amount of this is available to users through its APIs. From a social media analytics perspective, this is really exciting because this treasure trove of data, with easy to access APIs and powerful open source libraries from R, gives us enormous potential and opportunities to get valuable information from analyzing it in various ways.

We will follow a structured path in this chapter and cover the following major topics sequentially to ensure that you do not get overwhelmed with too much content at once:

- Accessing Facebook data
- Analyzing your personal social network
- Analyzing an English football social network
- Analyzing brand page engagements of some English football clubs

We will use libraries like `Rfacebook`, `igraph` and `ggplot2` to retrieve, analyze and visualize data from Facebook. The rest of this book assumes that you have a Facebook account which is necessary to access data from the APIs and analyze it. If you do not have an account, do not despair. You can use the data and code files from this chapter to follow along with hands-on examples to gain a better understanding of the concepts of social network and engagement analysis.

Accessing Facebook data

You will find a lot of content in several books and on the web about various techniques to access and retrieve data from Facebook. There are several official ways of doing this, which include using the Facebook Graph API either directly through low level `HTTP` based calls or indirectly through higher level abstract interfaces belonging to libraries like `Rfacebook`.

 Some alternative ways of retrieving Facebook data would be to use registered applications on Facebook like *Netvizz* or the *GetNet* applications built by Lada Adamic, used in her very popular *Social Network Analysis* course. (Unfortunately `http://snacourse.com/getnet` has not worked since Facebook completely changed its API access permissions and privacy settings).

Unofficial ways include techniques like web scraping and crawling to extract data. Do note though that Facebook considers this to be a violation of its terms and conditions of accessing data and you should try and avoid crawling Facebook for data, especially if you plan to use it for commercial purposes. In this section, we will take a closer look at the Graph API and the `Rfacebook` package in R. The main focus will be on how you can extract data from Facebook using both of them.

Understanding the Graph API

To start using the Graph API, you would need to have an account on Facebook to be able to use the API. You can access the API in various ways. You can create an application on Facebook by going to `https://developers.facebook.com/apps/` and then create a long-lived OAuth access token using the `fbOAuth(...)` function from the `Rfacebook` package. This enables R to make calls to the Graph API and you can also store this token on the disk and load it for future use. An easier way is to create a short-lived token which would let you access the API data for about two hours by going to the Facebook Graph API Explorer page, which is available at `https://developers.facebook.com/tools/explorer`, and getting a temporary access token there.

The following snapshot shows how to get an access token for the Graph API from Facebook:

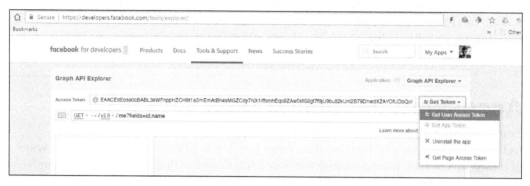

Facebook's Graph API explorer

On clicking **Get User Access Token** in the preceding snapshot, it will present a list of checkboxes with various permissions which you might need for accessing data including user data permissions, events, groups, pages, and other miscellaneous permissions. You can select the ones you need and click on the **Get User Access Token** button in the prompt. This will generate a new access token and you can directly copy and use it to retrieve data in R. Before going into that, we will take a closer look at the Graph API explorer. This allows you to access the API directly from your web browser and is helpful if you want to do some quick exploratory analysis. A part of it is shown in the previous snapshot. The current version of the API at the time of writing this book is v2.8, which you can see in the snapshot beside the GET resource call. Interestingly, the Graph API is so named because Facebook itself can be considered as a huge social graph where all the information can be classified into three categories:

- **Nodes**: These are basically users, pages, photos and so on. Nodes indicate a focal point of interest which is connected to other points.
- **Edges**: These connect various nodes together forming the core social graph and these connections are based on various relations like friends, followers and so on.
- **Fields**: These are specific attributes or properties about nodes; an example would be a user's address, birthday, name and so on.

As we mentioned before, the API is HTTP based and you can make HTTPGET requests to nodes or edges and all requests for data are passed to graph.facebook.com. Each node usually has a specific identifier and you can use it for querying information about a node as depicted in the following snippet:

```
GET graph.facebook.com
   /{node-id}
```

You can also use edge names in addition to the identifier to get information about the edges of the node. The following snippet depicts how you can do the same:

```
GET graph.facebook.com
    /{node-id}/{edge-name}
```

The following snapshot shows us how we can get information about our own profile:

Querying your details in the Graph API explorer

Now, suppose I wanted to retrieve information about a Facebook page, *Premier League* which represents the top tier competition in English Football, using its identifier, and also take a look at its liked pages. I can do the same using the following request:

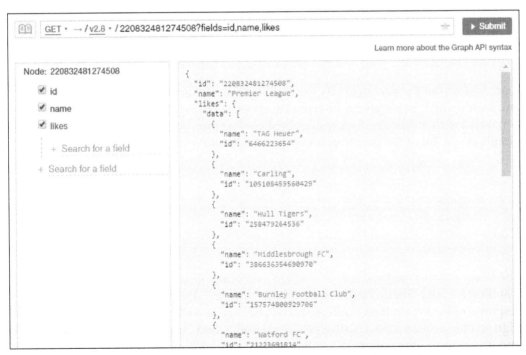

Querying information about a Facebook page using the Graph API explorer

You can clearly see the node identifier, page name and likes for the page, *Premier League*. It must be clear by now that all API responses are returned in the very popular JSON format which is easy to parse and format as needed for analysis. Besides this, there also used to be another way of querying the social graph in Facebook, which was known as FQL or Facebook Query Language, a SQL-like interface for querying and retrieving data. Unfortunately, Facebook seems to have deprecated its use so covering it now is out of our scope. Now that you have a firm grasp of the syntax of the Graph API and have also seen a few examples of how to retrieve data from Facebook, we will take a closer look at the Rfacebook package.

Understanding Rfacebook

Since we will be accessing and analyzing data from Facebook using R, it makes sense to have some robust mechanism to directly query Facebook and retrieve data instead of going to the browser every time as we did in the earlier section. Fortunately, there is an excellent package in R called Rfacebook which has been developed by Pablo Barberá. You can either install it from CRAN or get the most up-to-date version from GitHub. The following snippet demonstrates how you can do this. Remember, you might need to install the devtools package, if you don't have it already, to download and install the latest version of the Rfacebook package from GitHub:

```
install.packages("Rfacebook") # install from CRAN
# install from GitHub
library(devtools)
install_github("pablobarbera/Rfacebook/Rfacebook")
```

Once you install the package, you can load up the package using load(Rfacebook) and start using it to retrieve data from Facebook by using the access token you generated earlier. The following snippet shows us how you can access your own details as we did in the previous section, but this time by using R:

```
> token = 'XXXXXX'
> me <- getUsers("me", token=token)
> me$name
[1] "Dipanjan Sarkar"
> me$id
[1] "1026544"
```

The beauty of this package is that you get the results in curated and neatly formatted DataFrames, and you do not need to spend extra time trying to parse the raw JSON response objects from the Graph API. The package is well documented and has high level functions for accessing personal profile data on Facebook as well as page and group level data points. We will now take a quick look at Netvizz, a Facebook application, which can also be used to extract data easily from Facebook.

Understanding Netvizz

The Netvizz application was developed by Bernhard Rieder and is a tool which can be used to extract data from Facebook pages and groups, get statistics about links, and extract social networks from Facebook pages based on liked pages from each connected page in the network. You can access Netvizz at https://apps.facebook.com/netvizz/ and on registering the application on your profile, you will be able to see the following screen:

Netvizz v1.41

Netvizz is a tool that extracts data from different sections of the Facebook platform - in particular groups and pages - for research purposes. File outputs can be easily analyzed in standard software.

For **questions**, please consult the **FAQ** and **privacy** sections. Non-commercial use only.

This is a new version of Netvizz designed to work with Facebook's API v2.6. Please check the **FAQ** for how to report problems.

The following modules are currently available:

group data - creates networks and tabular files for user activity around posts on **groups**
page data - creates networks and tabular files for user activity around posts on **pages**
page like network - creates a network of **pages** connected through the likes between them
page timeline images - creates a list of all images from the "Timeline Photos" album on **pages**
search - interface to Facebook's **search function**
link stats - provides statistics for **links** shared on Facebook

Big pages or groups can take some time to process (minutes or hours). **Be patient and try not to reload!**

The Netvizz application interface

From the preceding app screenshot, you can see that there are various links based on the type of operation you want to execute to extract data. Feel free to play around with this tool. We will be using its **page like network** capability in one of our analyzes in a future section.

Data access challenges

There are several challenges with regards to accessing data from Facebook. Some of the major issues and caveats are:

- Facebook will keep evolving and updating its data access APIs and this can and will lead to changes and deprecation of older APIs and access patterns (just like FQL was deprecated).

- The scope of data available keeps changing with time with the evolution of Facebook's API and privacy settings. For instance, we can no longer get details of all our friends from the API.

- Libraries and tools built on top of the API tend to break with changes to Facebook's APIs. This has happened before with `Rfacebook` as well as Netvizz. Lada Adamic's GetNet application stopped working permanently when Facebook changed the way apps are created and the permissions they require. You can get more information about it here `http://thepoliticsofsystems.net/2015/01/the-end-of-netvizz/`

So, what was used in the book today for data retrieval might not be working completely tomorrow if there are any changes in the APIs, though it is expected it will be working fine for at least the next couple of years. However, to prevent any hindrance on analyzing Facebook data, we have provided the datasets we used in most of our analyzes except personal networks so that you can still follow along with each example and use-case. Personal names have been anonymized wherever possible to protect their privacy. Now that we have a good idea about Facebook's Graph API and how to access data, let's analyze some social networks!

Analyzing your personal social network

As we had mentioned before, Facebook is a massive social graph, connecting billions of users, brands and organizations. Consider your own Facebook account if you have one. You will have several friends who are your immediate connections, they in turn will have their own set of friends, and you might be friends with some of them and so on. You and your friends form the nodes of the network and edges determine the connections. In this section, we will analyze a small network of you and your immediate friends and also look at how we can extract and analyze some properties from the network. Before we jump into our analysis, we'll start by loading the necessary packages needed, which are mentioned in the following snippet, and store the Facebook Graph API access token in a variable:

```
library(Rfacebook)
library(gridExtra)
library(dplyr)
# get the Graph API access token
token = 'XXXXXXXXXX'
```

You can refer to the file `fb_personal_network_analysis.R` for code snippets used in the examples used in this section.

Basic descriptive statistics

In this section, we will try to get some basic information and descriptive statistics from our personal social network on Facebook. To start with let us look at some details of our own profile on Facebook using the following code:

```
# get my personal information
me <- getUsers("me", token=token,
                private_info = TRUE)
> View(me[c('name', 'id', 'gender', 'birthday')])
```

This shows us a few fields from the DataFrame containing our personal details retrieved from Facebook. We use the `View` function which basically invokes a spreadsheet-style data viewer on R objects like DataFrames:

	name	id	gender	birthday
1	Dipanjan Sarkar	1020 6544	male	12/18/1990

Now, let us get information about our friends in our personal network. Note that Facebook currently only lets you access information about those friends who have allowed access to the Graph API, so you may not be able to get information on all friends in your friends list. We have anonymized the names in this code for privacy reasons:

```
anonymous_names <- c('Johnny Juel', 'Houston Tancredi',...,
                    'Julius Henrichs', 'Yong Sprayberry')
# getting friends information
friends <- getFriends(token, simplify=TRUE)
friends$name <- anonymous_names
# view top few rows
> View(head(friends))
```

This gives us a peek at some people from our list of friends that we just retrieved from Facebook:

	name	id
1	Johnny Juel	5702!
2	Houston Tancredi	5875.
3	Eddie Artist	6225.
4	Paula Bauder	10152
5	Noble Towe	7100
6	Ira Denman	716

Let's now analyze some descriptive statistics based on personal information regarding our friends, such as where they are from, their gender and so on:

```
# get personal information
friends_info <- getUsers(friends$id, token, private_info = TRUE)

# get the gender of your friends
>View(table(friends_info$gender))
```

This gives us the gender of my friends. It looks like more male friends have authorized access to the Graph API in my network!

1	female	3
2	male	37

```
# get the location of your friends
>View(table(friends_info$location))
```

This depicts the location of my friends (wherever available) in the following DataFrame.

1	Bangalore, India	18
2	Kansas, US	5
3	Manchester, UK	4
4	Melbourne, Australia	3
5	Mumbai, India	3
6	Noida, India	2
7	Malaysia	2
8	Singapore	2

```
# get relationship status of your friends
> View(table(friends_info$relationship_status))
```

From the statistics in the following table I can see that a lot of my friends have got married over the past couple of years. Boy, that does make me feel old!

1	In a relationship	10
2	Married	13
3	Single	17

Suppose I want to look at the relationship status of my friends grouped by gender; we can do the same using the following snippet:

```
# get relationship status of friends grouped by gender
View(table(friends_info$relationship_status, friends_info$gender))
```

The following table gives us the desired results and you can see the distribution of friends by their gender and relationship status:

1	In a relationship	female	0
2	Married	female	2
3	Single	female	1
4	In a relationship	male	10
5	Married	male	11
6	Single	male	16

Analyzing mutual interests

Facebook is a wonderful platform to socialize and express your interests and communicate with people with similar interests on virtually any topic under the sun using pages. Here we will analyze mutual interests between my own friends and look at their top most liked pages on Facebook and then I will see if I have any of these interests. To start with, we define a function to extract and combine page likes by friends in my social network in the following snippet:

```
# extract top liked pages in your network
get_friends_likes <- function(id, token){
  df <- try(getLikes(user=id, token=token, n=1000))
  if(inherits(df, "try-error"))
  {
    #inset error handling code if needed
    # I am skipping this because I just need valid page likes
  }else{
    return(df)
  }
}
```

Next, we get page likes of all my friends using their node identifiers and the preceding function as follows:

```
 # get node ids of friends
ids <- friends$id
# get likes of all friends
likes_df <- data.frame()
for (id in ids){
  likes_df <- rbind(likes_df, get_friends_likes(id, token))
}
```

You might get some errors for friends who haven't given permissions to the API to view their likes. For others, this snippet will retrieve all page likes and store them in the `likes_df` DataFrame. Next, we aggregate all the liked pages and then view total pages liked by all my friends and the top liked pages among all my friends:

```
# aggregate liked pages
friend_likes <- tbl_df(likes_df) %>% count(names, sort=TRUE)
friend_likes <- as.data.frame(friend_likes)
colnames(friend_likes) <- c('names', 'freq')

# view total pages liked by all friends
> nrow(friend_likes)
[1] 4822
```

```
# view top liked pages among my friends
> View(head(friend_likes[order(friend_likes$freq,
decreasing=TRUE),],10))
```

This gives us the following table of the top ten Facebook pages which are most liked by my friends:

	names	freq
1	Facebook	12
2	IIIT Bangalore	11
3	Sachin Tendulkar	10
4	Premier League	8
5	Swami Vivekananda	8
6	A.R. Rahman	8
7	The Hindu	8
8	La Liga	8
9	Bill Gates	7
10	Coursera	7

Well, looks like Facebook is the most liked page and I do have quite a number of friends who love football in my friend list just like I do! I can also see my university listed there along with other interesting personalities like Sachin Tendulkar, Swami Vivekananda, A.R. Rahman and Bill Gates.

Now, what if I really wanted to see how many of these pages have also been liked by me and thus get some insights into which are the top liked pages between both me and my friend network. The following code snippet helps us achieve that:

```
# get my likes
my_likes <- get_friends_likes("me", token)
# view total liked pages by me
> nrow(my_likes)
[1] 1765

# get liked pages in common with my friends
my_liked_pages <- my_likes$names
common_likes <- friend_likes[friend_likes$names %in% my_liked_pages,]

# get total mutual liked pages between me and my friends
> nrow(common_likes)
```

```
[1] 402

# get top mutually liked pages
> View(head(common_likes[order(common_likes$freq,
decreasing=TRUE),],10))
```

From the preceding output, we can see that I have `402` liked pages which are in common with a total of `4822` different pages which have been liked by my friends. The preceding code depicts the top ten mutually liked pages in the following table:

	names	freq
2	Facebook	12
3	IIIT Bangalore	11
5	Sachin Tendulkar	10
6	Premier League	8
10	La Liga	8
17	Swami Vivekananda	8
20	Coursera	6
21	Google	6
22	Indian Cricket Team	6
23	Intel	6

Go ahead, give this a spin, and see what are the most common interests among you and your friends. Can you find out which friends have interests similar to you?

Build your friend network graph

Here we will build a graph depicting your friend network on Facebook and we will be using it in subsequent sections for analysis and visualizations. The following snippet helps in building your friend network graph:

```
# load dependencies
library(igraph)

# get friend network
>friend_network <- getNetwork(token, format="adj.matrix")
  |==================================================| 100%
# anonymize friend names
```

```
anonymize_names <- function(friend_network, names=anonymous_names){
  rownames(friend_network) <- names
  colnames(friend_network) <- names
  return(friend_network)
}
friend_network <- anonymize_names(friend_network=friend_network)

# get singleton friends (only friends with me)
singletons <- rowSums(friend_network)==0
# view total singletons
> table(singletons)
singletons
FALSE   TRUE
   36      4


# remove singleton friends from graph
friend_network_graph <- graph.adjacency(friend_network[!singletons,!s
ingletons])
```

This gives us an `igraph` object containing our friend network graph and we can view its details using the following code:

```
> # view graph details
> str(friend_network_graph)
IGRAPH DN-- 36 136 --
+ attr: name (v/c)
+ edges (vertex names):
Houston Tancredi -> Noble Towe
Eddie Artist -> Paula Bauder, Johann Paul........
```

From the preceding output, we see that our network has 36 nodes and 136 edges. We will now visualize this graph in the next section before diving into further details like looking at various properties in the graph.

Visualizing your friend network graph

Here we will visualize the friend network graph which we created in the earlier section. We use the following code snippet:

```
tkplot(friend_network_graph,
       vertex.size = 15,
       vertex.color="lightblue",
       vertex.frame.color= "white",
       vertex.label.color = "black",
       vertex.label.family = "sans",
```

```
edge.width=1,
edge.arrow.size=0,
edge.color="black",
edge.curved=TRUE,
layout=layout.fruchterman.reingold)
```

This gives us an interactive graph as depicted in the following figure and you can move around the nodes and play around with it and see how many connections are there between various nodes. Can you identify the most influential people here?

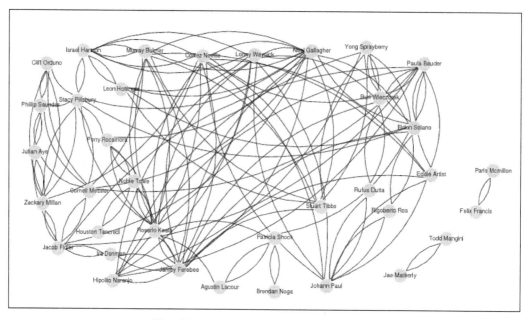

Visualizing my personal friends' social network

The graph has one major component and two other components where a pair of friends are connected to each other but they are not friends with anyone else in the network.

Analyzing node properties

There are various properties in the social network with regard to nodes that can measure and indicate important and influential nodes, how information might typically flow in the network, and so on. Remember the graph visualization depicting the network in the earlier section? We will be analyzing specific properties like betweenness, degree, closeness and so on, which you can consider by looking at the visualization time and again to see if it makes sense. These are also often called as measures of centrality or importance in the graph.

Degree

The degree of a node is denoted by the number of edges adjacent to the node, which is the sum of the indegree and outdegree of the node assuming it is a directed graph. Indegree is denoted by the total number of incoming edges to the node and Outdegree is the total number of outgoing edges from the node. The following snippet shows us how to get these statistics:

```
# get total degree of nodes
degree_fng <- degree(friend_network_graph, mode="total")
degree_fng_df <- data.frame(Name=V(friend_network_graph)$name,
                            "Degree"=as.vector(degree_fng))
degree_fng_df <- degree_fng_df[order(degree_fng_df$Degree,
                                     decreasing=TRUE),]
# get total indegree of nodes
indegree_fng <- degree(friend_network_graph, mode="in")
indegree_fng_df <- data.frame(Name=V(friend_network_graph)$name,
                              "Indegree"=as.vector(indegree_fng))
indegree_fng_df <- indegree_fng_df[order(indegree_fng_df$Indegree,
                   decreasing=TRUE),]
# get total outdegree of nodes
outdegree_fng <- degree(friend_network_graph, mode="out")
outdegree_fng_df <- data.frame(Name=V(friend_network_graph)$name,
                               "Outdegree"=as.vector(outdegree_fng))
outdegree_fng_df <- outdegree_fng_df[order(outdegree_fng_df$Outdegree,
                                           decreasing=TRUE),]
```

We can now look at the top influential nodes in terms of degree. The following code shows us the frequency of nodes having various degrees: the higher the degree, the greater the possibility of the node being influential since it is connected to more people. We can see that there are two nodes with a degree of 15 from the following table:

```
# view frequency table of nodes with various degrees
> table(degree_fng)
degree_fng
 2  3  4  5  6  7  8  9 10 11 12 13 14 15
 6  1  3  1  5  2  3  3  3  2  3  1  1  2
```

The `degree_distribution(...)` function gives us a numeric vector of the same length as the maximum degree plus one from the preceding graph. The first element of the result is the relative frequency of zero degree nodes; the second value indicates frequency of nodes with degree one, and so on:

```
> degree_distribution(friend_network_graph)
 [1] 0.00000000 0.00000000 0.16666667 0.02777778 0.08333333
 [6] 0.02777778 0.13888889 0.05555556 0.083333330.08333333
[11] 0.08333333 0.05555556 0.08333333 0.02777778 0.02777778 0.05555556
```

From the preceding output, as expected we see maximum relative frequency for nodes having degrees 2 and 6. The following snippet shows us the nodes with maximum degree, indegree and outdegree respectively:

```
# degree stats
if (dev.cur()!=1){dev.off()}
grid.table(head(degree_fng_df, 10),
          rows=NULL)
# indegree stats
if (dev.cur()!=1){dev.off()}
grid.table(head(indegree_fng_df, 10),
          rows=NULL)
# outdegree stats
if (dev.cur()!=1){dev.off()}
grid.table(head(outdegree_fng_df, 10),
          rows=NULL)
```

This gives us three tables which are depicted in the following figure showing the top ten influential people with respect to total degree, indegree and outdegree respectively:

Name	Degree	Name	Indegree	Name	Outdegree
Neal Gallagher	15	Eddie Artist	5	Neal Gallagher	10
Jamey Ferebee	15	Paula Bauder	5	Jamey Ferebee	10
Rosario Keala	14	Phillip Saunder	5	Rosario Keala	9
Cortez Neville	13	Eldon Solano	5	Cortez Neville	8
Eldon Solano	12	Lonny Waynick	5	Eldon Solano	7
Lonny Waynick	12	Cornell Messier	5	Lonny Waynick	7
Murray Bulmer	12	Neal Gallagher	5	Murray Bulmer	7
Paula Bauder	11	Leon Hottinger	5	Paula Bauder	6
Stacy Pillsbury	11	Stacy Pillsbury	5	Stacy Pillsbury	6
Jacob Fidler	10	Burl Wieczorek	5	Jacob Fidler	5

Degree measures of friends in my network

We can see from the preceding table that these people have the maximum edges or connections with others and you can verify the same from the network graph visualization we plotted earlier.

Closeness

The closeness measure is another measure of centrality for nodes, where it indicates how long information might take to arrive at various nodes. We compute a normalized closeness score here, where each node's closeness is computed as the inverse of the sum of shortest distances between the node and all other nodes, and then multiplied by the total number of nodes – 1 in the graph. We will look at this in more detail in the next section when we analyze a much bigger graph. For now, you should remember that, the higher the score in this case, more central the node will be in the network, and hence the more influential:

```
# closeness stats
closeness_fng <- closeness(friend_network_graph, mode="all",
normalized=TRUE)
closeness_fng_df <- data.frame(Name=V(friend_network_graph)$name,
"Closeness"=as.vector(closeness_fng))
closeness_fng_df <- closeness_fng_df[order(closeness_fng_df$Closeness,
decreasing=TRUE),]
if (dev.cur()!=1){dev.off()}
grid.table(head(closeness_fng_df, 10),rows=NULL)
```

This gives us the top ten friends with the highest closeness and the most central nodes in the network as depicted in the following table:

Name	Closeness
Neal Gallagher	0.1758794
Cortez Neville	0.1758794
Jamey Ferebee	0.1741294
Eldon Solano	0.1724138
Rosario Keala	0.1724138
Murray Bulmer	0.1715686
Lonny Waynick	0.1699029
Stacy Pillsbury	0.1699029
Cornell Messier	0.1674641
Paula Bauder	0.1658768

Friends with the highest closeness

Betweenness

The betweenness measure is another centrality measure depicting brokerage potential. Node betweenness can be defined as the number of geodesics or shortest paths going through it. In simple terms, it is the number of times that any node needs to go through a given node to reach any other node by the shortest path. We will define this mathematically in the next section when we analyze a network of Facebook pages. The following snippet computes betweenness for my friends in the network:

```
# betweenness
betweenness_fng <- betweenness(friend_network_graph)
betweenness_fng_df <- data.frame(Name=V(friend_network_graph)$name,
         "Betweenness"=as.vector(betweenness_fng))
betweenness_fng_df <- betweenness_fng_df[order(betweenness_fng_
df$Betweenness,
                                    decreasing=TRUE),]
if (dev.cur()!=1){dev.off()}
grid.table(head(betweenness_fng_df, 10),
         rows=NULL)
```

This gives us the top ten friends with the highest betweenness score representing influential members who can acquire the most information:

Name	Betweenness
Rosario Keala	160.91726
Zackary Millan	110.83373
Stacy Pillsbury	110.41687
Paula Bauder	109.17143
Eldon Solano	99.08433
Jacob Fidler	96.87500
Jamey Ferebee	84.67063
Lonny Waynick	84.56091
Cortez Neville	82.50397
Israel Hartson	77.05833

Friends with the highest betweenness

Can you find out if there is any correlation between these measures? Can these data points be visualized in any way to understand their relationship? We will discuss all this in the next use-case when we also discuss ways to visualize and measure correlations among different measures of centrality in networks. The answers to the previous questions are given in the code files for our more inquisitive readers who can check them out immediately.

Analyzing network communities

In any social network, various nodes are connected to each other based on relationships. However, it is a fact that there are specific groups or clusters of nodes that are more densely connected to each other compared to the rest of the nodes. These are called communities in the network, just like we have communities in our society. There are various ways to detect and analyze communities in a social network. We will cover a few of them here.

Cliques

In graph theory, a clique is basically a subset of the nodes in the graph where every distinct pair of nodes in the clique is adjacent; that is, its induced subgraph is complete. A maximum clique in a graph is one that cannot be another clique because it has more nodes than the maximum clique. You can draw an analogy for this as a fully connected subgraph in the social network, where the nodes represent people who all know each other. Taking a simple example, consider a subgraph such that:

- A is friends with B and C
- B is also friends with C
- D is also friends with B and C but not with A

This makes this subgraph have a maximum clique of three having the nodes A, B and C or D, B and C. If D was to be friends with A now, this would make it a fully connected graph and thus the maximum clique size would be now be four, consisting of A, B, C and D.

The following snippet gives us the size of the largest clique:

```
> clique_num(friend_network_graph)
[1] 4
```

Now let us get all the cliques of size 4 using the following snippet:

```
> cliques(friend_network_graph, min=4, max=4)
[[1]]
+ 4/36 vertices, named:
[1] Phillip Saunder Cornell Messier Stacy Pillsbury Cliff Orduno
[[2]]
+ 4/36 vertices, named:
[1] Neal Gallagher Murray Bulmer  Jamey Ferebee  Stuart Tibbs
[[3]]
+ 4/36 vertices, named:
[1] Neal Gallagher Cortez Neville Jamey Ferebee  Stuart Tibbs
```

You can see three cliques being output with my friends, and if you look at the network visualization from before, you will notice these people are all friends with each other thus obeying the clique properties.

Communities

We will try to find communities or clusters of friends who are more connected together using the greedy optimization of the modularity score algorithm in `igraph`, which basically tries to extract dense subgraphs or communities such that it gets the maximum modularity score. This is basically a measure of how good the different clusters or subgraphs are in a given graph, and how much distance apart they are from each other:

```
# build clusters from the network graph
friend_network_graph <- graph.adjacency(friend_network[!singletons,!s
ingletons],
                                         mode='undirected')
layout <- layout_with_fr(friend_network_graph,
                         niter=500, start.temp=5.744)
fc <- cluster_fast_greedy(friend_network_graph)
# get community details
communities <- data.frame(layout)
names(communities) <- c("x", "y")
communities$cluster <- factor(fc$membership)
communities$name <- fc$names
```

From the preceding code snippet, we get cluster or community labels for each node using the greedy algorithm. Now we can analyze the results as follows:

```
# get number of nodes per cluster
> table(communities$cluster)

 1  2  3  4  5  6
11  6  8  7  2  2


# view friends per community
> groups(fc)
$`1`
 [1] "Eddie Artist"     "Paula Bauder"     "Eldon Solano"     "Rufus
Dutta"       "Burl Wieczorek"
 [6] "Hipolito Naranjo" "Cortez Neville"   "Jamey Ferebee"
"Rigoberto Ros"    "Yong Sprayberry"
[11] "Johann Paul"
$`2`
[1] "Lonny Waynick"  "Neal Gallagher" "Leon Hottinger" "Murray Bulmer"
"Stuart Tibbs"   "Israel Hartson"
$`3`
[1] "Ira Denman"      "Phillip Saunder" "Julian Aye"      "Cornell
Messier" "Stacy Pillsbury"
[6] "Zackary Millan"  "Jacob Fidler"    "Cliff Orduno"
$`4`
[1] "Houston Tancredi" "Noble Towe"       "Patricia Shook"   "Perry
Rocamora"    "Brendan Noga"
[6] "Agustin Lacour"   "Rosario Keala"
$`5`
[1] "Todd Mangini" "Jae Matherly"


# get modularity score
> modularity(fc)
[1] 0.3795085
```

The following code helps us in visualizing the previous communities that we extracted from our friend network in different ways to understand them better:

```
library(ggplot2)
comm_plot <- ggplot(communities, aes(x=x, y=y, color=cluster,
label=name))
comm_plot <- comm_plot + geom_label(aes(fill = cluster),
                                    colour="white")

comm_plot
```

This gives us the following figure showing the clusters in different coloured boxes:

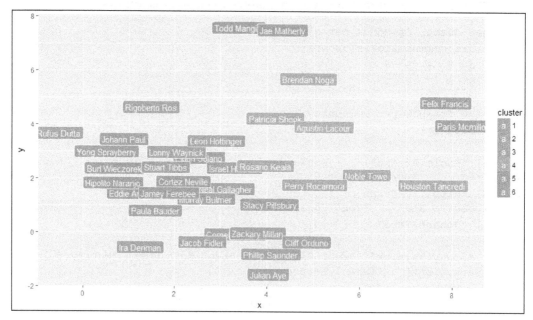

Visualizing communities of friends

We can view the complete social network, along with the different communities that we saw previously, using the following snippet:

```
plot(fc, friend_network_graph,
     vertex.size=15,
     vertex.label.cex=0.8,
     vertex.label=fc$names,
     edge.arrow.size=0,
     edge.curved=TRUE,
     vertex.label.color="black",
     layout=layout.fruchterman.reingold)
```

This creates a plot depicting my social network of friends and various communities amongst them:

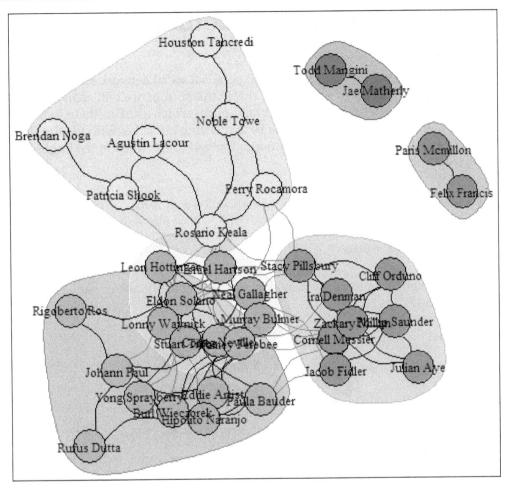

Visualizing my friend network including communities

You can now see each community prominently based on the enclosed boundaries and the color codes for each community and its people. Do you notice any specific reason behind specific communities in your friend network?

Analyzing an English football social network

In the previous section, we analyzed a small personal social network and got a good grasp of the basic concepts of social networks. In this section, we will analyze a much larger social network of Facebook brand pages which are directly or indirectly associated with English football. We will be associating ourselves with the **English Premier League** (EPL) which is the top tier of football competition in the English football league system.

> English Premier League is a corporation with 20 football clubs who act as member shareholders. A football season in the EPL typically runs from August to May where each team plays a total of 38 matches.

The following figure depicts the official logo of the English Premier League for the season of 2016-17:

The English Premier League brand logo

We shall be extracting a huge network of Facebook pages related to the EPL and then analyzing it in detail to understand social networks better. Without further ado, let's get started! You can refer to the file `fb_pages_network_analysis.R` for code snippets used in the examples depicted in this section, *Getting the data*.

I have used the Netvizz application to extract the page network from Facebook. The root page is *Premier League* available at `https://www.facebook.com/premierleague/`. It has a node identifier of `220832481274508`. You can go to the Netvizz **Page Like Network Module** and extract the data as shown in the following snapshot:

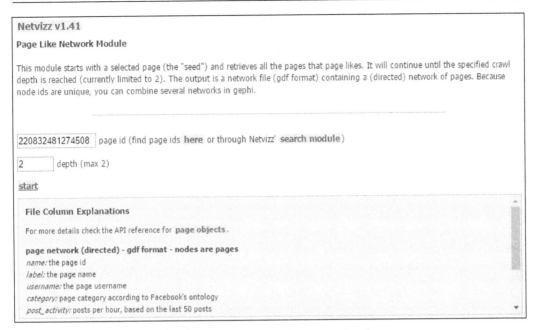

Netvizz v1.41

Page Like Network Module

This module starts with a selected page (the "seed") and retrieves all the pages that page likes. It will continue until the specified crawl depth is reached (currently limited to 2). The output is a network file (gdf format) containing a (directed) network of pages. Because node ids are unique, you can combine several networks in gephi.

220832481274508   page id (find page ids **here** or through Netvizz' **search module**)

2   depth (max 2)

start

File Column Explanations

For more details check the API reference for **page objects**.

page network (directed) - gdf format - nodes are pages
name: the page id
label: the page name
username: the page username
category: page category according to Facebook's ontology
post_activity: posts per hour, based on the last 50 posts

Netvizz's Page Like Network extraction interface

Once you extract the page like network data, it is available as a .gdf graph file, which I've reformatted and cleaned up a little bit, including changing the node identifier numbers because R has problems dealing with large number identifiers. Finally I opened this file using *Gephi*, a popular Graph visualization platform available at https://gephi.org/ and saved it as a .gml file named pl.gml. This is available along with the code files of this chapter. We will be using this file for our analysis in this section.

To start our analysis, we will first load the necessary dependencies and our Facebook pages social network using the following snippet:

```
# load dependencies
library(Rfacebook)
library(gridExtra)
library(igraph)
library(ggplot2)

# read in the graph
pl_graph <- read.graph(file="pl.gml", format="gml")
```

Basic descriptive statistics

We will look at some basic descriptive statistics pertaining to our social network in this section starting with the total nodes and edges in our network:

```
# inspect the page graph object
> summary(pl_graph)
IGRAPH D--- 582 2810 --
+ attr: id (v/n), label (v/c), graphics (v/c), fan_count (v/c),    |
category (v/c), username(v/c), users_can_post (v/c),
| link (v/c), post_activity (v/c), talking_about_count (v/c),
| Yala (v/c), id (e/n), value (e/n)
```

We can see that our social network in this case has a massive 582 node pages and 2810 edge connections. Quite a step-up from the last graph! The following snippet creates a DataFrame of some basic statistics of the Facebook pages from some metadata which was extracted when getting the page network data:

```
pl_df <- data.frame(id=V(pl_graph)$id,
                    name=V(pl_graph)$label,
                    category=V(pl_graph)$category,
                    fans=as.numeric(V(pl_graph)$fan_count),
         talking_about=as.numeric(V(pl_graph)$talking_about_count),
         post_activity=as.numeric(V(pl_graph)$post_activity),
                    stringsAsFactors=FALSE)
> View(pl_df)
```

The following table depicts a part of the DataFrame we built for the different pages in the network:

id		name	category	fans	talking_about	post_activity
1	10	Premier League	Sports League	39301910	634081	0.31
2	20	TAG Heuer	Jewelry/Watches	2823063	30796	0.14
3	30	Carling	Food & Beverage Company	200508	12078	0.03
4	40	Hull Tigers	Sports Team	1000560	40500	0.23
5	50	Middlesbrough FC	Sports Team	431967	25042	0.29
6	60	Burnley Football Club	Sports Team	352042	3279	0.19
7	70	Watford FC	Sports Team	362231	11308	0.11
8	80	AFC Bournemouth	Sports Team	326942	12651	0.54
9	90	Leicester City Football Club	Sports Team	6554721	218176	0.51
10	100	Crystal Palace Football Club	Sports Team	1004518	18338	0.27

Let's now look at various statistics of the network:

```
# aggregate pages based on their category
if (dev.cur()!=1){dev.off()}
grid.table(as.data.frame(sort(table(pl_df$category),
```

```
            decreasing=TRUE) [1:10]]), rows=NULL,
            cols=c('Category', 'Count'))

# top pages based on their fan count (likes)
if (dev.cur()!=1){dev.off()}
grid.table(pl_df[order(pl_df$fans, decreasing=TRUE),
            c('name', 'category', 'fans')][1:10,],
         rows=NULL)

# top pages based on total people talking about them
if (dev.cur()!=1){dev.off()}
grid.table(pl_df[order(pl_df$talking_about, decreasing=TRUE),
            c('name', 'category', 'talking_about')][1:10,],
         rows=NULL)

# top pages based on page posting activity
if (dev.cur()!=1){dev.off()}
grid.table(pl_df[order(pl_df$post_activity, decreasing=TRUE),
            c('name', 'category', 'post_activity')][1:10,],
         rows=NULL)
```

This gives us the following four tables showing top page categories, pages based on fans (likes), talking about and posting activity respectively:

Category	Count	name	category	fans
Athlete	151	Cristiano Ronaldo	Athlete	118925300
Sports Team	77	FC Barcelona	Sports Team	95491169
Community	31	Manchester United	Sports Team	72214897
Product/Service	26	UEFA Champions League	Sports League	60636892
Non-Profit Organization	21	Neymar Jr.	Athlete	59214746
Company	20	David Guetta	Musician/Band	54789663
Local Business	16	Chelsea Football Club	Sports Team	47253090
Games/Toys	15	Nike Football	Product/Service	42498785
Sports League	14	Nike Football	Product/Service	42498683
Travel Company	13	Nike Football	Product/Service	42498679

name	category	talking_about	name	category	post_activity
Cristiano Ronaldo	Athlete	3532172	SportPesa Care	Product/Service	21.74
FC Barcelona	Sports Team	1633078	GiveMeSport - Football	News/Media Website	10.54
Manchester United	Sports Team	1618239	Virgin Media	Telecommunication Company	9.94
Chelsea Football Club	Sports Team	1301568	Neymar Jr.	Athlete	8.77
UEFA Champions League	Sports League	1168555	Delta	Travel Company	2.83
Neymar Jr.	Athlete	1085169	Juan Mata	Athlete	2.37
Etihad Stadium	Stadium	1043577	The Sims	Games/Toys	2.23
Sergio Ramos	Athlete	1027324	Sky Sports	TV Network	2.18
LaLiga	Sports League	970684	ESPN UK	Media/News Company	2.02
Stamford Bridge	Stadium	862744	Sergio Ramos	Athlete	1.67

Do you notice any correlation between page fans and fans\people talking about the pages? The following snippet helps us visualize this:

```
# check correlation between fans and talking about for pages
clean_pl_df <- pl_df[complete.cases(pl_df),]
rsq <- format(cor(clean_pl_df$fans, clean_pl_df$talking_about) ^2,
              digits=3)
corr_plot <- ggplot(pl_df, aes(x=fans, y=talking_about))+ theme_bw() +
  geom_jitter(alpha=1/2) +
  scale_x_log10() +
  scale_y_log10() +
  labs(x="Fans", y="Talking About") +
  annotate("text", label=paste("R-sq =", rsq), x=+Inf, y=1,
           hjust=1)
corr_plot
```

This gives us the following scatter plot where R-square is the square of the correlation coefficient:

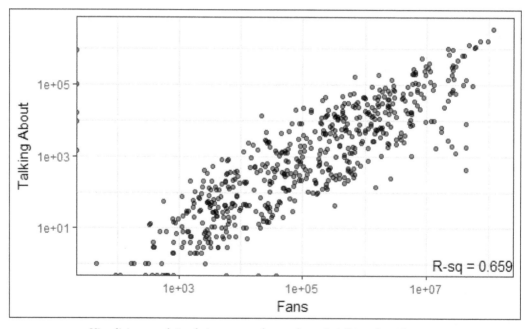

Visualizing correlation between page fans and people talking about the page

The plot shows a strong correlation between page fans and people talking about the page depicted by the data points on the plot as well as the R-square value.

Visualizing the network

We will now visualize the network in a similar way to what we did for our friend network. However, in this case, we are dealing with over 580 page nodes and visualizing them all on a small plot area would mess up the plot and not convey much useful information. Therefore, we will apply a degree filter to the plot and plot only important nodes having a degree of at least 30:

```
# plot page network using degree filter
degrees <- degree(pl_graph, mode="total")
degrees_df <- data.frame(ID=V(pl_graph)$id,
                         Name=V(pl_graph)$label,
                         Degree=as.vector(degrees))
ids_to_remove <- degrees_df[degrees_df$Degree < 30, c('ID')]
ids_to_remove <- ids_to_remove / 10

# get filtered graph
filtered_pl_graph <- delete.vertices(pl_graph, ids_to_remove)

# plot the graph
tkplot(filtered_pl_graph,
       vertex.size = 10,
       vertex.color="orange",
       vertex.frame.color= "white",
       vertex.label.color = "black",
       vertex.label.family = "sans",
       edge.width=0.2,
       edge.arrow.size=0,
       edge.color="grey",
       edge.curved=TRUE,
       layout = layout.fruchterman.reingold)
```

This gives us the following page network connected by mutual likes as depicted in the following figure:

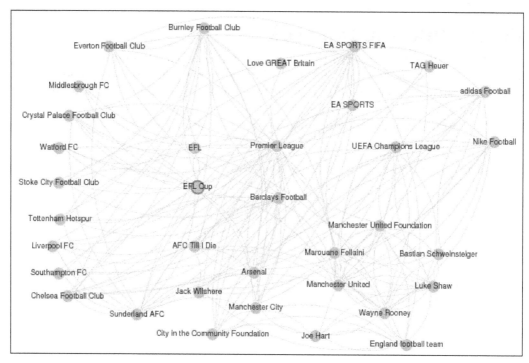

Visualizing the Premier League football social network

You can see the *Premier League* page at the center of the network and connected by various other competitions like the Champions League, Europa League and different football clubs as well as players and sponsors. Use this plot as a reference whenever we are analyzing the network in detail in the subsequent sections, especially with regard to influential pages, communities and so on.

Analyzing network properties

In this section, we will try to analyze the network as a whole and extract useful insights with regard to the network. These include various properties and attributes like diameter, density, coreness and so on. The basic idea here is to get an in-depth idea about the structure of our network and its various elements.

Diameter

The diameter of a network is basically the length of the longest geodesic or path between two nodes in the network based on the number of edges between them. In our case, we are dealing with a directed graph, so remember that when trying to find out the diameter using the following snippet:

```
# diameter (length of longest path) of the network
> diameter(pl_graph, directed=TRUE)
[1] 7

# get the longest path of the network
> get_diameter(pl_graph, directed=TRUE)$label
[1] "Sports Arena Hull" "Hull Tigers" "Teenage Cancer Trust"
[4] "Celtic FC" "Dafabet UK" "Premier League" "Carling"
[8] "Alice Gold"
```

We can see that the diameter of our network is 7 and the longest path is also depicted in the preceding network.

Page distances

Considering we have each page as a node or vertex in our social network graph, we can compute distances between nodes as well as find out what the average distance is between two nodes in the network. The following snippets help us achieve this:

```
# mean distance between two nodes in the network
> mean_distance(pl_graph, directed=TRUE)
[1] 3.696029

# distance between various important pages(nodes)
node_dists <- distances(pl_graph, weights=NA)
labels <- c("Premier League", pl_df[c(21, 22, 23, 24, 25), 'name'])
filtered_dists <- node_dists[c(1,21,22,23,24,25), c(1,21,22,23,24,25)]
colnames(filtered_dists) <- labels
rownames(filtered_dists) <- labels
if (dev.cur()!=1){dev.off()}
grid.table(filtered_dists)
```

In the preceding code snippet we basically try to find out the distance between some important nodes in the network (top football clubs) from the root page *Premier League* and we get the following table showing the required page distances:

	Premier League	Manchester United	Manchester City	Liverpool FC	Arsenal	Chelsea Football Club
Premier League	0	1	1	1	1	1
Manchester United	1	0	2	2	2	2
Manchester City	1	2	0	2	2	2
Liverpool FC	1	2	2	0	2	2
Arsenal	1	2	2	2	0	2
Chelsea Football Club	1	2	2	2	2	0

Distances between several Facebook pages related to Premier League football

Density

The density of the graph is the ratio of the number of actual edges in the graph to the total number of possible edges in the graph. Mathematically, it can be denoted as:

$$ND(G) = \frac{|E|}{|V| \times |V| - 1}$$

Here *ND(G)* denotes the network density of the graph *G(V,E)* with vertices *V* and edges *E* such that $|E|$ denotes the total number of edges in the graph and $|V|$ denotes the total number of vertices or nodes in the network. The following snippet shows us how to get the density of the network and also verifies it with the preceding mathematical equation:

```
# edge density of the graph
> edge_density(pl_graph)
[1] 0.008310118

# Verify edge density of the graph
> 2801 / (582*581)
[1] 0.008283502
```

We get the density of our network, and it's pretty close to our manual computation using the formula depicted previously.

Transitivity

The transitivity of the network is also defined as the clustering coefficient and gives a measure of the probability that the adjacent nodes of a network are connected. For instance, if page A is connected to B and B to C, what is the probability of A being connected to C. The following snippet computes the transitivity of our network:

```
# transitivity - clustering coefficient
> transitivity(pl_graph)
[1] 0.163949
```

Coreness

The coreness is a useful measure to understand which pages are present at the heart or core of the network and which pages are at the edge or periphery of the network. This can be computed using K-core decomposition which has two major principles:

- The k-core of a graph is the maximal subgraph in which each node has at least a degree of k

- The coreness measure of any page is k if it belongs to a k-core subgraph but not a (k+1)-core subgraph

The following snippet helps us compute the coreness of our network:

```
# compute coreness
page_names <- V(pl_graph)$label
page_coreness <- coreness(pl_graph)
page_coreness_df = data.frame(Page=page_names,
                              PageCoreness=page_coreness)


# max coreness
> max(page_coreness_df$PageCoreness)
[1] 11
```

To view important pages at the core of the network and unimportant pages at the periphery of the network, use the following snippet:

```
# view the core of the network
View(head(page_coreness_df[
  page_coreness_df$PageCoreness == max(page_coreness_
df$PageCoreness),], 20))

# View the periphery of the network
View(head(page_coreness_df[
  page_coreness_df$PageCoreness == min(page_coreness_
df$PageCoreness),], 20))
```

This gives us the following two tables showing the core and periphery pages in the network:

Core Pages			Periphery Pages		
	Page	PageCoreness		Page	PageCoreness
1	Premier League	11	34	Henrik Lundqvist	1
6	Burnley Football Club	11	37	Cara Delevingne	1
10	Crystal Palace Football Club	11	38	La Carrera Panamericana	1
11	West Ham United	11	39	Patrick Dempsey	1
12	Southampton FC	11	40	Dempsey Racing	1
14	Everton Football Club	11	52	The Carling Local at V Festival	1
15	Nike Football	11	57	Tigers Trust	1
16	West Bromwich Albion	11	59	Hull Tigers Commercialâ€™	1
17	Tottenham Hotspur	11	60	Hull Tigers Arabic	1
18	Swansea City Football Club	11	61	Andy Dawson Testimonial	1
19	Sunderland AFC	11	84	Safehands Nursery at Barnoldswick	1
20	Stoke City Football Club	11	88	Liv Fox Photography	1
21	Manchester United	11	89	Split Screen Wedding Dreams	1
22	Manchester City	11	94	Alex O'Neill Photography	1
23	Liverpool FC	11	95	Pier Fun Casinos Event Management Ltd	1

Facebook pages which are at the core and periphery of the Premier League network

You can see from these tables that all the football clubs in the Premier League have the highest coreness along with the *Premier League* page itself, which is expected; in addition, various pages have some relationship with the Premier League, like same country, sponsors, regions, cities, and popular people. These pages are part of the peripheral pages since they have the fewest connections when compared to other more influential nodes in this football social network.

Analyzing node properties

Just like we analyzed various node properties in the previous social network, we will do the same here using various measures of centrality including several new ones to find out influential and important pages. Let's get started!

Degree

The degree of a node is defined as the number of edges adjacent to the node, which is the sum of the indegree and outdegree, as we've discussed earlier. Therefore, the greater the degree of a page node, the greater influence it will have on the network and vice-versa. So, important and influential pages will be the first to hear or spread information quickly compared to other pages. The following snippet computes the degree of pages in our network. We will show the output together after computing betweenness and closeness:

```
# compute degree
degree_plg <- degree(pl_graph, mode="total")
degree_plg_df <- data.frame(Name=V(pl_graph)$label,
                            Degree=as.vector(degree_plg))
degree_plg_df <- degree_plg_df[order(degree_plg_df$Degree,
decreasing=TRUE),]
```

Now we will compute the closeness of various pages in the network.

Closeness

The term closeness is defined as how long it might take for information to arrive at various page nodes in the network. Theoretically, it can be defined as the distance (shortest) from the node under analysis to all other nodes in the network. So, the larger the distance sum, the less central is the node. However ,we compute the normalized closeness score by taking the reciprocal of this distance and multiplying it by the total number of nodes –1 in the network. Mathematically this can be denoted as:

$$Cl(x) = \frac{|V-1|}{\sum_{i=1}^{|v|} sdist(i,x) \forall (i \neq x)}$$

Here, $Cl(x)$ denotes closeness for the node x; $sdist(i,x)$ is the shortest distance between nodes i and x; and $|V|$ is the total number of nodes in the network. The higher the score in this case, the more central and influential is the page node. The following snippet computes closeness of the pages in our network:

```
# compute closeness
closeness_plg <- closeness(pl_graph, mode="all", normalized=TRUE)
closeness_plg_df <- data.frame(Name=V(pl_graph)$label,
                            Closeness=as.vector(closeness_plg))
closeness_plg_df <- closeness_plg_df[order(closeness_plg_df$Closeness,
                                        decreasing=TRUE),]
```

Next, we will compute betweenness of the pages in the network and then we will finally compare the scores and correlate them.

Betweenness

The term betweenness is basically defined as the number of geodesic or shortest paths passing through a page node thus indicating the number of times a node needs to go through a given node to reach any other node in the network using the shortest path. Mathematically, this can be denoted by:

$$Bw(x) = \sum_{i,j \in v} \frac{nsdist(i,j)x}{nsdist(i,j)}$$

Here, $Bw(x)$ indicates betweenness for the node x, such that $nsdist(i,j)\_x$ denotes the total number of shortest path connecting i and j that pass through x; and $nsdist(i,j)$ denotes the total number of shortest path connecting i and j in the whole network. The following snippet helps us compute betweenness for the page nodes in the network:

```
# Betweenness
betweenness_plg <- betweenness(pl_graph)
betweenness_plg_df <- data.frame(Name=V(pl_graph)$label,
Betweenness=as.vector(betweenness_plg))
betweenness_plg_df <- betweenness_plg_df[order(betweenness_plg_
df$Betweenness,
                                    decreasing=TRUE),]
```

Now we can view the top ten influential pages based on degree, betweenness and closeness using the following snippet:

```
# view top pages based on above measures
View(head(degree_plg_df, 10))
View(head(closeness_plg_df, 10))
View(head(betweenness_plg_df, 10))
```

The following three tables are consolidated into a single figure where we can look across the top influential pages on the basis of degree, betweenness and closeness respectively:

	Name	Degree		Name	Closeness		Name	Betweenness
22	Manchester City	109	1	Premier League	0.5340074	1	Premier League	96082.15
24	Arsenal	92	19	Sunderland AFC	0.4874161	22	Manchester City	32242.45
15	Nike Football	91	6	Burnley Football Club	0.4805624	19	Sunderland AFC	24583.19
19	Sunderland AFC	91	26	Barclays Football	0.4723577	24	Arsenal	22258.68
25	Chelsea Football Club	90	129	EFL Cup	0.4611111	6	Burnley Football Club	21872.56
1	Premier League	85	366	606	0.4469231	15	Nike Football	21232.93
21	Manchester United	84	243	EA SPORTS FIFA	0.4418251	21	Manchester United	19781.41
6	Burnley Football Club	82	150	The Offside Rule (We Get It!) Podcast	0.4411541	243	EA SPORTS FIFA	19013.00
14	Everton Football Club	65	156	The H and C News Football Pie League	0.4365139	25	Chelsea Football Club	18181.46
23	Liverpool FC	59	22	Manchester City	0.4342302	2	TAG Heuer	16698.68

Top influential pages with the highest degree, closeness and between

Do you see any common pages in all the three tables in the previous figure? Do you think there might be some correlation between these measures? Think about these questions for a while and try to see if you can find some answers.

Visualizing correlation among centrality measures

While analyzing our previous social network, we did mention an exercise for you about thinking of ways in which we could visualize and measure the correlation among our various measures of centrality. In this section, we will try to visualize and compute the correlation between the centrality measures that we computed for our network in the previous section.

```
plg_df <- data.frame(degree_plg, closeness_plg, betweenness_plg)

# degree vs closeness
rsq <- format(cor(degree_plg, closeness_plg) ^2, digits=3)
corr_plot <- ggplot(plg_df, aes(x=degree_plg, y=closeness_plg))+
theme_bw() +
  geom_jitter(alpha=1/2) +
  scale_y_log10() +
  labs(x="Degree", y="Closeness") +
  annotate("text", label=paste("R-sq =", rsq), x=+Inf, y=1, hjust=1)
corr_plot
```

This gives us the following figure with the R-square value, which is the squared value of the correlation coefficient between degree and closeness for our network:

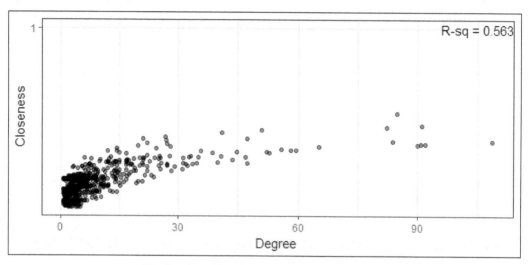

Visualizing correlation between degree and closeness

From the preceding figure, we can see that there is a strong correlation between degree and closeness and the correlation coefficient is the square root of the R-square value which gives us 0.75 indicating a strong correlation. Let's now look at the correlation between degree and betweenness:

```
# degree vs betweenness
rsq <- format(cor(degree_plg, betweenness_plg) ^2, digits=3)
corr_plot <- ggplot(plg_df, aes(x=degree_plg, y=betweenness_plg))+
theme_bw() +
  geom_jitter(alpha=1/2) +
  scale_y_log10() +
  labs(x="Degree", y="Betweenness") +
  annotate("text", label=paste("R-sq =", rsq), x=+Inf, y=1, hjust=1)
corr_plot
```

This gives us the following plot of degree versus betweenness and depicts the R-squared value:

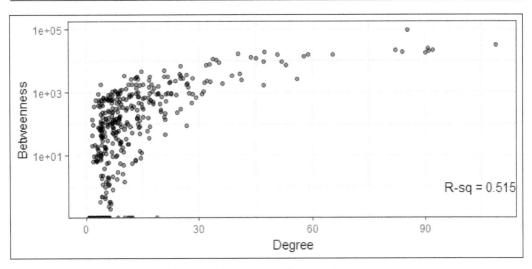

Visualizing correlation between degree and betweenness

The preceding figure shows us that there is a strong correlation between degree and betweenness, and that the correlation coefficient has a value of 0.72 approximately.

Eigenvector centrality

The eigenvector centrality scores usually correspond to the values of the first eigenvector of the graph adjacency matrix in the network. These scores are computed by a reciprocal process, such that the centrality of each page node is directly proportional to the sum of the centralities of those nodes to which it is connected. So, pages with high eigenvector centralities are connected to many other page nodes, which, in turn, are connected to many others, and the process goes on. In simple terms, eigenvector centrality can be defined as is a measure of being well-connected to the other well-connected nodes. The following snippet computes the eigenvector centrality for pages in our network:

```
# Eigenvector Centrality
evcentrality_plg <- eigen_centrality(pl_graph)$vector
evcentrality_plg_df <- data.frame(Name=V(pl_graph)$label,
                            EVcentrality=as.vector(evcentrality_
plg))
evcentrality_plg_df <- evcentrality_plg_df[order(evcentrality_plg_
df$EVcentrality,
                            decreasing=TRUE),]
View(head(evcentrality_plg_df, 10))
```

This gives us the following table showing top ten influential pages on the basis of eigenvector centrality:

	Name	EVcentrality
1	Premier League	1.0000000
21	Manchester United	0.9756104
22	Manchester City	0.9193786
24	Arsenal	0.7601505
262	Wayne Rooney	0.7497510
15	Nike Football	0.7217245
25	Chelsea Football Club	0.6871378
19	Sunderland AFC	0.6842139
445	UEFA Champions League	0.6432694
6	Burnley Football Club	0.6300486

Top influential pages with highest eigenvector centrality

Interestingly, if you look at this table, all these pages have a high value of the degree measure. Do you think there is a strong correlation between eigenvector centrality and degree? Try finding out!

PageRank

The PageRank measure gives an approximate probability value of a message arriving on a particular page node. This is computed using the Google PageRank algorithm invented by Google founders, Sergey Brin and Lawrence Page. Mathematically this is defined as:

$$PR(p_x) = \frac{1-d}{N} + d \sum_{pi \in M(p_x)} \frac{PR(p_i)}{L(p_i)}$$

In the preceding formula, $p_1, p_2, \cdots, p_x, \cdots, p_N$ are the various page nodes in the network, N is the total number of pages in the network, d is the damping factor usually set to 0.85, $M(p_x)$ is the set of pages having links to p_x and $L(p_i)$ is the total number of outgoing links on page p_i. For more details, you can refer to the original paper on PageRank at http://infolab.stanford.edu/~backrub/google.html. The following snippet computes the PageRank score for various page nodes in our network:

```
# Pagerank
pagerank_plg <- page_rank(pl_graph)$vector
```

```
pagerank_plg_df <- data.frame(Name=V(pl_graph)$label,
                              PageRank=as.vector(pagerank_plg))
pagerank_plg_df <- pagerank_plg_df[order(pagerank_plg_df$PageRank,
                              decreasing=TRUE),]
View(head(pagerank_plg_df, 10))
```

The following table depicts the top ten important pages on the basis of their PageRank score:

	Name	PageRank
15	Nike Football	0.027226678
24	Arsenal	0.019968333
21	Manchester United	0.018352130
25	Chelsea Football Club	0.017139476
22	Manchester City	0.013780236
558	adidas Football	0.013302024
245	PSG - Paris Saint-Germain	0.011784058
1	Premier League	0.011723774
445	UEFA Champions League	0.009690068
264	Nike	0.008748710

Top influential pages with highest PageRank score

It looks like Adidas and Nike are quite influential pages in this case along with some top level football clubs in the Premier League!

HITS authority score

The **Hyperlink-Induced Topic Search (HITS)** authority score developed by Jon Kleinberg is another algorithm which is used to rank web pages like PageRank. The authority scores of the page nodes can be computed as the principal eigenvector of $t(M) \times M$, where M is the adjacency matrix of the network. The following snippet computes the authority score of the pages in the network using the HITS algorithm:

```
# Kleinberg's HITS Score
hits_plg <- authority_score(pl_graph)$vector
hits_plg_df <- data.frame(Name=V(pl_graph)$label,
                          AuthScore=as.vector(hits_plg))
hits_plg_df <- hits_plg_df[order(hits_plg_df$AuthScore,
decreasing=TRUE),]
View(head(hits_plg_df, 10))
```

The following table depicts the top ten influential pages based on the HITS authority score.

	Name	AuthScore
21	Manchester United	1.0000000
24	Arsenal	0.9619702
1	Premier League	0.9178324
22	Manchester City	0.8847690
25	Chelsea Football Club	0.8299846
14	Everton Football Club	0.6517946
17	Tottenham Hotspur	0.6220038
23	Liverpool FC	0.5799794
459	England football team	0.5277520
18	Swansea City Football Club	0.4647856

Top influential pages with highest HITS authority score

This time, it looks like the top ten are all English football clubs or teams, apart from our root page. Quite interesting!

Page neighbours

We can also find out the neighboring pages from a root page by leveraging igraph's `neighbor (...)` function. The following snippet depicts the same for our root page *Premier League* and one of the football clubs, *Southampton FC*, more popularly known as *Saints FC*:

```
# finding neighbours of page vertices
> pl_neighbours <- neighbors(pl_graph, v=which(V(pl_
graph)$label=="Premier League"))
> pl_neighbours
+ 26/582 vertices:
 [1]  2  3  4  5  6  7  8  9 10 11 12 13 14 15 16 17 18 19 20 21 22 23
24 25 26 27

> pl_neighbours$label
 [1] "TAG Heuer" "Carling""Hull Tigers""Middlesbrough FC"
 [5] "Burnley Football Club" "Watford FC" "AFC Bournemouth"
"Leicester City Football Club"
 [9] "Crystal Palace Football Club" "West Ham United"
"Southampton FC" "Love GREAT Britain"
```

```
[13] "Everton Football Club" "Nike Football" "West Bromwich Albion"
"Tottenham Hotspur"
[17] "Swansea City Football Club" "Sunderland AFC"
"Stoke City Football Club" "Manchester United"
[21] "Manchester City" "Liverpool FC" "Arsenal"
"Chelsea Football Club"
[25] "Barclays Football" "EA SPORTS"

> pl_neighbours <- neighbors(pl_graph, v=which(V(pl_
graph)$label=="Southampton FC"))
> pl_neighbours
+ 19/582 vertices:
 [1]   26 126 185 186 187 188 189 190 191 192 193 194 195 196 197 198
199 200 201

> pl_neighbours$label
 [1] "Barclays Football" "The Emirates FA Cup" "JÃ©rÃ©my Pied"
 [4] "Virgin Media" "Under Armour (GB, IE)" "Radhi JaÃ¯di"
 [7] "Oriol Romeu Vidal" "NIX Communications Group" "JosÃ© Fonte"
[10] "OctaFX" "Florin Gardos" "Harrison Reed"
[13] "Ryan Bertrand" "Garmin" "James Ward-Prowse"
[16] "Benali's Big Race" "Southampton Solent University - Official"
"Sparsholt Football Academy"
[19] "Saints Foundation"
```

If you look more closely at the neighbouring pages in each case you will see that they make a lot of sense. In the first case, they are all football clubs or sponsors related to the Premier League. In the second case, they are all players, sponsors, or other entities related to Saints FC.

Analyzing network communities

Just as in our previous social network, we will try to extract and analyze specific clusters or communities in our page network graph, such that each community is more strongly connected compared to the rest of the network.

Cliques

As we've mentioned before, a clique is basically a subset of the nodes in the graph such that they are connected, and a maximum clique in a graph has the maximum number of connected nodes. Let us look closely at the maximum cliques in our football pages social network:

```
# get the size of the max clique
> clique_num(pl_graph)
```

```
[1] 10
# get count of max cliques of size 10
> count_max_cliques(pl_graph, min=10, max=10)
[1] 2

# get the max cliques and their constituent pages
clique_list <- cliques(pl_graph, min=10, max=10)
for (clique in clique_list){
  print(clique$label)
  cat('\n\n')
}
```

This gives us two cliques having ten pages each as shown in the following figure:

```
[1] "Manchester United"        "Adnan Januzaj"         "Wayne Rooney"      "Juan Mata"
[5] "Bastian Schweinsteiger"   "David De Gea"          "Luke Shaw"         "Daley Blind"
[9] "Marouane Fellaini"        "Manchester United Foundation"


[1] "Manchester United"        "Wayne Rooney"          "Juan Mata"         "Bastian Schweinsteiger"
[5] "David De Gea"             "Luke Shaw"             "Daley Blind"       "Chevrolet FC"
[9] "Marouane Fellaini"        "Manchester United Foundation"
```

Can you detect any relationship between pages in the cliques, Manchester United fans? Well they are all players, sponsors, or entities closely linked with the Manchester United football club! That's definitely a justification of why this is a clique.

Communities

We will now try to find communities or clusters of pages that are more connected by using the fast greedy clustering algorithm from the igraph package. Before we do that, we need to curate our network and keep only the important pages to reduce the size of our network, otherwise visualizing it would be really difficult on smaller plots. We use the following snippet for the same to remove nodes of lower degrees:

```
# filtering graph to get important nodes based on degree
degrees <- degree(pl_graph, mode="total")
degrees_df <- data.frame(ID=V(pl_graph)$id,
                         Name=V(pl_graph)$label,
                         Degree=as.vector(degree_plg))
ids_to_remove <- degrees_df[degrees_df$Degree < 30, c('ID')]
ids_to_remove <- ids_to_remove / 10

filtered_pl_graph <- delete.vertices(pl_graph, ids_to_remove)
fplg_undirected <- as.undirected(filtered_pl_graph)
```

We now apply the `fast greedy clustering algorithm` which tries to maximize the cluster modularity score which we had discussed earlier when we analyzed communities in our personal friend network:

```
# fast greedy clustering
fgc <- cluster_fast_greedy(fplg_undirected)
layout <- layout_with_fr(fplg_undirected,
                         niter=500, start.temp=5.744)
communities <- data.frame(layout)
names(communities) <- c("x", "y")
communities$cluster <- factor(fgc$membership)
communities$name <- V(fplg_undirected)$label

# get total pages in each cluster
> table(communities$cluster)
 1  2  3
15 10 10

# get page names in each cluster
community_groups <- unlist(lapply(groups(fgc),
                    function(item){
                      pages <- communities$name[item]
                      i <- 1; lim <- 4; s <- ""
                      while(i <= length(pages)){
                        start = i
                        end = min((i+lim-1),
                                  length(pages))
                        s <- paste(s,
                  paste(pages[start:end], collapse=", "))
                        s <- paste(s, "\n")
                        i=i+lim
                      }
                      return(substr(s, 1, (nchar(s)-2)))

                    })
)
if (dev.cur()!=1){dev.off()}
grid.table(community_groups)
```

This gives us the following table depicting each community and its constituent pages:

Premier League, Middlesbrough FC, Burnley Football Club, Watford FC Crystal Palace Football Club, Love GREAT Britain, Everton Football Club, Tottenham Hotspur Sunderland AFC, Stoke City Football Club, Liverpool FC, Chelsea Football Club Barclays Football, EFL, EFL Cup
TAG Heuer, Southampton FC, Manchester United, Wayne Rooney Bastian Schweinsteiger, Luke Shaw, Marouane Fellaini, Manchester United Foundation UEFA Champions League, adidas Football
Nike Football, Manchester City, Arsenal, EA SPORTS EA SPORTS FIFA, Jack Wilshere, Joe Hart, City in the Community Foundation England football team, AFC Till I Die

We can now get the modularity score of the network using the following code:

```
# get modularity score
> modularity(fgc)
[1] 0.2917283
```

To visualize the clusters in the network, we can use the following snippet:

```
# visualize clusters in the network
comm_plot <- ggplot(communities, aes(x=x, y=y, color=cluster,
label=name))
comm_plot <- comm_plot + geom_label(aes(fill = cluster),
                                    colour="white")
comm_plot
```

This gives us the following plot showing the different pages based in their cluster color:

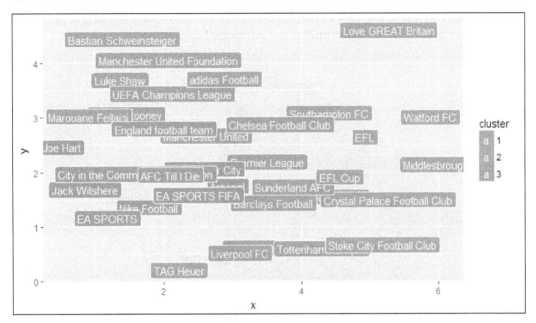

Visualizing communities of football pages related to the Premier League

We can now visualize the whole network along with its various communities using the following code:

```
plot(fgc, fplg_undirected,
     vertex.size=15,
     vertex.label.cex=0.8,
     vertex.label=fgc$names,
     edge.arrow.size=0,
     edge.curved=TRUE,
     vertex.label.color="black",
     layout=layout.fruchterman.reingold)
```

This gives us the following plot depicting the complete network with all the pages, their connections, and the communities we computed earlier:

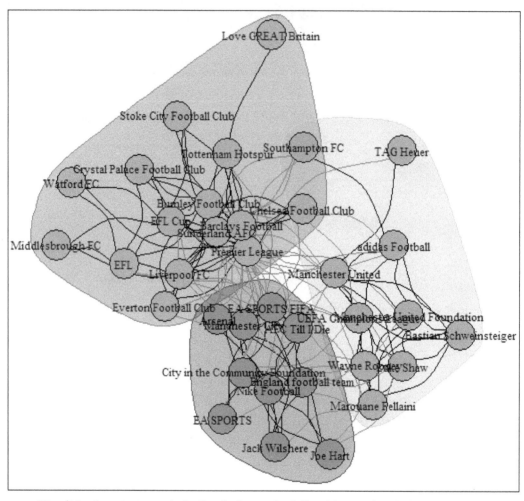

Visualizing important pages in the Premier League football social network including communities

Do you notice any specific reason for these communities being formed? Try the edge betweenness clustering algorithm using the `cluster_edge_betweenness(...)` function from the `igraph` package. You can refer to the code files for the solution if needed. Do you notice any difference in the communities being formed? Why do you think it exhibits such behavior?

Analyzing English Football Club's brand page engagements

Continuing our analysis of Facebook pages, let us now focus our analysis on brand page engagements. Each page on Facebook belonging to a commercial entity is basically a prestigious brand and keeping proper engagement with its followers on Facebook is very important. In this section, we will pick up three prestigious top tier football clubs from the Premier League and analyze their brand page engagements, trending posts and influential users using various analyzes and visualizations by retrieving data from their Facebook pages. We will also be using a `multiplot(...)` function for depicting multiple `ggplot2` plots together. The code is present in the `multiple_plots.R` code file which you can load along with the other dependencies as shown here:

```
library(Rfacebook)
library(ggplot2)
library(scales)
library(dplyr)
library(magrittr)
source('multiple_plots.R')
```

The code used for analysis in this section is available under the file named `fb_page_data_analysis.R` in the code files for this chapter, in case you want to open it and follow along. Now, let's look at how we can retrieve page data from Facebook.

Getting the data

You can use the `Rfacebook` package to get data from any Facebook page using the `getPage(...)` function. The following snippet gets data for three popular football clubs from the English Premier League. Besides being popular, there is also serious rivalry and competition between them, which is one of the reasons for choosing them. I have retrieved posts starting from 1st January, 2014 till 17th January, 2017. Some of the posts from a couple of the pages in the 2015-16 time period were not retrieved because of a Facebook post privacy issue rather than a library issue. However, we will analyze whatever data we were able to retrieve for the time period:

```
# get facebook token
token = 'XXXXXXXXX'

# get page stats
man_united <- getPage(page='manchesterunited', n=100000,
                      token=token, since='2014/01/01',
                      until='2017/01/17')
```

```
man_city <- getPage(page='mancity', n=100000,
                        token=token,since='2014/01/01',
                        until='2017/01/17')
arsenal <- getPage(page='Arsenal', n=100000,
                        token=token,since='2014/01/01',
                        until='2017/01/17')

# save data for later use
save(man_united, file='man_united.RData')
save(man_city, file='man_city.RData')
save(arsenal, file='arsenal.RData')
```

I have saved the page posts in the previously mentioned files for your ease and they are included with the code files for this chapter. You can use the following snippet to load the data directly into R:

```
# load data for analysis
load('man_united.RData')
load('man_city.RData')
load('arsenal.RData')
```

Curating the data

Now that we have the data loaded in R, we will curate the data by following some steps to filter specific columns in the data, and we'll also format the post creating a timestamp and adding new fields as needed. The steps are shown in the following snippet:

```
# combine data frames
colnames <- c('from_name', 'created_time', 'type',
                'likes_count', 'comments_count', 'shares_count',
                'id', 'message', 'link')
page_data <- rbind(man_united[colnames], man_city[colnames],
arsenal[colnames])
names(page_data)[1] <- "Page"
# format post creation time
page_data$created_time <- as.POSIXct(page_data$created_time,
format = "%Y-%m-%dT%H:%M:%S+0000",
tz = "GMT")
# add new time based columns
page_data$month <- format(page_data$created_time, "%Y-%m")
page_data$year <- format(page_data$created_time, "%Y")
```

You can now view the total number of combined posts from all three Facebook pages using the following command:

```
# total records
> nrow(page_data)
[1] 12537
```

Let's deep dive into analyzing this data in the next sections!

Visualizing post counts per page

We can visualize the total number of posts made by each of the football clubs'
Facebook pages by using the following code snippet and by leveraging `ggplot2`:

```
# post counts per page
post_page_counts <- aggregate(page_data$Page, by=list(page_data$Page),
length)
colnames(post_page_counts) <- c('Page', 'Count')
ggplot(post_page_counts, aes(x=Page, y=Count, fill=Page)) +
  geom_bar(position = "dodge", stat="identity") +
  geom_text(aes(label=Count),  vjust=-0.3, position=position_
dodge(.9), size=4) +
  scale_fill_brewer(palette="Set1")  +
  theme_bw()
```

This gives us the following plot depicting post counts per football club:

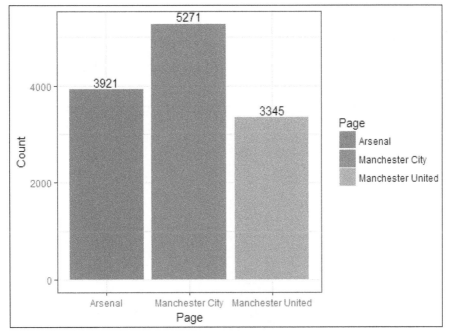

Post counts per page

Manchester City is the page with the highest number of posts compared to the other two. Surprisingly **Manchester United** has fewer posts, even though it has more fans and people talking about it on Facebook. There could be two reasons for this, either Manchester United posts less frequently than the other two pages, or we were unable to retrieve some of the posts for this page due to the post privacy issue mentioned earlier.

Visualizing post counts by post type per page

We can visualize the post counts per page by post types or categories. To do this, we use the following code snippet:

```
# post counts by post type per page
post_type_counts <- aggregate(page_data$type, by=list(page_data$Page,
page_data$type), length)
colnames(post_type_counts) <- c('Page', 'Type', 'Count')
ggplot(post_type_counts, aes(x=Page, y=Count, fill=Type)) +
  geom_bar(position = "dodge", stat="identity") +
  geom_text(aes(label=Type),  vjust=-0.5, position=position_dodge(.9),
size=3) +
  scale_fill_brewer(palette="Set1")  +
  theme_bw()
```

This gives us the following plot showing posts grouped by post type for each brand page:

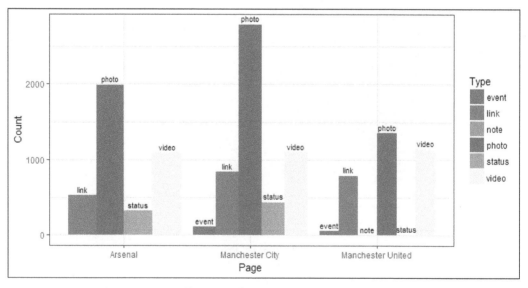

Post counts by post type per page

We can see that photos and videos are the media which are used the most by each page, to engage with their fans.

Visualizing average likes by post type per page

Let's visualize some user engagement with the brand pages now. To start with, we can compute the mean likes per post in each page by post type and then visualize it. Basically, the higher average likes per post means more fans are engaging actively with the page. Grouping them by post type would enable us to get insights as to which types of media are getting the most likes from the football club fans. The following snippet helps us achieve this:

```
# average likes per page by post type
likes_by_post_type <- aggregate(page_data$likes_count,
                                by=list(page_data$Page, page_
data$type), mean)
colnames(likes_by_post_type) <- c('Page', 'Type', 'AvgLikes')
ggplot(likes_by_post_type, aes(x=Page, y=AvgLikes, fill=Type)) +
  geom_bar(position = "dodge", stat="identity") +
  geom_text(aes(label=Type),  vjust=-0.5, position=position_dodge(.9),
size=3) +
  scale_fill_brewer(palette="Set1")  +
  theme_bw()
```

This gives us the following plot showing mean user likes grouped by post type per page:

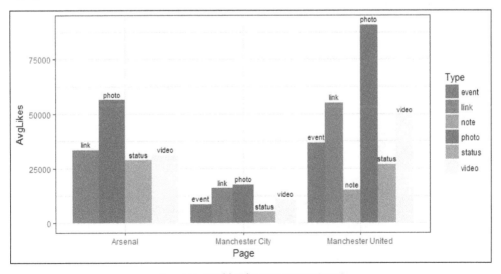

Average user likes by post type per page

Interesting, right? We can now see how Manchester United's strong fan base has an impact here. It has a massive count with regards to mean likes for each post type compared to the other football clubs. This clearly indicates that more club fans and page followers lead to more user engagement with the club's page posts based on post likes. Besides this, we also see that photos are the most liked media. Glory Glory Manchester United indeed!

Visualizing average shares by post type per page

Let's now visualize user engagement with the brand pages based on mean shares grouped by post type and compare it across all the football club brand pages. The following snippet helps us achieve this:

```
# average shares per page by post type
shares_by_post_type <- aggregate(page_data$shares_count,
                            by=list(page_data$Page, page_
data$type), mean)
colnames(shares_by_post_type) <- c('Page', 'Type', 'AvgShares')
ggplot(shares_by_post_type, aes(x=Page, y=AvgShares, fill=Type)) +
  geom_bar(position = "dodge", stat="identity") +
  geom_text(aes(label=Type),  vjust=-0.5, position=position_dodge(.9),
size=3) +
  scale_fill_brewer(palette="Set1")  +
  theme_bw()
```

This gives us the following visualization showing average post share counts per page grouped by post type:

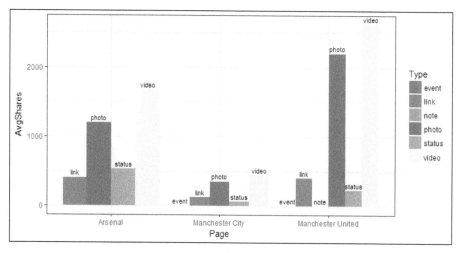

Average user shares by post type per page

No surprises here for Manchester United's landslide victory over the other two clubs in terms of user engagement based on post shares. However, do you notice an interesting pattern here across all three clubs compared to the previous plot? Videos are clearly shared more than photos. This provides an interesting aspect of user behavior. It's highly likely that fans want their friends and other fans to see short videos posted by the clubs about their training sessions, match highlights, and daily news related to the club, and hence the high counts in video shares.

Visualizing page engagement over time

Let's now visualize each brand page's engagement over time, based on their posts. We can do this by aggregating post counts per page over time and then visualizing it with the help of the following snippet:

```
# page engagement over time
page_posts_df <- aggregate(page_data[['type']], by=list(page_
data$month, page_data$Page), length)
colnames(page_posts_df) <- c('Month', 'Page', 'Count')
page_posts_df$Month <- as.Date(paste0(page_posts_df$Month, "-15"))
ggplot(page_posts_df, aes(x=Month, y=Count, group=Page)) +
  geom_point(aes(shape=Page)) +
  geom_line(aes(color=Page)) +
  theme_bw() + scale_x_date(date_breaks="3 month", date_labels='%m-
%Y') +
  ggtitle("Page Engagement over time")
```

This gives us the following plot depicting the total posts per page over a period:

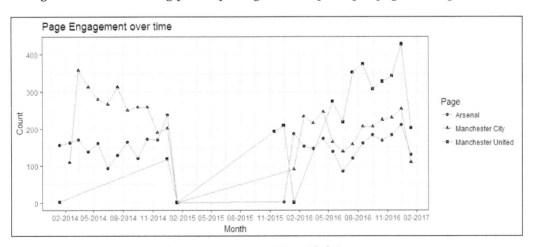

Page engagements over time with their users

The drop in posts in 2015 could be due to the page privacy issue mentioned earlier regarding inaccessible posts. Ignoring that, we can see that Manchester City and Arsenal have a higher post count in 2014, but that Manchester United slowly picks up the pace and beats them from May 2016 onwards.

Visualizing user engagement with page over time

Let's now visualize user engagement with each brand page over time based on likes, shares, and comments on various page posts. The steps are shown in the following snippet:

```
## user engagement with page over time
# create metric aggregation function
aggregate.metric <- function(metric, data) {
  m <- aggregate(data[[paste0(metric, "_count")]], list(month =
data$month),
                 mean)
  m$month <- as.Date(paste0(m$month, "-15"))
  m$metric <- metric
  return(m)
}

# get aggregated stats per page
mu_df <- subset(page_data, Page=="Manchester United")
mu_stats_df.list <- lapply(c("likes", "comments", "shares"),
aggregate.metric, data=mu_df)
mu_stats_df <- do.call(rbind, mu_stats_df.list)
mu_stats_df <- mu_stats_df[order(mu_stats_df$month), ]

afc_df <- subset(page_data, Page=="Arsenal")
afc_stats_df.list <- lapply(c("likes", "comments", "shares"),
aggregate.metric, data=afc_df)
afc_stats_df <- do.call(rbind, afc_stats_df.list)
afc_stats_df <- afc_stats_df[order(afc_stats_df$month), ]

mc_df <- subset(page_data, Page=="Manchester City")
mc_stats_df.list <- lapply(c("likes", "comments", "shares"),
aggregate.metric, data=mc_df)
```

```
mc_stats_df <- do.call(rbind, mc_stats_df.list)
mc_stats_df <- mc_stats_df[order(mc_stats_df$month), ]

# build visualizations on aggregated stats per page
p1 <- ggplot(mu_stats_df, aes(x=month, y=x, group=metric)) +
  geom_point(aes(shape = metric)) +
  geom_line(aes(color = metric)) +
  theme_bw() + scale_x_date(date_breaks="3 month", date_labels='%m-
%Y') +
  scale_y_log10("Avg stats/post", breaks = c(10, 100, 1000, 10000,
50000)) +
  ggtitle("Manchester United")

p2 <- ggplot(afc_stats_df, aes(x=month, y=x, group=metric)) +
  geom_point(aes(shape = metric)) +
  geom_line(aes(color = metric)) +
  theme_bw() + scale_x_date(date_breaks="3 month", date_labels='%m-
%Y') +
  scale_y_log10("Avg stats/post", breaks = c(10, 100, 1000, 10000,
50000)) +
  ggtitle("Arsenal")

p3 <- ggplot(mc_stats_df, aes(x=month, y=x, group=metric)) +
  geom_point(aes(shape = metric)) +
  geom_line(aes(color = metric)) +
  theme_bw() + scale_x_date(date_breaks="3 month", date_labels='%m-
%Y') +
  scale_y_log10("Avg stats/post", breaks = c(10, 100, 1000, 10000,
50000)) +
  ggtitle("Manchester City")

# view the plots together
multiplot(p1, p2, p3)
```

This gives us a nice multi-plot comparing three visualizations for user engagement across time for each of the three brand pages:

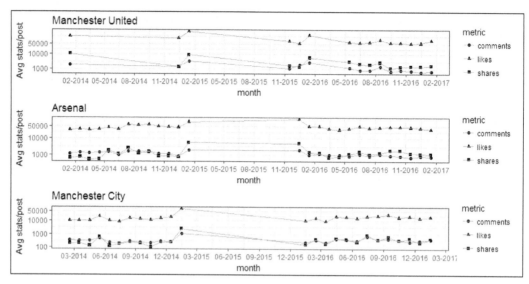

User engagements with pages over time

We can see that Manchester United and Arsenal have a higher user engagement over time compared to Manchester City.

Trending posts by user likes per page

Let's now see if we can get the top stories per year for each page based on user likes, in order to find out which were the most trending or viral posts annually. The following snippet helps us achieve this:

```
# trending posts by likes per page
trending_posts_likes <- page_data %>%
                        group_by(Page, year) %>%
                        filter(likes_count == max(likes_count))
trending_posts_likes <- as.data.frame(trending_posts_likes)
View(trending_posts_likes[,c('Page', 'year', 'month', 'type',
'likes_count', 'comments_count',
'shares_count','message', 'link')])
```

This gives us the following table showing the most trending posts per page based on likes:

	Page	year	month	type	likes_count	comments_count	shares_count	message
1	Manchester United	2017	2017-01	photo	366400	2504	9381	Two Premier League awards in December! <ed><U+00A...
2	Manchester United	2016	2016-12	photo	656353	6601	29237	Congratulations to Cristiano Ronaldo... Ballon d'Or win...
3	Manchester United	2015	2015-12	photo	801468	21413	34063	Happy birthday, Sir Alex!
4	Manchester United	2014	2014-12	photo	601320	16598	13978	Happy birthday, Sir Alex Ferguson! We hope you have a ...
5	Manchester City	2017	2017-01	photo	85490	515	1659	<ed><U+00A0><U+00BD><ed><U+00B2><U+0099>
6	Manchester City	2016	2016-07	video	300005	17245	76050	When Pep Guardiola stunned City fan Braydon Bent! <e...
7	Manchester City	2015	2015-01	photo	74606	1047	2443	Wishing all City fans a very happy New Year! Here's to a ...
8	Manchester City	2014	2014-06	photo	228690	7189	5088	Feliz cumpleaños Sergio! Join us in wishing Sergio Ague...
9	Arsenal	2017	2017-01	photo	169899	2772	11838	That's what we <U+2764><U+FE0F><U+FE0F> to see! ...
10	Arsenal	2016	2016-06	photo	354423	3317	13556	Rest in peace, Champ.
11	Arsenal	2015	2015-12	photo	143412	871	2283	NA

Top trending page posts by year and user like counts

You can see that Manchester United's beloved manager and legend Sir Alex Ferguson gets the highest likes on his birthday posts. Manchester City gets the highest likes on the birthday post for its star striker, Sergio Aguero. Their new coach, Pep Guardiola, also receives quite a lot of attention. Arsenal's cover photo was most liked in 2015, and their star player, Alexis Sanchez, is popular with their fans based on the likes he gained when he joined the club.

Trending posts by user shares per page

Let's now see if the top trending stories per year for each page based on user shares are any different compared to those based on likes. The following snippet gives us the top annual trending posts per page based on user shares:

```
# trending posts by shares per page
trending_posts_shares <- page_data %>%
                    group_by(Page, year) %>%
                    filter(shares_count == max(shares_count))
trending_posts_shares <- as.data.frame(trending_posts_shares)
View(trending_posts_shares[,c('Page', 'year', 'month', 'type',
'likes_count', 'comments_count',
'shares_count','message', 'link')])
```

The following table depicts the top trending annual posts per page based on shares:

	Page	year	month	type	likes_count	comments_count	shares_count	message	link
1	Manchester United	2017	2017-01	video	262038	3247	14986	On this day in 2008 - <U+26BD> <U+FE0F> <U+26BD> ...	https://www.fac
2	Manchester United	2016	2016-05	photo	327285	17059	137536	We are delighted to announce Jose Mourinho is our ne...	https://www.fac
3	Manchester United	2015	2015-12	photo	801468	21413	34063	Happy birthday, Sir Alex!	https://www.fac
4	Manchester United	2014	2014-01	photo	269723	3191	20394	Happy New Year, from everyone at Manchester United.	https://www.fac
5	Manchester City	2017	2017-01	photo	79888	10518	7020	FT	Everton 4-0 City Ugh.	https://www.fac
6	Manchester City	2016	2016-07	video	300005	17245	76050	When Pep Guardiola stunned City fan Braydon Bent! <e...	https://www.fac
7	Manchester City	2015	2015-01	photo	74606	1047	2443	Wishing all City fans a very happy New Year! Here's to a ...	https://www.fac
8	Manchester City	2014	2014-07	photo	27941	2659	29643	SHARE TO WIN: Share this photo and you could be one ...	https://www.fac
9	Arsenal	2017	2017-01	video	76750	4663	27510	This is amazing... watch Arsenal and Dunking Devils war...	https://www.fac
10	Arsenal	2016	2016-01	video	263978	11998	48981	No Per? No problem - Theo finds a fan for his celebrator...	https://www.fac
11	Arsenal	2015	2015-12	photo	131529	3063	7484	Happy New Year to Arsenal fans around the world!	https://www.fac
12	Arsenal	2014	2014-05	photo	266363	8825	44301	NA	https://www.fac

Top trending page posts by year and user share counts

Do you notice any difference in the posts this time compared to the trending posts based on likes? Interestingly New Year greeting posts get a lot of shares across all three clubs. So do United and City coaches. Do you notice any other interesting patterns? Everton 4 – 0 City was a surprise result in 2017 for Manchester City and it is one of the most shared posts!

Top influential users on popular page posts

Let's take a couple of trending posts and try to see who the most influential users from their post comments are. We can do this by simply taking the total number of likes on their comment by other users. We will extract comments for one United and one Arsenal post using the following snippet:

```
# extract post comment data
mu_top_post_2015 <- getPost(post='7724542745_10153390997792746',
token=token, n=5000, comments=TRUE)
afc_top_post_2014 <- getPost(post='20669912712_10152350372162713',
token=token, n=5000, comments=TRUE)

# save the data for future analysis
save(mu_top_post_2015, file='mu_top_post_2015.RData')
save(afc_top_post_2014, file='afc_top_post_2014.RData')
```

The data is saved and available for analyzes along with the code files of this chapter, so you can choose to skip the preceding steps and directly load the data to start analyzing it using the following snippet:

```
# load top post comments
load('mu_top_post_2015.RData')
```

```
load('afc_top_post_2014.RData')

# get top influential users for United post
> mu_top_post_2015$post[, c('from_name', 'message')]
         from_name                        message
1 Manchester United Happy birthday, Sir Alex!
mu_post_comments <- mu_top_post_2015$comments
View(mu_post_comments[order(mu_post_comments$likes_count,
                      decreasing=TRUE),][1:10,
c('from_name', 'likes_count', 'message')])
```

This gives us the following table depicting top influential users based on total likes on their comments:

	from_name	likes_count	message
1	Vu Nguy<U+1EC5>n Thanh Tu<U+1EA5>n	4153	Happy birthday to the greatest of all time !!!
4	Đ<U+1ED6> KIM PHÚC	1103	Happy birthday Sir Alex <3
3	Ariwa Michael Odinakachukwu	485	happy birthday sir come back...we need you
2	Okweni Nelson Ogheneovo	476	Happy birthday grt man that man united even miss
8	Yappey Calo	244	Happy birthday Maax Mohamed . The biggest fan of Ma...
3466	Vaishnavi Desai	147	happy birthday sir Alex....u r the best n ull alwz be...man...
5	Ernie Mcracken	88	Happy birthday sir Alex Miss you so much Not a day goe...
7	Matt Gill	88	Happy birthday Sir Alex, a legend for Manchester United...
6	Pankaj Singh	84	On your Birthday, Sir Alex, I am going to present my smal...
196	Lenq Nesh	41	Happy Birthday To The Legend Sir Alex Ferguson <3 Plea...

Top influential users based on comment like counts for Manchester United's trending post

Let's now look at the top influential users for the Arsenal post using the following snippet:

```
# get top influential users for Arsenal post
> afc_top_post_2014$post[, c('from_name', 'message')]
   from_name
message
Arsenal Alexis Sanchez in his new PUMA #Arsenal training kit!\n\
n#SanchezSigns

afc_post_comments <- afc_top_post_2014$comments
View(afc_post_comments[order(afc_post_comments$likes_count,
                      decreasing=TRUE),][1:10,
c('from_name', 'likes_count', 'message')])
```

This gives us the following table showing the top influential users based on likes received on their comments:

	from_name	likes_count	message
2	Alex Peters	1578	Please tell me I wasnt the only one to be constantly chec...
1	Albeiro Molano	1145	grande alexis 100%
5	Promise Kofi Quampah	207	
6	Kim Akim Joachim	176	arsenal is always on my mind
3	Damon Selman-Carrington	172	As a Barcelona fan I am really excited by this move. Sanc...
4	Alex Dougherty	154	`biggest mistake of his life` That's exactly what everyon...
7	Griffin Lee	94	James Blasina omg finally a world class striker
8	Tom Immins	85	Ramsey to Ozil, Ozil to Walcott, Walcott to Sanchez...GO...
9	Iqbal Umar	71	
10	Jack Parkes	34	

Top influential users based on comment like counts for Arsenal's trending post

All the comments are about praising Alexis Sanchez on signing for the Gunners (Arsenal). This is just scratching the surface of what can be done with this data. Try and see if you can come up with more interesting patterns and insights.

Summary

I really appreciate and commend your efforts to stay with me to the end of this chapter. We went on a long and fruitful journey looking at the possibilities of tapping the potential goldmine that exists in Facebook's data stores. We looked at the Graph API and the Rfacebook package and harnessed it efficiently to extract and curate data from Facebook. We covered several important use-cases to understanding the basic use of the Graph API, analyzing your own personal social network of friends, and even learnt concepts of social network analysis by leveraging the `igraph` package. We built on these concepts and analyzed an even larger social network of Facebook brand pages related to English Football and applied more advanced concepts of social network analysis. Finally, we looked at Facebook page data and analyzed brand page and user engagements on Facebook, based on several different attributes and variables. We also mined trending posts and influential users from this data. You now know how to use the Graph API efficiently and how to build great visualizations to depict valuable insights from Facebook data. I encourage you to play around more with the code snippets from this chapter and build more use-cases and problems to solve on your own!

4
Foursquare – Are You Checked in Yet?

Foursquare is a search and discovery platform which helps users with their social endeavors. It uses the user's information including previous history, demographic information, location, and so on, to suggest locations of interest to the user. In simple terms, it can be viewed as an application dishing out aggregated location knowledge custom built to an individual's tastes. It is very much akin to the oracle on your shoulder to whom you can ask the important question: *"What should I do?"* and then decide whether to act on that information.

In this chapter, we will try to learn how we can leverage Foursquare data to gain some meaningful insights to the user's behavior. We will try to build some use cases which will help us in demonstrating the actual process of answering relevant questions starting from the data.

To summarize, broadly we will be covering the following topics:

- Understanding Foursquare data and working with its data APIs
- Finding category trends along major cities and providing an example of a recommender system built on that data
- Performing sentiment analysis and then using that analysis for performing an extended study
- Finding a next venue graph and giving some insights into it
- Discussing the challenges of Foursquare data and especially the JSON issues

A very important idea in this chapter is using the data to form a relevant use case about business problems. We will solve one of them, the recommender system, and will discuss others wherever they arise. A very important issue in this chapter pertains to data wrangling, which will become quite important in any real-life analytics process and also in the subsequent chapters of this book.

Foursquare – the app and data

Foursquare was founded in 2009 by *Dennis Crowley* and *Naveen Selvadurai*. It was a reimagined version of a similar service, Dodgeball, founded by Crowley in his graduate studies days. Dodgeball was an attempt to help the user interact with his neighborhood using his phone and primarily using SMS messages:

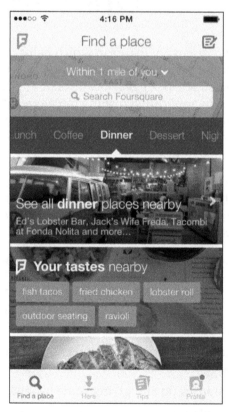

Foursquare main page. Image source: By Source (WP:NFCC#4), Fair use,
https://en.wikipedia.org/w/index.php?curid=43651932

Foursquare continued that paradigm and tried to use the new features of smartphones for achieving the same interaction, the most important of these features being the GPS.

The initial rise to fame of Foursquare was related to its innovative *check-in* feature, which allowed a user to share his/her location at any venue. This feature was quite similar to Facebook's own check-in feature. Although with the launch of Foursquare 8.0, the check-in feature has been removed from the Foursquare application.

A unique feature of Foursquare data is the tips users can leave for the venue. Like tweets, tips are required to be short, concise text information about the venue instead of long, free form reviews that are generally found on most sites.

An important thing to keep in mind, for the check-in data, is that now Foursquare doesn't allow a user to check-in, the data about the venues would be a bit dated. Nevertheless, it is important for insights into the venues as we will witness in the coming pages.

Foursquare APIs – show me the data

All major social media services provide a good set of APIs to third parties for accessing their data. The intent of these APIs is to give access to programmers for consuming their data and building products using this data.

Foursquare also has a rich set of APIs in keeping with this tradition.

We will go over the main end points (which we will be using) of Foursquare API, including:

- **Venues**: Venues are the major data provided by Foursquare. They contain data about the locations of interest. The data collected about these venues includes contacts, location, stats, verification, and so on. Each venue can also have a manager configured who can manage information about that particular venue.

- **Users**: This end point gives information about the users of Foursquare. Like Twitter, a Foursquare user can be any entity. In recent times, this end point has become very restricted as you can only extract user information of your friends.

- **Check-ins**: This is one of the most important data end points. It contains the metadata associated with each check-in made using Foursquare. It captures information related to venue, user, timestamp, and location of the check-in.

- **Tips**: Tips are the small reviews type text that Foursquare users can give for the venues. This end point provides all the metadata related to any tip left for a venue.

- **Events**: Venue manager can post events which relate to their venue. This end point provides all the information related to these events. In a third-party application, these events can be used to provide suggestions to the users.

These APIs have extensive documentation which can be used to retrieve more information about them. A thorough understanding of these APIs will help in having a complete knowledge of the data that we are using for our studies.

Creating an application – let me in

Like the steps followed in the previous chapters, the starting point to our analysis is the application which we will use to access the APIs. Again like most other social media applications, Foursquare also uses an OAuth-based access to its APIs. We would encourage you to go through the terms and conditions of the data access as you don't want to be caught in any legal tangles.

The steps to the app created are quite simple:

1. Create a Foursquare account (if you don't already have one).
2. Log in to the app management console at: `https://foursquare.com/developers/apps`
3. Once logged in, click on **Create a new app button**. Fill in the required fields and then click on **Create App**. This will complete the app creation process:

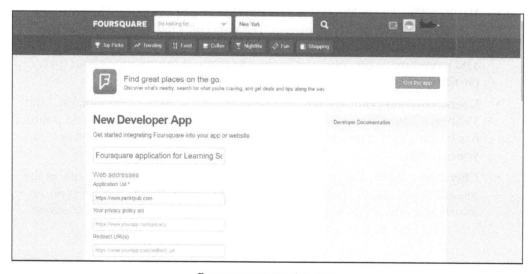

Foursquare app creation page

Once you have completed the app creation process, you will be taken to the app details page. This page will have the most important information you will need for data access. This includes the **CLIENT_ID** and **CLIENT_SECRET** information for your app. Every API call we make will use these two pieces of information. This is used to collect and monitor API access by the Foursquare team:

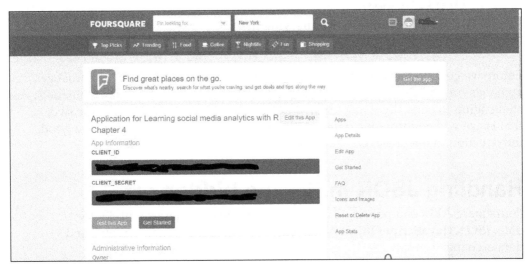

Foursquare app's details

Now we have all the information, we need to proceed with our data access. Now we will use the relevant API end point to query for the data we need for our purpose.

One important aspect of an API-driven data access is the applicable fair use policy. Please get acquainted with the limits that apply to you, otherwise you risk actions being placed against your account, including restriction or even blocking of your account.

Data access – the twist in the story

The process until now has been pretty much similar to the data access process that we followed in the previous chapter. This is where the similarities end. Foursquare doesn't have any R package that we can use for a simplified data access. Foursquare data can only be used by directly querying the API end points. This is where the major complication of the data extraction process arises.

The general process that we will follow for our data extraction process will follow the following steps:

1. Find the required end points for the required data.
2. Construct the required URL for data access using **CLIENT_ID** and **CLIENT_SECRET**.
3. Get the JSON response by querying the URL.
4. Parse the JSON response into a tabular format.

Before we get into the process of getting data from Foursquare APIs, we must get an hands-on introduction to JSON data. JSON data is notoriously easy but equally challenging to parse. To make for an efficient process, we will combine the two, that is, we will go through a data extraction example which will also give a good introduction to the process of JSON parsing.

Handling JSON in R – the hidden art

Foursquare API's end point will always respond to our queries with JSON data. **JSON (JavaScript Object Notation)** is a flexible, easy, and widely used data exchange format.

We will use an example in which we will extract all the categories in which Foursquare venues data is organized. We will start by installing the required packages. We will be using the packages `dplyr`, `tidyjson`, `magrittr`, and `RCurl`. So let's get started with the whole process.

Getting category data – introduction to JSON parsing and data extraction

The data we are interested in is the categories that exist on Foursquare.

A quick check in the API documentation reveals that the end point we are looking for is:

```
https://api.foursquare.com/v2/venues/categories?v=20131016
```

This API URL will not directly work for us so we need to enrich it with our
CLIENT_ID and **CLIENT_SECRET** information. So we will initialize a
parameterized `uri` to which we can then add the required information:

```
#Sequence for extracting all categories in foursquare
json_res <- NULL

# Initialize the necessary authorization information

token="xxxxxxxxxxxxxxxxxxxxxxxxxxxxxxxxxxxxxxxxxxxxxxxxxx"
secret="xxxxxxxxxxxxxxxxxxxxxxxxxxxxxxxxxxxxxxxxxxxxxxxxxx"

#Create the necessary API endpoint URL
uriTemplate <-"https://api.foursquare.com/v2/venues/
categories?v=20131016&client_id=%s&client_secret=%s"

#Update the API URL with authorization information
apiurl<- sprintf(uriTemplate, token,secret)

#Call the end point for JSON response
json_res <- getURL(apiurl, .mapUnicode=TRUE)
```

Once our `apiurl` is ready, we use the `getURL` function to get the required JSON
response. It contains three major objects, namely `meta`, `notifications`, and
`response`. `Meta` contains the metadata about the API request and the notification
object is more of a concern for the Foursquare developers. The `response` object
contains the data we have requested. As different APIs will have different `response`
objects, we will have to write custom code for each data point we want to use. Before
we start parsing the `response` object, it is important to check the `meta` object for
some metadata information, that is, we want to make sure it was a valid response:

```
# Code snippet for extracting the result of an API query
json_res %>% enter_object("meta") %>% spread_values(result =
jnumber("code"))
```

This is where the effectiveness of tidyjson comes in handy. We need to understand how we got to this particular data, as this will form the basis of our future parsing process. The JSON response to our API request looks like this:

```
□ {
    "meta": □ {
        "code": 200,
        "requestId": "58a05a0ddb04f577fb8a600d"
    },
    "notifications": □ [
        □ {
            "type": "notificationTray",
            "item": □ {
                "unreadCount": 0
            }
        }
    ],
    "response": □ {
        "categories": □ [
            □ {
                "id": "4d4b7104d754a06370d81259",
                "name": "Arts & Entertainment".
```

JSON response for categories response

Now the parsing process can be explained in terms of *actions* or *verbs* that can be applied to the response. Here we want to enter the meta object and then extract the numeric value of the key code. So this is exactly what we write using the code. Likewise, this applies in the preceding JSON response, if we want to get the values of the type token. In the JSON, we have three objects: meta, notifications, and response. For the type, we will enter the notification object followed by extracting the textual value of the type. The code enter_object("notifications") will allow us to enter the notifications object. Once we are *in the object*, we can directly refer to the value and the code spread_values(type_value = jstring("type")) will allow us to extract the value of the key "type" in the variable type. Take a look at the code again and it will be clear now.

The different result codes for the Foursquare APIs can be found at this link: https://developer.foursquare.com/overview/responses. You can use them accordingly to add some reliability to your code.

Now extracting this value was quite easy as we only had a single key inside the meta object. The task becomes a little tougher when we have nested objects and arrays. The data of importance for us is contained in the response object.

Let's take a look at what is contained in that object:

```json
"response": ⊟ {
  "categories": ⊟ [
    ⊟ {
      "id": ████████████████████9",
      "name": "Arts & Entertainment",
      "pluralName": "Arts & Entertainment",
      "shortName": "Arts & Entertainment",
      "icon": ⊞ {},
      "categories": ⊟ [
        ⊞ {},
        ⊞ {},
        ⊞ {},
        ⊟ {
          "id": "████████████████████",
          "name": "Art Gallery",
          "pluralName": "Art Galleries",
          "shortName": "Art Gallery",
          "icon": ⊟ {
            "prefix": "https://ss3.4sqi.net/img/categories_v2/arts_entertainment/artgaller
",
            "suffix": ".png"
          },
          "categories": ⊟ []
        },
```

Nested JSON objects

The `response` object contains an array of categories and one of the keys in each of these categories is a list of categories. Puzzled? This is a nested JSON where the first category is a type of major category and the categories nested in that are the sub-categories of the major category. You can imagine it as a *Parent category-Child category* relationship. The following is the code that we will use to extract these nested relationships while maintaining the relationships in our output:

```r
#Parsing the JSON object for extracting the data frame
category_df <- as.data.frame(json_res %>% enter_object("response")
           %>% enter_object("categories")
           %>% gather_array()
           %>% spread_values(super_cat_id = jstring("id"), super_
cat_name = jstring("name"))
           %>% enter_object("categories")
           %>% gather_array()
           %>% spread_values(cat_id = jstring("id"), cat_name =
jstring("name"), cat_pluralName = jstring("pluralName"), cat_shortName
= jstring("shortName"))
```

```
            %>% enter_object("categories")
            %>% gather_array()
            %>% spread_values(cat_id2 = jstring("id"), cat_name2
= jstring("name"), cat_pluralName2 = jstring("pluralName"), cat_
shortName2 = jstring("shortName")))

#Removing extra variables from the data frame
category_df$array.index <- NULL
category_df$document.id <- NULL
```

The preceding code looks a little bit puzzling for sure. So let's dissect it a bit. The key is to follow the same *verb*-based paradigm as we did in our simple example. We want to enter the `response` object and then enter the `categories` object. This `categories` object is an array, that is, a list of categories. So we will have to gather all these categories together, which is done using the `gather_array()` function. If there was only one level of category, we could have captured the relevant values (using the spread `values` function) and be done with it. But we also want to capture the nested categories within these top level ones. Now, before we descend down into the next level of category, we also want to capture the relevant information about the top level. So we capture the relevant top level values using the `spread_values()` function. Then we repeat the process of going down one more level as we did earlier.

 tidyjson is a pretty powerful and easy to understand package to handle JSON objects. The intuitive syntax is a great help for getting data out of JSON objects having a tough structure, which often is the case.

We can keep repeating this process if we have a lot of nesting in our JSON objects. Thankfully, this is not the case for most of our data.

The output of this snippet is very much similar to the tabular data format which we want to achieve. It looks like this:

super_cat_id	super_cat_name	cat_id	cat_name	cat_pluralName	cat_shortName
4d4b7104d754a06370d81259	Arts & Entertainment	56aa371be4b08b9a8d5734db	Amphitheater	Amphitheaters	Amphitheater
4d4b7104d754a06370d81259	Arts & Entertainment	4fceea171983d5d06c3e9823	Aquarium	Aquariums	Aquarium
4d4b7104d754a06370d81259	Arts & Entertainment	4bf58dd8d48988d1e1931735	Arcade	Arcades	Arcade
4d4b7104d754a06370d81259	Arts & Entertainment	4bf58dd8d48988d1e2931735	Art Gallery	Art Galleries	Art Gallery
4d4b7104d754a06370d81259	Arts & Entertainment	4bf58dd8d48988d1e4931735	Bowling Alley	Bowling Alleys	Bowling Alley
4d4b7104d754a06370d81259	Arts & Entertainment	4bf58dd8d48988d17c941735	Casino	Casinos	Casino
4d4b7104d754a06370d81259	Arts & Entertainment	52e81612bcbc57f1066b79e7	Circus	Circuses	Circus
4d4b7104d754a06370d81259	Arts & Entertainment	4bf58dd8d48988d18e941735	Comedy Club	Comedy Clubs	Comedy Club
4d4b7104d754a06370d81259	Arts & Entertainment	5032792091d4c4b30a586d5c	Concert Hall	Concert Halls	Concert Hall
4d4b7104d754a06370d81259	Arts & Entertainment	52e81612bcbc57f1066b79ef	Country Dance Club	Country Dance Clubs	Country Dance Club
4d4b7104d754a06370d81259	Arts & Entertainment	52e81612bcbc57f1066b79e8	Disc Golf	Disc Golf Courses	Disc Golf
4d4b7104d754a06370d81259	Arts & Entertainment	56aa371be4b08b9a8d573532	Exhibit	Exhibits	Exhibit
4d4b7104d754a06370d81259	Arts & Entertainment	4bf58dd8d48988d1f1931735	General Entertainment	General Entertainment	Entertainment

Output JSON parser

Once we have the required data parsed, all we need to do is to convert it into a DataFrame and we can use it for our analytics workflows.

Revisiting the analytics workflow

By now we have completely established the overall process of deriving relevant insights from our target data. We will revisit the key steps in the process to give the users a light refresher into it again. We have the following four stages in any workflow:

- **Data access**: This step involves creating the required credentials for data access and completing the basic prerequisites for data access.

- **Data processing and normalization**: In this stage, we will use the data access we secured to extract the relevant data and wrangle it into usable formats. The complex parsing process that we evolved in the last section was an apt example.

- **Data analysis**: This is the stage where we use the data and perform various operations such as summarizing, and aggregating on it to find out the questions which we can pose on the dataset.

- **Insights**: This is the most important stage of any analytics workflow. Here we summarize our findings and finalize the findings that we were able to extract from the dataset. This is where the value part of the data is realized.

Category trend analysis

Foursquare is essentially a collection of real-life locations databases and their interaction with the actual users of those locations. How the users interact with these venues is the kind of data which encapsulates a lot of interesting information, both about the venues and the users. For our opening analysis into the Foursquare data, we will try to answer some questions about the choices of users in different cities across the world. We will learn how to extract data relevant to our analysis, how to ask the relevant questions and answer them using visualizations, and lastly, how to fit a usable analytics use case around the data. So let's dive in!

Getting the data – the usual hurdle

We want to get check-in data for some important cities across the globe and then use that data to find out what are the category trends are in those cities. Then we will proceed further with that data and try to build a recommender system which will tell us which restaurant category to venture into if we want to make it big in any of those cities.

The first step in any analytical process is identifying the data that we will need to perform the necessary analysis. In our particular case, the data that we will need is the check-in data for all the venues in the identified cities. Once we have this outline of thedata required, we will check how to actually extract that data.

The required end point

The first point in our data extraction process is always identifying the required API end point using the API documentation. After digging through the API documentation, we found the following end point to be of interest to us:

```
https://api.foursquare.com/v2/venues/
explore?v=20131016&ll=40.00%2C%20-74.8
```

This end point will give us the venue information around the longitude and latitude supplied (here latitude = 40.00 and longitude = -74.8). So this is the end point that we can use for getting data about locations of a city. But the twist is that actually getting all the data for a city is still a mystery to us.

Getting data for a city – geometry to the rescue

The idea to extract venue data for a city is a tricky one. As the API will only give you the location data for a sphere around a point, the idea must involve tracing that sphere across the city and collecting the corresponding data points.

To extract data for a city we will use the following strategy:

1. Start with the city's central latitude and longitude.
2. Get the venue detail around those centers.
3. Get the radial distance around the city center and get new centers.
4. Extract data for these new centers.
5. Repeat the process for a sufficient number of times to cover an approximate large area around a city center.

The scheme described in these steps is visually represented in the following figure. The idea is to start with **C1** (city center) and then use it to find **C2** (new centers):

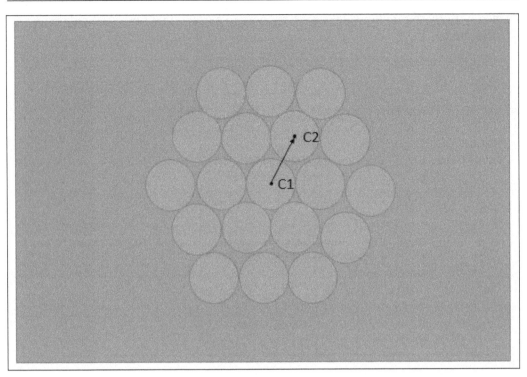

City data extraction

So this is the theoretical idea.

Let's look at the code that will achieve this data extraction. We have written three utility functions for this data extraction:

- `explore_around_point`: This is the most basic function for our data extraction. It takes a longitude, latitude pair and gives data about that center in a fixed radius.

- `span_a_arc`: This function takes the starting center and then spans an arc around that center. As an output, it generates the next pair of candidate centers.

- `get_data_for_points`: This function invokes the necessary function to extract data for a collection of centers.

Armed with these functions, let's see how we can extract data for a particular city, say Istanbul:

```
#City data extraction for Istanbul
#Get longitude latitude for Istanbul
istanbul_city_center = cbind(28.9784,41.0082)
colnames(istanbul_city_center) = c("lon","lat")


#Name the output csv file
file_level1 = "istanbul_data_l1.csv"
file_level2 = "istanbul_final_data.csv"
#Function to repeatedly generate the new centres and get data for
these centres
# Takes the number of levels we want to traverse as an argument
get_data_for_city <- function(city_center, levels_to_traverse = 2){
 new_centers_l1 = span_a_arc(city_center)
 out_df = data.frame()
 df_cent = explore_around_point(city_center)
 out_df = rbind(out_df, df_cent)
 df_l1 = get_data_for_points(new_centers_l1)
 out_df = rbind(out_df, df_l1)
 for(j in 1:levels_to_traverse){
  new_centers_lu = c()
  df_l2 = data.frame()
  for(i in 1:nrow(new_centers_l1)){
   new_cent = span_a_arc(new_centers_l1[i,], start_deg = -25, end_deg
= 25, degree_step = 25)
   new_centers_lu = rbind(new_centers_lu, new_cent)
   df_l2 = get_data_for_points(new_centers_lu)
   sum_points = sum_points + nrow(new_centers_lu)
   new_centers_l1 = new_centers_lu
   out_df = rbind(out_df, df_l2)
   write.csv(out_df, file = file_level2, row.names = FALSE)
  }
 }
 write.csv(out_df, file = file_level2, row.names = FALSE)
 return(out_df)
}# Function call for final data collection
final_data_istanbul = get_data_for_city(istanbul_city_center, levels_
to_traverse = 2)
```

Once we execute this snippet of code, we will get the data about Istanbul in a neatly formatted DataFrame. These steps can be repeated for different city centers by supplying the necessary longitudes and latitudes. The extracted DataFrame for the Istanbul data looks like this:

	venue.name	venue.id	venue.statž	venue.usersCount	venue.tipCount	venue.categoryid
3729	Istiklal Caddesi	4b50966af964a520632827e3	3972957	1107739	4774	4bf58dd8d48988d1f9931735
3730	Istiklal Caddesi	4b50966af964a520632827e3	3972957	1107739	4774	4bf58dd8d48988d1f9931735
3731	Istiklal Caddesi	4b50966af964a520632827e3	3972957	1107739	4774	4bf58dd8d48988d1f9931735
3732	Istiklal Caddesi	4b50966af964a520632827e3	3972957	1107739	4774	4bf58dd8d48988d1f9931735
3725	Kapaliçarsi	4c09fd76009a0f476ac2e8bf	1144926	400184	1663	4deefb944765f83613cdba6e
3726	Kapaliçarsi	4c09fd76009a0f476ac2e8bf	1144926	400184	1663	4deefb944765f83613cdba6e
3727	Kapaliçarsi	4c09fd76009a0f476ac2e8bf	1144926	400184	1663	4deefb944765f83613cdba6e
3728	Kapaliçarsi	4c09fd76009a0f476ac2e8bf	1144926	400184	1663	4deefb944765f83613cdba6e
3715	Galata Kulesi	4b732d5bf964a52011a02de3	732496	510733	1885	4deefb944765f83613cdba6e
3716	Galata Kulesi	4b732d5bf964a52011a02de3	732496	510733	1885	4deefb944765f83613cdba6e
3717	Galata Kulesi	4b732d5bf964a52011a02de3	732496	510733	1885	4deefb944765f83613cdba6e
3718	Galata Kulesi	4b732d5bf964a52011a02de3	732496	510733	1885	4deefb944765f83613cdba6e
3719	Galata Kulesi	4b732d5bf964a52011a02de3	732496	510733	1885	4deefb944765f83613cdba6e

Istanbul data

We note that some venues' data have been repeated. This is the side effect of the crude algorithm that we have developed. We will fix it up in the analysis step.

Analysis – the fun part

Now that we have gone through the nitty gritty process of data collection, it is time for the fun part: the analysis of the data. As part of our illustrative data collection and analysis process, we have collected data for a total of seven cities. The first step in performing any kind of analysis on all that data is to combine the data together (we had persisted all the data that we extracted in the previous step).

This can be achieved with the following snippet of code:

```
# Getting data for all the city we have extracted data for
city_names <- c("ny", "istanbul", "paris", "la", "seattle", "london",
"chicago")
all_city_data_with_category <- data.frame()
for ( city in city_names){
    #combine all cities data and remove duplicated
    city_data <- read.csv(file = paste(city,"_final_data.csv", sep =
''),stringsAsFactors = FALSE)
    # Removing duplicated data points
    city_data <- city_data[!duplicated(city_data$venue.id),]
    # Combining with the category ids
    city_data_with_category <- join_city_category(city_data)
    city_data_with_category["cityname"] <- city
    all_city_data_with_category <- rbind(all_city_data_with_category,
city_data_with_category)
}
```

Now we have all the data in the combined DataFrame, `all_city_data_with_category`. This DataFrame will form the basis of all our future analysis. The customary `head` function on this DataFrame returns the following information:

```
> head(all_city_data_with_category)
                       venue.name            venue.id venue.stats venue.usersCount
1               Pasanella & Sons 4b61d830f964a52088262ae3         816              527
2               Noodle Village ç²¥é°µè»'  49d3deadf964a5201d5c1fe3        6160             3113
3 Smorgasbar @ Seaport Smorgasburg 51a0e3c2498e8382f6b3a3bf        6838             4911
4           South Street Seaport Museum 4ab67030f964a520187720e3        1606             1157
5                        Dumplings 4ae775c8f964a52087ab21e3         247              128
6                        Bocadillo 577a8f47498ebddf91b56bbd         164               92
  venue.tipCount        venue.categoryid             super_cat_id        super_cat_name
1             24 4bf58dd8d48988d119951735 4d4b7105d754a06378d81259        Shop & Service
2            103 4bf58dd8d48988d145941735 4d4b7105d754a06374d81259                  Food
3             66 4bf58dd8d48988d117941735 4d4b7105d754a06376d81259         Nightlife Spot
4             14 4bf58dd8d48988d190941735 4d4b7104d754a06370d81259 Arts & Entertainment
5              5 4bf58dd8d48988d145941735 4d4b7105d754a06374d81259                  Food
6              6 4bf58dd8d48988d1db931735 4d4b7105d754a06374d81259                  Food
             cat_name        cat_pluralName cat_shortName cityname
1    Food & Drink Shop    Food & Drink Shops  Food & Drink       ny
2     Asian Restaurant     Asian Restaurants         Asian       ny
3                  Bar                  Bars           Bar       ny
4               Museum               Museums        Museum       ny
5     Asian Restaurant     Asian Restaurants         Asian       ny
6 Spanish Restaurant Spanish Restaurants       Spanish       ny
> |
```

All city data

Basic descriptive statistics – the usual

Now that we have our data all extracted and processed in a neat tabular format, we can get started with some visualizations to get some more knowledge about the categories and their distribution across all the cities.

Let's start by finding out which cities among these have the most data of interest to us (all through our analysis, we will use the `venue.stats` as our metric of interest as it represents the total check-in at the venue):

```
summary_df <- all_city_data_with_category %>%
       group_by(cityname) %>%
       summarise(total_checkins = sum(venue.stats), city_user=
sum(venue.usersCount), city_tips = sum(venue.tipCount))
ggplot(summary_df, aes(x=cityname, y=total_checkins)) +
 geom_bar(stat="identity") +
 ggtitle("City wise check-ins") +
  theme(plot.title = element_text(lineheight=.8, face="bold",hjust =
0.5))
```

The preceding code snippet produces the distribution of `venue.stats` for each of the cities. The bar graph gives us important information about which city is the most popular when it comes to total check-in counts:

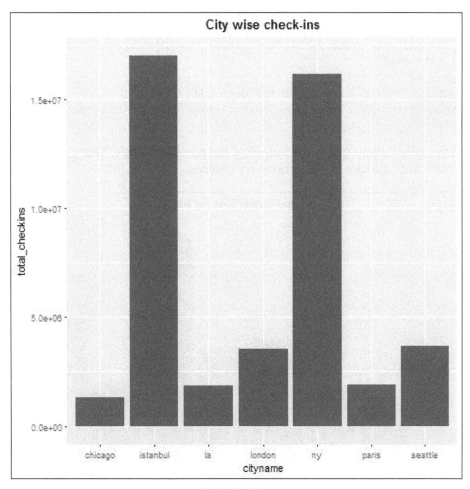

Total check-ins

With a single look at the graph, we have a first little hint of an insight. Istanbul is the city having most check-ins after New York, which straight away seem different from the general perception. And it highlights the importance of making data-based decisions instead of perception-based decisions, analytics 101 in our first plot.

Now let's find out how we are doing in these cities in terms of the major categories that we have. This will tell us which city has the most widespread representation in terms of the total categories, so we can assume this to be indicative of being a diverse city. Going by the general perception, we would expect New York to be one of the most diverse cities. Let's find out if the data supports this perception or not:

```
# Total category count for different cities
cat_rep_summary <- all_city_data_with_category %>%
                group_by(cityname) %>%
```

```
                         summarise(city_category_count = n_distinct(cat_
name))
ggplot(cat_rep_summary, aes(x=cityname, y=city_category_count),
col(cityname))+
  geom_bar(stat="identity")+
  ggtitle("Total categories for each city") +
  theme(plot.title = element_text(lineheight=.8, face="bold",hjust =
0.5))
```

We get the following graph as the output of the preceding code. This graph tells us which city offers the most diverse category choices:

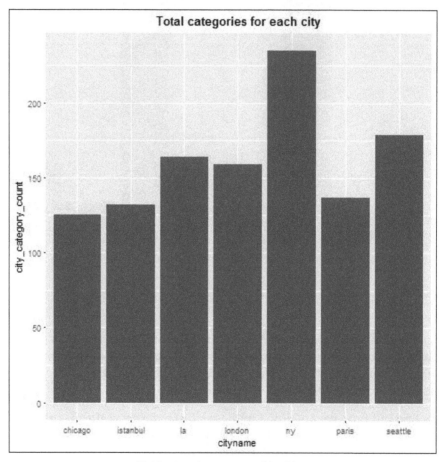

Total categories represented in cities

So our perception in this case is backed up by the data that we have. New York indeed is the city with the most diverse range of categories.

Now we want to focus on this data a bit; we want to see how the total categories represented in a city are distributed across the various major categories that Foursquare provides. We will plot the percentage distribution of total check-ins across all the major categories and try to come up with a visual representation of the most dominant category for each city:

```
# Distribution of city check-ins across the major categories
super_cat_summary_detail <- all_city_data_with_category %>%
    group_by(cityname,super_cat_name) %>%
    summarise(city_category_count = sum(venue.stats)) %>%
    mutate(category_percentage = city_category_count/sum(city_
category_count))

# For brevity we will only plot the two cities with most check-ins
p5 <- ggplot(subset(super_cat_summary_detail, cityname %in% c("ny",
"istanbul")), aes(x=super_cat_name, y=category_percentage))
(p5 <- p5 + geom_bar(stat="identity") +
    theme(axis.text.x=element_text(angle=90,hjust=1,vjust=0.5)) +
        facet_wrap(~cityname, ncol = 1)) +
    ggtitle("category distribution for NY and Istanbul") +
    theme(plot.title = element_text(lineheight=.8, face="bold",hjust =
0.5))90,hjust=1,vjust=0.5)) +
        facet_wrap(~cityname, ncol = 1))
```

The graph generated by the code is given here. This graph informs us about the differences/similarities that exist between the two cities we have selected:

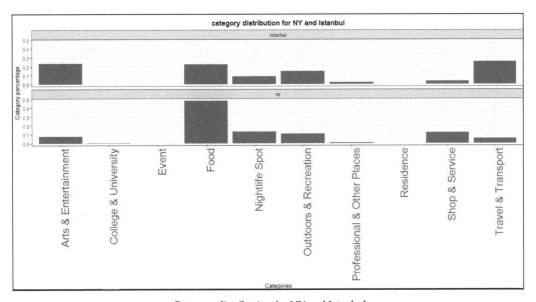

Category distribution for NY and Istanbul

A detailed inspection of the accompanying plot again reveals a lot of information. The major category, **Food**, is the major category across both the cities which is not really a huge surprise.

From the plot, you can determine that Istanbul is a city you can easily associate with **Arts & Entertainment** and **Travel & Transport**. Whereas New York is the city for **Nightlife Spot** and **Shop & Service**. Also you can easily spot that Istanbul has no representation in the **College & Universities** category. So either the students are not checking-in or they are not really attending the educational institutes. Well this is a question the present data cannot answer. Analytics can only deduce insight for which we have accompanying data.

Before we move on to build a recommendation engine on top of our categories data, we will draw one more plot. Until now we have been focusing on the super categories only but those are the umbrella categories. Now we want to see how the breakup is among the top children categories.

For drawing this plot, we will do a city-wise summarization on the category name using the following code snippet:

```
# Top 5 category distribution for each city
cat_summary_detail <- all_city_data_with_category %>%
    group_by(cityname,cat_name) %>%
    summarise(city_category_count = sum(venue.stats)) %>%
    mutate(category_percentage =
city_category_count/sum(city_category_count)) %>%
    top_n(5)
p5 <- ggplot(cat_summary_detail, aes(x=cat_name, y=category_
percentage))
(p5 <- p5 + geom_bar(stat="identity") +
    ylab("Check-in percentage") + xlab("Categories") +
    theme(axis.text.x=element_text(angle=90,hjust=1,vjust=0.5)) +
    facet_wrap(~cityname, ncol = 1)) +
    ggtitle("category distribution for all cities") +
    theme(plot.title = element_text(lineheight=.8, face="bold",hjust
= 0.5))
```

The resultant plot of this code section highlights the top five categories of all the cities. This plot again throws some obvious answers and some puzzling information. Spend a moment studying the plot:

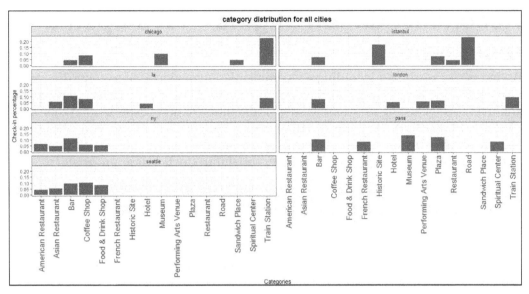

Category distribution for all cities

The most obvious information from the plot is that only one category is common across all the cities which is, no prize for guessing, **Bar**. It highlights the universality of alcohol, even when we have Istanbul in the mix. The second highlight is the prominence of the **Transport** category for New York and Chicago, which when investigated further can be traced to their iconic stations. The next genuine surprise comes in the form of the most dominant category in Istanbul, which is a road, but when you look inside the data you find out one of the most important tourist attractions in Istanbul is İstiklal Avenue.

This section helps us in uncovering a lot of surprises and obvious information using just simple bar plots and hence it helps us establish an important caveat of data analytics:

 Never under estimate the power of basic descriptive statistics.

Recommendation engine – let's open a restaurant

An important reason for including a recommendation engine as one of our use cases is to emphasize how we can link the existing data to frame it as an analytics problem and then to use existing solutions to solve it reliably. We don't expect to have cutting edge accuracy with this recommendation engine but we use it to give you a healthy learning of working on such problems as and when they arrive. Before we dive into building a recommendation engine, a (very) brief introduction is appropriate.

Recommendation engine – the clichés

Recommendation engines (or systems) are one of the most recognized machine learning applications in the industry today. To say that a lot of people equate recommendation engines to machine learning won't be an exaggeration. They command such immense visibility for a simple reason: they integrate with business and they work. A recommendation engine is ubiquitous in today's technology landscape. They are present on e-commerce sites, financial applications, search engines, and even dating websites.

The basic idea of a recommendation engine is pretty simple: it tries to predict your rating for an item which you have not rated yet and on the basis of those predicted ratings it tries to suggest the items *which you may like*. Sounds familiar, right? Well that's another testament to the extent of their spread.

Framing the recommendation problem

In the last section, we underlined the importance of descriptive statistics and the inferences that can be derived with simple plots and summaries. A common conundrum for analytics professionals is to move past the descriptive summaries because, although immensely useful, these representations are not often a complete solution. The next important paradigm for getting more out of your data is your problem definition aptitude. These often are not so obvious extensions to data which you can form once you have a good understanding of the data and also of the potential uses of the data. So the question pertinent to us, given our dataset, is: *What more can we do with our data??*

The answer to the preceding question will always depend on the data. In our case, a simple problem can be:

We want to open a restaurant in one of those cities. Can we use the data in some way to recommend to us the category of restaurant most likely to succeed?

Building our restaurant recommender

A problem definition is often a hard problem as this requires an intimate understanding of the data and potential problems which can be solved using it. Once we have a well-defined problem, the solution building part is quite straightforward using the excellent tools that R provides (well mostly, if not always). So let's dive into our data once again to trace the possible problems that we may have in building a recommendation engine.

The typical data required for a recommendation engine is shown in the following table:

	Item1	Item2	Item3	Item4	Item5	Item6	Item7	Item8	Item9
User1	2	?	4	5	3	?	?	1	1
User2	1	1	5	?	?	5	5	3	2
User3	?	?	?	?	2	3	4	5	1

But we don't have any concept of *User* or *Item*. For our framing of problem, the *Cities* will be our users and *Restaurant Categories* will be our items. So we will have ratings for various categories from the cities and then we will build a system which will predict the ratings of unknown restaurant categories across the cities.

The next piece of the puzzle is the ratings. We don't have any concept of ratings in our dataset so how are we going to find the ratings? This is a tricky question but the good news is that there is no fixed rule as to how you will arrive at the ratings; all you need is a logical way of defining them.

For example, we can define the ratings for restaurants by following these steps:

1. Find out the total check-ins for all the categories in the super category, *Food*.
2. Replace check-in counts with the percent of total check-ins.
   Mathematically, this is:

   Percent (check-in) = Number (check-in)/total check-in for Food category

3. Find out the range of values of the percent ratings.

4. Divide the range of percent ratings in five equal sections.

5. Assign the ratings using these sections, that is, a value in section 1 is a rating of 1 and so on.

This explains the two major adaptations we have to do to our data to mould it in to a format which we can use for building our recommendation engine. Let us now focus on the kind of recommendation engine we will use.

We will use a class of recommendation engine which is based on *Matrix Factorization*. Explaining the inner workings of this kind of recommendation engine is beyond the scope of this book (you can pick up the book by the authors of this book for a detailed understanding of it). The basic idea of a matrix factorization-based recommendation engine is to partition the *User X Rating* matrix as a product of two different matrices. Once we have achieved that factorization, the recommendation generation step for any unknown data will be simply the inner products between those two matrices. The output will give us the predicted ratings for any new data point, given some existing data.

Now that we have the process identified, we can start with the development of our recommendation engine.

The first thing which is required before we start building our recommendation engine is the necessary data wrangling to bring the data in the required format:

```
# Select the relevant data and subset for "Food" Category
selected_cols <- c("cityname", "cat_name", "venue.stats")
reco_data <- all_city_data_with_category[all_city_data_with_
category$super_cat_name == "Food",selected_cols]
# Change the format of data
reco_data_reshaped <- reshape(reco_data,
                              timevar = "cat_name",
                              idvar = c("cityname"),
                              direction = "wide")
# Substitute the NAs with 0
reco_data_reshaped[is.na(reco_data_reshaped)] <- 0
reco_final <- cbind(reco_data_reshaped[,"cityname"],round(reco_
data_reshaped[,(!colnames(reco_data_reshaped) %in% c("cityname"))]/
rowSums(reco_data_reshaped[,(!colnames(reco_data_reshaped) %in%
c("cityname"))]), 4))
colnames(reco_final)[1] <- "cityname"
```

This brings the data in the familiar format as shown in the following table:

	cityname	venue.stats.Asian Restaurant	venue.stats.Spanish Restaurant	venue.stats.Dessert Shop	venue.stats.Caribbean Restaurant	venue.stats.Mexican Restaurant
2	ny	0.0183	0.0005	0.0102	0.0023	0.0990
3800	istanbul	0.0267	0.0000	0.0010	0.0002	0.0000
4767	paris	0.0082	0.0732	0.0097	0.0000	0.0173
6356	la	0.0670	0.0000	0.0005	0.0051	0.0226
7378	seattle	0.0130	0.0202	0.0169	0.0652	0.0009
8775	london	0.0205	0.0352	0.0025	0.0246	0.0719
10080	chicago	0.0015	0.0000	0.0003	0.0477	0.0053

Recomputed check-ins data

Now we need to convert this data into a ratings data. To achieve that, we have written a utility which we will apply to each row of the DataFrame to arrive at the ratings for each restaurant. The package we are using for our recommendation system requires the data in a particular format. We will convert the check-in data into ratings and arrive at the necessary data format:

```
# Converting percents into ratings and recosystem required format

# Transposing the ratings data and adding the city name
reco_ratings <- t(reco_ratings)
city_id_name_map <- as.factor(reco_final[,"cityname"])
colnames(reco_ratings) <- colnames(reco_final[,(!colnames(reco_final)
%in% c("cityname"))])
reco_ratings <- cbind(as.data.frame(reco_final[,"cityname"]), reco_
ratings)
colnames(reco_ratings)[1] <- "cityname"
rest_type_id = colnames(reco_final)[!(colnames(reco_ratings) %in%
c("cityname"))]

# Changing format of data so that each row becomes,
# city, restaurant type, rating
reco_rating_long <-reshape(reco_ratings,varying = !(colnames(reco_
final) %in% c("cityname")), v.names = "rating", direction = "long")
reco_rating_long[,"id"] <- NULL
colnames(reco_rating_long)[2] <- "restaurant_type"
reco_rating_long$cityname <-as.numeric(reco_rating_long$cityname)
```

This leads to data in the following format (which is the format required by recosystem). The data points with NAs are the ratings that we will try to predict using our recommender system. We have saved the necessary data to map the city name and restaurant types from their numerical equivalent so don't be alarmed by that transformation:

cityname	restaurant_type	rating
5	1	4
2	1	5
6	1	4
3	1	5
7	1	4
4	1	4
1	1	1
5	2	2
2	2	NA

Formatted check-ins data

Now we can use the recosystem package to arrive at our necessary recommendation system. The code we have used is very much similar to the usage notes given by the package developers:

```
# Seperate the training data and predcition data and persist them as
files
reco_rating_long_predict <- reco_rating_long[is.na(reco_rating_
long$rating),]
reco_rating_long_train <- reco_rating_long[!is.na(reco_rating_
long$rating),]
write.table(reco_rating_long_train, file = "restaurant_reco_train.
txt", quote = FALSE,sep = " ", row.names = FALSE, col.names = FALSE)
write.table(reco_rating_long_predict, file = "restaurant_reco_test.
txt", quote = FALSE,sep = " ", row.names = FALSE, col.names = FALSE)
```

```
# Train a recommendation system using recosystem
r = Reco()
train_set = data_file("restaurant_reco_train.txt")

# Setting sme parameters for our enging
opts = r$tune(train_set, opts = list(dim = c(10, 20, 30), lrate =
c(0.1, 0.2),
                                     costp_l1 = 0, costq_l1 = 0,
                                     nthread = 1, niter = 10))

# training the recommentdation engines
r$train(train_set, opts = c(opts$min, nthread = 1, niter = 50))
pred_file = tempfile()
test_set = data_file("restaurant_reco_test.txt")

# Generating predictions for our cities
r$predict(test_set, out_file(pred_file))
pred_ratings <- scan(pred_file)

# Getting the string values for restaurant type and city name as they
# were replaced by numeric values earlier
reco_rating_long_predict$predicted_ratings <- as.data.frame(pred_
ratings)
reco_rating_long_predict$restaurant_type_name <-rest_type_id[reco_
rating_long_predict$restaurant_type]
reco_rating_long_predict$restauracity_name <-rest_type_id[reco_rating_
long_predict$cityname]
reco_rating_long_predict$city_name <- city_id_name_map[reco_rating_
long_predict$cityname]
reco_rating_long_test[,c("cityname", "restaurant_type",
"rating","restauracity_name")] <- NULL
# The results of our recommendation engine for New York City
View(subset(reco_rating_long_test, city_name %in% "ny"))
```

A little note about the training process.

Please bear in mind that training a model is a very involved process. Traditionally we will have a test set train set split, multiple iterations, and hyper parameters tunings to arrive at the best possible model. We have skipped these steps as we want to illustrate the process instead of dwelling over the results.

A sample of ratings recommendations generated by our recommendation system for New York is as follows:

predicted_ratings.pred_ratings	restaurant_type_name	city_name
3.922040	venue.stats.Swiss Restaurant	ny
3.746480	venue.stats.Irish Pub	ny
3.670470	venue.stats.Australian Restaurant	ny
3.288700	venue.stats.Austrian Restaurant	ny
3.245940	venue.stats.Fish & Chips Shop	ny
3.213090	venue.stats.American Restaurant	ny
3.150580	venue.stats.Spanish Restaurant	ny
3.147840	venue.stats.Modern European Restaurant	ny
3.138350	venue.stats.Portuguese Restaurant	ny
3.080260	venue.stats.Soup Place	ny

Restaurant prediction for New York

Ideally, we would have a rigorous validation process to accept the suggestions made by our recommendation system, which once again is beyond the scope of this book. But we can validate the recommendations with some general sense. We don't need a validation process to find that an Irish pub is a good idea for New York!!

This concludes our first use case for Foursquare data analysis. We learned how to get data using complex APIs and parse it into the required format. We also learned the use of descriptive statistics and a recommendation system on our collected data.

The sentimental rankings

In the first use case, we explored the venue data from Foursquare and built some analysis and a proper solution on top of that data. In this section, we will focus on the textual aspect of the Foursquare data. We will extract the tips generated for a venue by users and perform some basic analysis on them. Then we will try to build a use case in which we will use those tips to arrive at a decision.

Extracting tips data – the go to step

By now we know the analysis work flow off by heart and as always the first step is getting to the required data. We have already detailed the steps involved in data extraction with Foursquare APIs. So instead of restating the obvious, we will start with the process of data extraction.

We have written two utility functions for the extraction of tips data from the identified end point:

- `extract_all_tips_by_venue`: This function takes the ID of the venue as an argument and extracts the JSON object containing all the tips for that venue
- `extract_tips_from_json`: This function will extract the tweets from the JSON object generated in the previous step

Let's take an example of the extraction of tips data. We will find out the ID of the venue by browsing to the Foursquare page. This is the URL for the Vasa Museum in Stockholm:

`https://foursquare.com/v/vasamuseet/4adcdaeff964a520135b21e3`

The identified bold area in the URL is the ID that our function will need for data extraction:

```
# Extract data for Vasa Museum
vasa_museum_id = "4adcdaeff964a520135b21e3"
tips_df <- extract_all_tips_by_venue(vasa_museum_id)
```

The resultant DataFrame will look like this:

tip_id	tip_text	tip_user_gender
5260e0ab11d2cffe485e9eb5	Join our tour Stockholm Must Sees and skip the line a...	none
51bf73d4498e1757060897fe	*** : Construit en 1628, le Wasa a parcouru 1,5km ava...	male
572873be498e6a3ca2b93c5e	its amazing to see Vasa after 333 years staying unde...	female
56882608498e9a34f506b7fc	Interested in history or (old) technologies? This is th...	none
52167b6f11d27a67a4fa0a1f	One of the best museums I've been to. Excellent exh...	female
5585c23f498e693bc67c63da	Cool and worth the visit. Discount for students. It will...	male
54e0fedb498eed57395379eb	An entire salvaged 17th naval warship housed in the ...	male
57b702be498e840b547ba756	What a great museum <U+2764><U+FE0F> it's all abo...	male
5473023a498e9daa236f177f	The Vasa Ship, soon to be 400 years old, is one of th...	none
560a3c44498e70bb7343b116	I suggest to watch the movie about the salvage and t...	female
57497c89498e56b7a4610227	The museum has several levels so you can see the s...	female
5664ac59498ec523863853ee	A must see! The only place where you'll see a ship fr...	male
56ae709c498e5cc8e3bb99a2	A great museum. There is free English guided tour w...	female

Tips for Vasa Museum, Stockholm

In addition to the tips, we have also extracted the gender of the tip user. This will help us with some interesting insights once we get started with our analytics step with the data.

The actual data

This use case is an attempt to use the textual data and then use the sentiments arising out of that text to guide us in a decision-making process. For illustrating this concept, we have decided to pit the museum ratings from the popular travel site, TripAdvisor (`https://www.tripadvisor.com`) against the sentiment ratings from the users of Foursquare. We would like to find out if the sentiment of Foursquare users' tips are in agreement with the rankings given by TripAdvisor or not. This use case once again is a little bit speculative but it builds on the fundamentals of sentiment analysis we picked up in *Chapter 2, Twitter – What's Happening with 140 Characters*. The concepts and the idea behind sentiment analysis were explained in detail in *Chapter 2, Twitter – What's Happening with 140 Characters*, hence here we will get started with the use case directly. So let's see if the TripAdvisor ratings are validated by Foursquare users or not.

This is the list for the world's best museums according to TripAdvisor (`https://www.tripadvisor.in/TravelersChoice-Museums-cTop-g1`). We will manually compile this list in a DataFrame with the corresponding ranking.

This will be the final DataFrame for the museum rankings:

museum_name	trip_advisor_rank
mpma_ny_tips	1
art_institute_chicago_tips	2
hermitage_moscow_tips	3
musee_d_orsay_tips	4
nat_muse_anthro_tips	5
madrid_museum_tips	6
acropolis_museum_tips	7
vasa_museum_tips	8
louvre_tips	9

Museum rankings. Source https://www.tripadvisor.in/TravelersChoice-Museums-cTop-g1

The next step involves collecting the tips data for each of these museums. For this we will manually collect the Foursquare IDs for each of these museums and apply our tips extraction function on them. We have written a utility function which extracts data for each of these museums and then persists each of the DataFrame.

Analysis of tips

To perform analysis on the collective tips data, we will first start by concatenating the tips data for all the museums. We will assume that we have persisted data for each museum in a `.csv` file ending with `_tips`.

Using the following code, we will concatenate these files:

```
# Combine all the Tips data in a single data frame
tips_files <-list.files(pattern="*tips.csv")
complete_df <- data.frame()
for(file in tips_files)
{
    perpos <- which(strsplit(file, "")[[1]]==".")
    museum_name <- gsub(" ","",substr(file, 1, perpos-1))
    df <- read.csv(file, stringsAsFactors = FALSE)
    df$museum <- museum_name
    complete_df <- rbind(complete_df, df)
}
```

Now that we have all the data combined, we can get started with our analysis. Following up on the important caveat of the last section, we will start with some basic descriptive analysis.

Basic descriptive statistics

The first thing we want to see is how many tips there are for each of the museums. This is one of the initial requirements for the popularity of any venue.

Let us plot the number of total tips for each of these museums:

```
# Basic Descriptive statistics
review_summary <- complete_df %>% group_by(museum) %>% summarise(num_
reviews = n())
ggplot(data = review_summary, aes(x = reorder(museum, num_reviews), y
= num_reviews)) +
    geom_bar(aes(fill = museum), stat = "identity") +
    theme(legend.position = "none") +
    xlab("Museum Name") + ylab("Total Reviews Count") +
ggtitle("Reviews for each Museum") +
    theme(axis.text.x=element_text(angle=90,hjust=1,vjust=0.5)) +
coord_flip()
```

The accompanying graph reveals our first important finding. Although the Louvre, Paris is ranked quite low in the TripAdvisor ratings, the number of tips generated paints a different picture all together. It suggests that the Louvre should be the highest ranking museum. Another important difference is in the ranking of the National Museum of Anthropology, Mexico. Ranked 5th in the TripAdvisor, its popularity nose dives and it ends up at the bottom spot. These are some obvious outputs based on the number of tips, although we should not read much into it as we should be making such conclusions on the cumulative content of the tips and not just the number. Before we dig down to the level of sentiment of these tips, let us see if the rankings remain constant when we consider the gender of the user:

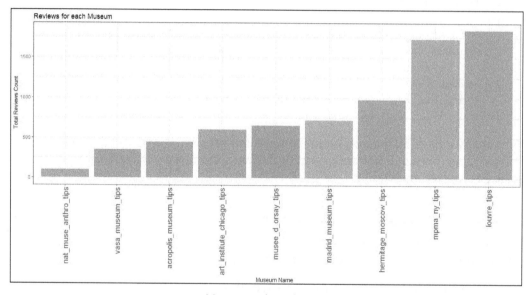

Museum rankings by tips

The plot for the three different genders (yes three because Foursquare also allows accounts having none as a gender), for the male and female gender the ranking is the same as the cumulative rankings. This tells us that gender is not a huge discriminant when it comes to leaving tips for a museum. Both genders are pretty consistent in their evaluation of the museums:

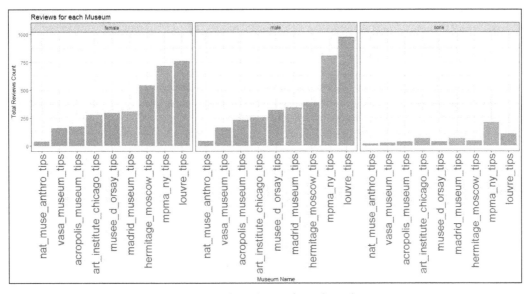

Museum rankings by tips for each gender

Next we want to examine the emotions that any visit to these museums generate. Are the emotions consistent across all the museums or can we identify different sentiments to attribute to different museums? To examine this, we will use the syuzhet package as we used in *Chapter 2, Twitter – What's Happening with 140 Characters*. We recall that given any text data, the syuzhet package helps us find the different sentiments reflected in that text. For the related information about the package and the working please refer to the excellent introduction provided in *Chapter 2, Twitter – What's Happening with 140 Characters*.

The following snippet will generate and plot a sentiment-based summary for each of our museums:

```
# Sentiments across different museums
sentiments_df <- get_nrc_sentiment(complete_df[,"tip_text"])
sentiments_df <- cbind(sentiments_df, complete_df[,c("tip_user_
gender","museum")])
sentiments_summary_df <-sentiments_df %>% select(-
c(positive,negative)) %>%
    group_by(museum) %>% summarise(anger = sum(anger),anticipation
= sum(anticipation),disgust = sum(disgust), fear= sum(fear) , joy =
sum(joy) , sadness = sum(sadness), surprise = sum(surprise), trust
=sum(trust))
```

```
sentiments_summary_df_reshaped <- reshape(sentiments_summary_
df,varying = c(colnames(sentiments_summary_df)[!colnames(sentiments_
summary_df) %in% c("museum")]), v.names = "count", direction =
"long",new.row.names = 1:1000)
sentiment_names <-c(colnames(sentiments_summary_df)
[!colnames(sentiments_summary_df) %in% c("museum")])
sentiments_summary_df_reshaped$sentiment <- sentiment_
names[sentiments_summary_df_reshaped$time]
sentiments_summary_df_reshaped[,c("time", "id")] <- NULL

p5 <- ggplot(sentiments_summary_df_reshaped, aes(x=sentiment,
y=count))
(p5 <- p5 + geom_bar(stat="identity") + theme(axis.text.x=element_text
(angle=90,hjust=1,vjust=0.5)) +
        facet_wrap(~museum, ncol = 1)) +
        ylab("Percent sentiment score") +
        ggtitle("Sentiment variation across museums")
```

The output of the preceding code snippet will give us a distribution of all the sentiments across the different museums. The plot is given here:

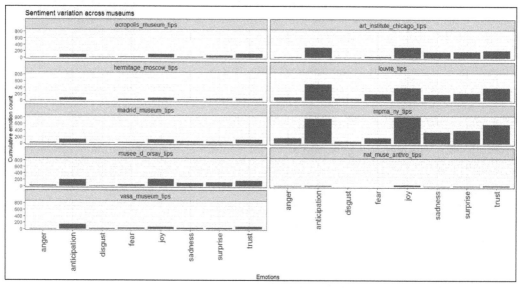

Sentiment score for each museum

A careful reading of the preceding plot reveals some important information about the sentiments dominating the tips for them. Anticipation, joy, and trust are the major sentiments across all the museum visitors, which is exactly what one would expect. It is nice to find corroborating data for our human intuitions. It also reveals something about the museums in New York and Paris: they often experience a sentiment of **disgust** and **anger** by the users visiting them, which is not something which you would expect when visiting the world's top most museums.

The final rankings

This sentiment analysis helps us get some insights into the museums and the sentiments associated with them but we can't use them directly to achieve our initial goal: building a sentiment-based ranking of the museums. To build that, we need a numerical definition of sentiment. Thankfully, the package which we are using has functions to do precisely that. To arrive at our rankings, we will associate a sentiment score with each of the textual tips and sum them to arrive at a cumulative total. Sounds nice but this approach has a flaw in it; we need to take into account the number of tips also. Otherwise, the museums with a large number of tips will be favored. To counter such fallacies, we will do a tip count-based normalization. This will remove the effect of the large number of tips for each of the museums. We will be left with a metric of *per tip sentiment score* which we can use to rank the museums:

```
# Sentiment analysis based ranking
#Ranking based on cumulative review sentiments
for (i in 1:nrow(complete_df)){
    review <- complete_df[i,"tip_text"]
    poa_word_v <- get_tokens(review, pattern = "\\W")
    syuzhet_vector <- get_sentiment(poa_word_v, method="bing")
    complete_df[i,"sentiment_total"] <- sum(syuzhet_vector)
}
rank_sentiment_score <- complete_df %>% group_by(museum) %>%
summarise(total_sentiment = sum(sentiment_total), total_reviews =
n()) %>% mutate(mean_sentiment = total_sentiment/total_reviews) %>%
arrange(mean_sentiment)
rank_sentiment_score$museum.rank <- rank(-rank_sentiment_score$mean_
sentiment)

rank_sentiment_score_gender <- complete_df %>% group_by(museum, tip_
user_gender)%>% summarise(total_sentiment = sum(sentiment_total),
total_reviews = n()) %>% mutate(mean_sentiment = total_sentiment/
total_reviews) %>% arrange(mean_sentiment)
```

```
rank_sentiment_score_gender_female <- subset(rank_sentiment_score_
gender, tip_user_gender == "female")
rank_sentiment_score_gender_female$museum.rank <- rank(-rank_
sentiment_score_gender_female$mean_sentiment)

rank_sentiment_score_gender_male <- subset(rank_sentiment_score_
gender, tip_user_gender == "male")
rank_sentiment_score_gender_male$museum.rank <- rank(-rank_sentiment_
score_gender_male$mean_sentiment)

rank_sentiment_score_gender_none <- subset(rank_sentiment_score_
gender, tip_user_gender == "none")
rank_sentiment_score_gender_none$museum.rank <- rank(-rank_sentiment_
score_gender_none$mean_sentiment)

# All the ranks in one data frame
combined_rank <- museum_tripadvisor %>% inner_join(rank_sentiment_
score[,c("museum", "museum.rank")])
colnames(combined_rank)[ncol(combined_rank)] <- "overall_sentiment_
rank"
combined_rank<- combined_rank %>% inner_join(rank_sentiment_score_
gender_female[,c("museum", "museum.rank")], by = "museum")
colnames(combined_rank)[ncol(combined_rank)] <- "female_sentiment_
rank"
combined_rank<- combined_rank %>% inner_join(rank_sentiment_score_
gender_male[,c("museum", "museum.rank")], by = "museum")
colnames(combined_rank)[ncol(combined_rank)] <- "male_sentiment_rank"
combined_rank<- combined_rank %>% inner_join(rank_sentiment_score_
gender_none[,c("museum", "museum.rank")], by = "museum")
colnames(combined_rank)[ncol(combined_rank)] <- "none_sentiment_rank"
```

This summarization helps us arrive at our new set of rankings based on the metric of mean sentiment score per user. So basically we are saying that based on the cumulative sentiments of tips generated for each of the museums, we can find out which museum can be ranked higher. We can contrast this with the ranks given by TripAdvisor to find out whether these ranks are in agreement or not. Furthermore, we are able to rank the museums based on the same metric for each gender.

Let's see how the results of this summarization look:

museum	trip_advisor_rank	overall_sentiment_rank	female_sentiment_rank	male_sentiment_rank	none_sentiment_rank
mpma_ny_tips	1	6	5	6	4
art_institute_chicago_tips	2	2	2	2	1
hermitage_moscow_tips	3	9	9	9	9
musee_d_orsay_tips	4	4	6	3	3
nat_muse_anthro_tips	5	1	1	1	5
madrid_museum_tips	6	8	7	8	8
acropolis_museum_tips	7	3	3	4	2
vasa_museum_tips	8	5	4	5	7
louvre_tips	9	7	8	7	6

Sentiment score for each museum

A word of caution. We saw how we can leverage the sentiment values to find out different interpretations of the same data. But we must keep in mind an important point that such sentiment summarization is quite useful but not 100% correct. Text is a tough subject to master based on statistics, so take such results with a pinch of salt and always have strict validation bounds around them.

This will formally conclude our text-based analysis on the tips data. We learned a fair deal about extracting sentiments from textual data and also how to use the numerical values of sentiments to perform important analytics.

Venue graph – where do people go next?

Our next use case on Foursquare data is geared more towards creative data extraction. We will demonstrate how the combination of some creativity with the basic data can give rise to unusual datasets. The base data of Foursquare is not really suitable for extracting a graph-based dataset. But a close examination of the APIs reveals an end point which will give the next five venues people go to from any given venue. This can be combined with a graph search algorithm such as a depth-first search to create a graph in which venues can be linked to the next possible venues.

To extract this data, we will use our two utility functions:

- `extract_venue_details`: This function will get us the venue details of each venue occurring in our traversal

- `extract_next_venue_details`: This function will get us information about the next five venues to which users go from a particular venue

- `extract_dfs_data`: This the implementation of a depth-first search in R which will take a vector of seed venues and a level of depth to which to search for new venues

For the data extraction, we will start with three different starting points (we will choose John F. Kennedy Airport, Central Park, and the Statue of Liberty as starting points in New York). With these starting points, we will use our utility functions to arrive at two DataFrame and persists them:

- `Edge_list` : This DataFrame will contain edges from the source venue to the next venue

- `Venue_detail`: This DataFrame will contain details about each of the nodes that occur in our edge list:

```
# Graph data extraction
jfk_id = "xxxxxxxxxxxxxxxxxxxxxxxxxx"
statue_ofLiberty_id = " xxxxxxxxxxxxxxxxxxxxxxxxx "
central_park_id = " xxxxxxxxxxxxxxxxxxxxxxxx "
venues_to_crawl = c(jfk_id,statue_ofLiberty_id,central_park_id)
extract_dfs_data(venues_to_crawl, depth = 10)
```

Once we have extracted the graph data, we can load and enhance data by finding out the distance between the nodes in each link. This information can serve as the edge weight and can be used in the graph-based analysis that we perform. So we will load up the two DataFrame that we persisted, perform a little cleanup, and then call our utility function to find the distance between each pair of nodes in the edge list:

```
# Load data sets
edges_list_final <- read_delim("edges_list_final.csv",";", escape_
double = FALSE, trim_ws = TRUE)
venue_details_final <- read_delim("venue_details_final.csv",",",
escape_double = FALSE, trim_ws = TRUE)
# Clean up the edge list to remove nodes for information was not
extracted
venue_details_final <- venue_details_final[!duplicated(venue_details_
final$venue.id),]
edges_list_final <-edges_list_final[edges_list_final$NodeFrom %in%
venue_details_final$venue.id,]
```

```
edges_list_final <-edges_list_final[edges_list_final$NodeTo %in%
venue_details_final$venue.id,]
edges_list_final$distance <- apply(edges_list_final, 1, get_distances_
between_nodes)
```

The distance that we will add between the two nodes is not the typical driving distance between them. We will use the longitude and latitude information of the venues to find out the distance as the crow flies. With the distance information added in, we can straight away do a little descriptive analysis. We can try to find out which are the venues in New York to which the maximum number of Foursquare users prefer starting from another venue. Also we can find the average distance that users will cover to reach these venues. The following snippet will find out the 10 most venues which end up being a target node:

```
# Most visited locations in New York
prominent_next_venues <- edges_list_final %>%
            group_by(NodeTo) %>%
            summarise(avg_distance_from_last_venue =
mean(distance),num_targets = n()) %>%
            arrange(desc(num_targets)) %>%
            top_n(10)
colnames(prominent_next_venues)[1]<- "venue.id"

prominent_next_venues <- prominent_next_venues %>%
                    inner_join(venue_details_final) %>%
                    select(venue.id, venue.name, avg_distance_
from_last_venue, num_targets)
```

The result is not a very surprising one. The popular places of New York are the ones people usually go to from other venues. The result in a DataFrame is as follows:

venue.id	venue.name	avg_distance_from_last_venue	num_targets
412d2800f964a520df0c1fe3	Central Park	1394.0244	80
49b7ed6df964a52030531fe3	Times Square	474.7327	76
3fd66200f964a520d7f11ee3	Bryant Park	276.5055	49
427c0500f964a52097211fe3	The Metropolitan Museum of Art (Metropolitan Museu...	796.4101	49
49b79f54f964a5202c531fe3	Rockefeller Center	373.2110	41
4b6b5abff964a520fb022ce3	National September 11 Memorial & Museum	690.7747	41
41102700f964a520d60b1fe3	Macy's	395.0770	39
4297b480f964a52062241fe3	American Museum of Natural History	500.0943	39
4b992b04f964a520726635e3	Barclays Center	373.1741	35
447bf8f1f964a520ec331fe3	Apple Fifth Avenue	556.5376	34
4531059cf964a520683b1fe3	Bloomingdale's	251.0266	34

Top venues in New York

We learned a great deal about analysis on graph data in the previous chapter, hence we will not be doing a repeat of all that analysis on this dataset again. The point of extracting a graph dataset out of Foursquare was to illustrate how we can get imaginative with our data extraction process also. This is the kind of creativity that makes social media analytics an exciting field of study.

> We have skipped repeating a great deal of analysis that can be done on the extracted venue graph data. But the data is in the same format as we used in the previous chapters. Users are encouraged to replicate the results obtained in the previous chapters on the current dataset. This will give you an intense flavor of actually working on some of these problems.

Challenges for Foursquare data analysis

The analysis on Foursquare data involved a bunch of challenges. Akin to the rest of our social media sources, we will try to enumerate the challenges associated with Foursquare data:

- **Data extraction**: The most obvious problem in dealing with Foursquare data analytics is the lack of a decent package. This makes the data extraction process extremely cumbersome and low level. This was one of the most remarkable challenges about the Foursquare application.

- **API changes**: All the social media services keep tinkering with their APIs frequently. This makes it a challenge for the developer to continually adapt to those changes. This often means a lot of code rewriting every time your favorite social media application launches some changes in its APIs. This constant tussle with the changes is at times extremely frustrating and time consuming.

- **Privacy**: Privacy is a glaringly important challenge in any social media analytics. We always strive to study the users collectively but we never want to intrude on the privacy of an individual user. This analysis versus privacy debate is relevant for not just social media applications but across all the services on the Internet. Not so long ago, Foursquare would have provided you with check-in details of any user but a bunch of mischievous people used that to detrimental effect. This usually leads to a restricted data access and weak analyzes.

These were some of the challenges that we faced along the path that we took for Foursquare data analysis. This is not an exhaustive list; there were many others, but most of those were dealt with by writing flexible code and being a little creative here and there.

Summary

Foursquare is an important social media source. The concept of check-in that Foursquare introduced was quite revolutionary at the time of launching. Now we find the check-in feature in Facebook also. This chapter helped us in understanding the basic flow of data extraction in absence of a neatly developed R package. We learned how to get creative with our data extraction process. We built up on the key concepts of sentiment and graph analytics introduced in previous chapters. A conscious effort was made to not repeat the obvious processes again but to build on those processes for building something relevant. The most important takeaway from this chapter is to learn how to form a problem definition. We introduced it with an example (recommendation engine) and the users are encouraged to find different such problems in the data that we extracted (hint: classification system). This chapter also prepared us for the upcoming challenges. The next social media sources are going to be challenging as we transition from the R packages to the low level APIs.

The next set of chapters will go into the diverse area of social data and help the users with their analytics work flows.

5
Analyzing Software Collaboration Trends I – Social Coding with GitHub

Technology has evolved with leaps and bounds over the last couple of decades. With better hardware, software, and data, we are finally seeing trends such as open source, big data, predictive analytics, artificial intelligence, and productivity tools. The rise of open source development has created a healthy collaborative culture in the software development landscape where pair programming, open source contributions, and problem redressal have helped developers build better software together. In the next couple of chapters, we will try to analyze trends in the software development and collaboration domain by focusing on two major platforms – GitHub and StackExchange.

To know about GitHub, we need to know about Git! If you are a software developer, tester, or have worked collaboratively with others in building software, you might be familiar with Git. In the year 2005, famous software engineer Linus Torvalds, more popularly known as the father of Linux, created Git with the purpose of collaborative development of the Linux kernel with other kernel developers. Git is a version control system and a source code management system which is mainly used in distributed and collaborative development projects. GitHub is nothing but a platform which is a web-based version of Git. It is a distributed version control system at heart which encourages social collaboration when developing software.

Another popular aspect of software collaboration include Question & Answer (Q&A) platforms such as StackOverflow, WikiAnswers, and StackExchange, where users can post various questions related to bugs, issues, and the problems they face in their day-to-day lives in building software, technology, and products. Thus platforms such as these have become indispensable to the community at large.

We will follow a structured two-chapter approach in this book focusing on two different software collaboration platforms. In this chapter, we will be focusing on GitHub, the most popular social coding and collaboration platform for developers. We will learn a bit about the various features of GitHub, understand ways to access GitHub data with the help of APIs, and also cover several major aspects of analyzing GitHub data including:

- Analyzing repository activity
- Retrieving trending repositories
- Analyzing repository trends
- Analyzing language trends
- Analyzing user trends

In the next chapter, we will focus on a popular Q&A platform for software and collaboration, StackExchange. We will learn about the StackExchange platform, look at various ways to access data including APIs and data dumps, and cover different aspects of analyzing the data by focusing on two interesting problems.

We will be using a suite of libraries in the following sections to retrieve, parse, analyze, and visualize data in R. While we will mention the libraries we use as necessary, in case you do not have any of them installed, remember to use the `install.packages(...)` function to install the necessary packages.

Environment setup

We will be using several R libraries or packages in this chapter as mentioned before. The major libraries which will be used along with their main utility are outlined in the following table. Feel free to use `install.packages(...)` to install them. For ease of usage, I have also created a file called `env_setup.R` which you can load into R and execute the necessary code present there to install all the necessary packages which will be used in this chapter. You can also find the package descriptions in more detail from the CRAN website at `https://cran.r-project.org/web/packages/available_packages_by_name.html`:

R package	Utility description
`httr`	Tools for working with APIs, URLs, and HTTP
`jsonlite`	Flexible, robust, high performance tools for working with JSON in R
`dplyr`	A fast, consistent tool for working with DataFrame-like objects, both in memory and out of memory
`ggplot2`	A system for declaratively creating graphics, plots, and visualizations based on The Grammar of Graphics

R package	Utility description
reshape2	A tool to flexibly restructure and aggregate data
hrbrthemes	A compilation of extra ggplot2 themes, scales, and utilities with an emphasis on typography
sqldf	A tool to manipulate R DataFrame using SQL
lubridate	Fast and user-friendly parsing and manipulation of date-time data
corrplot	Helps in visualization of correlation matrices
devtools	Collection of package development tools and utilities. Useful for installing packages from GitHub
data.table	Fast aggregation of large DataFrames

We will be using several functions from these packages to retrieve, analyze, and visualize our data in various scenarios in the following sections. An important point to note here is that I had to install the hrbrthemes package from its GitHub repository and you can use the following code snippet to do the same:

```
install.packages("scales")
install.packages('extrafontdb')
install.packages('Rttf2pt1')
devtools::install_github("hrbrmstr/hrbrthemes")
```

Before we start discussing data retrieval and analysis from GitHub, let us understand a bit more about GitHub and its major features.

Understanding GitHub

It's always advisable to be more familiar with the domain before processing or analyzing any data. Hence before understanding how to extract, process, and analyze data from GitHub, we will spend some time on understanding more about GitHub, its vision, and the major features which are used across the world by software and technology enthusiasts.

As mentioned before, the core of GitHub is a web-based service for hosting Git repositories. You can think of a repository as a directory or a folder containing multiple folders or subdirectories, code files, and other assets such as images, media, documents, and so on. People build software by collaborating together on various repositories which they create and maintain. Open source principles are promoted on GitHub and various open source projects and software are developed, improved, and maintained using GitHub. Anyone can be an open source contributor by talking to the members of a project maintained in a repository, adhering to the necessary coding standards, and being open to collaborative development, reviews, and feedback.

GitHub at its core uses Git functionality and hence it enables users to use all the features of distributed source code management and version control. The following are some of the concepts and terminology widely used in GitHub and the collaborative software development community:

- A repository is basically a container which contains all necessary code and assets for a software product or project.

- Repository forks are basically clones or copies of the parent or original repository. Any user can fork a repository and then modify it to add enhancements to suit their own needs as long as it adheres with the license.

- Repository stars are basically GitHub's version of Facebook likes or +1 from Google+. Users can star a repository if they like it. Then they become a stargazer of that repository. Often stargazer and fork counts are ways of finding out trending and popular repositories!

- Users can also create issues, feature requests, and file bugs and track them over a period of time.

- Each repository usually has one or multiple languages which are basically programming languages which were used to build the project.

- Adding new content to a repository is done through commits.

- When multiple users are modifying and adding content to a repository using commits, they usually send pull requests which consist of the necessary modifications.

- Pull requests are usually merged to the repository after due reviews and conflict resolutions.

- A repository might have multiple branches, where each branch can have the same or different code and assets. Each branch usually can focus on specific new content, features, or enhancements which can then be merged to the default master branch of the repository.

GitHub also offers a variety of interesting features and capabilities besides code hosting, version control, and management. Some of its popular features include the following:

- Ability to collaborate, develop, and manage code with the help of repositories which can be used by multiple users at any point in time without losing data.

- Ability to build beautiful markdown-based documentation, wikis, and readme files for various code repositories.

- GitHub pages to host personal websites or build websites for projects and repositories.

- Ability to track issues, bugs, and feature requests for various repositories and help improve and evolve software with time.

- Ability to search through code, repository lists, and users.

- Ability to get curated content of repositories as well as trending repositories by language over time.

- Visualizations and statistics with regard to commits, code frequency, punch cards, contributors, members, and networks.

- Feature-rich issue and enhancement tracking capabilities with abilities to review code, add comments, tag contributors, users, and assign tasks.

- E-mail notification capabilities.

- Ability to view CSV files, Jupyter notebooks, PSD files, images, and PDF documents directly from GitHub itself.

Thus you can guess by all the features and capabilities we listed that there is a lot which can be done with GitHub and it has really done a lot to make coding and software development more social, fun, and collaborative! Indeed, the official trademark mascot of GitHub, the Octocat is quite popular amongst the developer community and the logo can be observed in the following figure:

The very popular GitHub mascot—Octocat

GitHub also provides various other features including public and private repositories and special enterprise software development capabilities also known as GitHub enterprise, where it is usually hosted in private enterprise environments behind corporate firewalls. GitHub also has gists for hosting short snippets of code. Besides this, it also has Speaker Deck which can be used for hosting slide and presentation decks. Now that we are well acquainted with GitHub and collaborative software development, let's start our journey by retrieving some data from GitHub.

Accessing GitHub data

There are various ways to access data from GitHub just like we have seen in the previous chapters for other social media platforms. If you are using R, you can go ahead and use the rgithub package which provides a high level interface with several functions to retrieve data from GitHub. Besides that, you can also register an application with GitHub to get an OAuth-based access token which can be used to gain access to GitHub's own API. We will cover both mechanisms briefly in this section.

Using the rgithub package for data access

As we mentioned earlier, there is a specific package in R known as rgithub which provides high level functions and interfaces to access GitHub data. You can install and load the package in R using the following code snippet:

```
library(devtools)
install_github("cscheid/rgithub")
library(github)
```

Of course, you would then need a GitHub application ID and secret token to gain seamless access to the data without too many restrictions and rate limits. We will cover this in the next section. To get more information about this package you can head over to the official GitHub repository at https://github.com/cscheid/rgithub. The package has well-defined functions with proper names and you can start using them to retrieve data from GitHub. The following snippet shows an example of getting data pertaining to your repositories:

```
# assuming you get your app id and secret tokens from GitHub
ctx = interactive.login(client.id, client.secret)
repos = get.my.repositories(ctx)
```

While this is a good library, we did find it quite restrictive in terms of the flexibility of using the raw power of GitHub's API as well as a lack of proper documentation with regard to each of its functions, unlike what we have observed for other packages such as RFacebook. Hence, in this chapter, we will be using the GitHub's API directly in all our analyzes.

Registering an application on GitHub

The main intent of registering an application on GitHub is to access the official API provided by GitHub using authenticated requests. If you are already familiar with the GitHub API, you might know that you can still access and retrieve data without any authentication. The question which might come to mind is: why do we need any authentication then? The reason is to avoid excessive rate limiting and the ability to access more data with more API requests per hour. Without authentication, you can make 60 API requests per hour and with authentication, you can make up to 5,000 requests per hour free of charge. This is quite a substantial gain and hence we will spend some time to understand how to register an application and use its access tokens for data retrieval.

Of course, you would definitely need to have a GitHub account for this; it is assumed that you already have it. If not, head over to `https://github.com` and create a personal account; it's free if you host public repositories. Once you have an account, head over to the settings page which is available in the link at `https://github.com/settings/developers`, which basically points you to all your registered developer OAuth applications. The following snapshot depicts the settings page for all my registered GitHub applications:

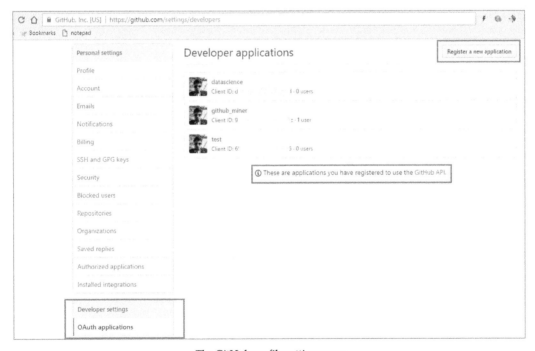

The GitHub profile settings page

The boxes in red point out the main areas which you should focus on. You can already see in the bottom left-hand menu that we are in the OAuth applications section under the settings. Existing applications, if any, are shown there, which have been registered to use the GitHub API as mentioned in the text at the bottom. For now, you need to look at the top right box which points to a button saying **Register a new application**. Click on the button and it should take you to the next page as depicted in the following snapshot:

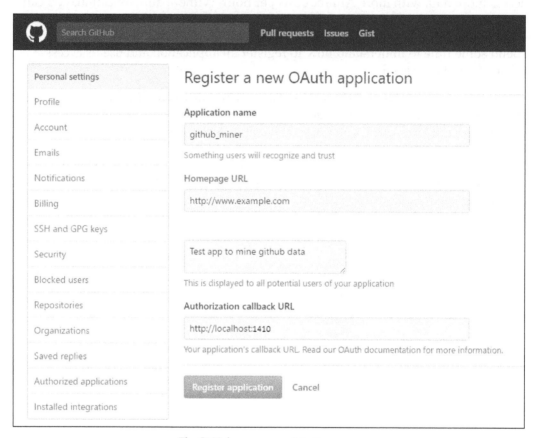

The GitHub new app registration page

You can give the application a name of your choice. Once you have registered your application, click on the **Register application** button. This should take you to the following screen which shows you the **Client ID** and **Client Secret** tokens:

Getting your GitHub app access tokens

Copy these tokens and store them somewhere so that we can start using them when we access the GitHub API.

Accessing data using the GitHub API

We are now ready to start using the GitHub API to access and retrieve data! The base URL for the API is always `https://api.github.com` and usually there are various end points which can be requested for based on the type of data we want to retrieve. GitHub's latest API is on version 3 at the time of writing this book and there is a dedicated section on the GitHub website containing detailed documentation of the API. Feel free to visit `https://developer.github.com/guides/getting-started` if you are interested in knowing in more detail about how the API works.

Any API end point typically returns data in JSON format which is usually a document of key and value pairs. We will use libraries such as `httr` and `jsonlite` to retrieve and parse the data into easy-to-use data formats such as R DataFrames. Let's take a simple example of trying to get relevant statistics for our personal GitHub account. First let us load the necessary packages we will be using:

```
library(httr)
library(jsonlite)
```

Now, let us create the necessary arguments we will be passing to the API, which will be our access token details:

```
auth.id <- 'XXXXXX'
auth.pwd <- 'XXXXXXXXXX'
api_id_param <- paste0('client_id=', auth.id)
api_pwd_param <- paste0('client_secret=', auth.pwd)
arg_sep = '&'
```

Now, if I want to get the statistics for my account, I will be using the following snippet where the base API URL points to my GitHub account user name:

```
base_url <- 'https://api.github.com/users/dipanjanS?'
my_profile_url <- paste0(base_url, api_id_param, arg_sep, api_pwd_
param)
response <- GET(my_profile_url)
```

On closer inspection of the `response` object, we observe the following output:

```
> response
Response [https://api.github.com/users/dipanjanS?client_
id=XXXXXX&client_secret=XXXXXXXXXX]
  Date: 2017-03-23 20:14
  Status: 200
  Content-Type: application/json; charset=utf-8
  Size: 1.45 kB
{
  "login": "dipanjanS",
  "id": 3448263,
  "avatar_url": "https://avatars2.githubusercontent.com/
u/3448263?v=3",
  "gravatar_id": "",
  "url": "https://api.github.com/users/dipanjanS",
  "html_url": "https://github.com/dipanjanS",
  "followers_url": "https://api.github.com/users/dipanjanS/followers",
  "following_url": "https://api.github.com/users/dipanjanS/following{/
other_user}",
  "gists_url": "https://api.github.com/users/dipanjanS/gists{/gist_
id}",
  ...
```

Remember our discussion about rate limits earlier? Well we can see how many requests per hour are allotted to us and how many are remaining using the following snippet:

```
> as.data.frame(response$headers)[,c('x.ratelimit.limit',
'x.ratelimit.remaining')]
  x.ratelimit.limit x.ratelimit.remaining
1             5000                  4999
```

Thus you can clearly see from the headers in our response object, that we have 5000 requests allocated to us out of which we used up one in the previous request. Try executing the same code with no authentication token and see how the rate limits differ.

We can parse the preceding JSON `response` object into a more suitable object such as a DataFrame using the following snippet:

```
me <- content(response)
me <- as.data.frame(t(as.matrix(me)))
View(me[,c('login', 'public_repos', 'public_gists', 'followers',
            'created_at', 'updated_at')])
```

This gives us the DataFrame as depicted in the following snapshot:

	login	public_repos	public_gists	followers	created_at	updated_at
1	dipanjanS	62	34	105	2013-02-01T11:52:11Z	2017-02-18T13:38:06Z

There is a better approach to get the same DataFrame using minimal code. We will use the `fromJSON(...)` function available in the `jsonlite` package as depicted in the following code snippet:

```
me <- fromJSON(my_profile_url)
me <- as.data.frame(t(as.matrix(me)))
View(me[,c('login', 'public_repos', 'public_gists', 'followers',
            'created_at', 'updated_at')])
```

This gives us the same DataFrame which we wanted for the stats pertaining to my GitHub account as depicted in the following snapshot:

	login	public_repos	public_gists	followers	created_at	updated_at
1	dipanjanS	62	34	105	2013-02-01T11:52:11Z	2017-02-18T13:38:06Z

This gives us a good peek at how to access and retrieve data from GitHub. We will now look at various ways to extract and analyze useful data from GitHub in the following sections by utilizing the aforementioned data access mechanisms in combination with the other packages we mentioned in the Environment setup section to produce insightful visualizations. We will start off by analyzing repository activity on GitHub.

Analyzing repository activity

We mentioned before that any collaborative software development is typically done in repositories on GitHub. A repository is typically a store for code, data, and other assets which can be accessed in a distributive manner by various collaborators across the world. In this section, we will analyze and visualize various parameters with regard to repository activity for one of the most popular open sourced operating systems, Linux. The GitHub repository for Linux can be accessed at `https://github.com/torvalds/linux` in case you want to view its components. With over 600,000 commits, it is one of the most popular open source repositories on GitHub. We will start by loading the necessary packages we will be using in this and in future sections and our GitHub access tokens. I have already placed them in the `load_packages.R` file available with the code files for this chapter. You can load it up using the following command:

```
source('load_packages.R')
```

Now we have the necessary packages loaded along with the access tokens and we can start accessing and analyzing the required repository activity data.

Analyzing weekly commit frequency

Commits are basically a mechanism to add new code and make changes to existing code files and assets in a repository. Here, we will analyze the weekly commit frequency for the `linux` repository. We will start by retrieving the weekly frequency data using the following snippet:

```
# get weekly commit data
base_url <- 'https://api.github.com/repos/torvalds/linux/stats/commit_
activity?'
repo_url <- paste0(base_url, api_id_param, arg_sep, api_pwd_param)
response <- fromJSON(repo_url)
```

The week field returned in the preceding response will be in epoch, so we will convert it into a more readable and understandable date-time format using the following code.

```
# convert epoch to timestamp
response$week_conv <- as.POSIXct(response$week, origin="1970-01-01")
```

We are now ready to visualize the weekly commit frequency and we can do this by using the following code:

```
# visualize weekly commit frequency
ggplot(response, aes(week_conv, total)) +
  geom_line(aes(color=total), size=1.5) +
  labs(x="Time", y="Total commits",
      title="Weekly GitHub commit frequency",
      subtitle="Commit history for the linux repository") +
  theme_ipsum_rc()
```

This gives us the following line chart showing the weekly commit frequency in the linux repository:

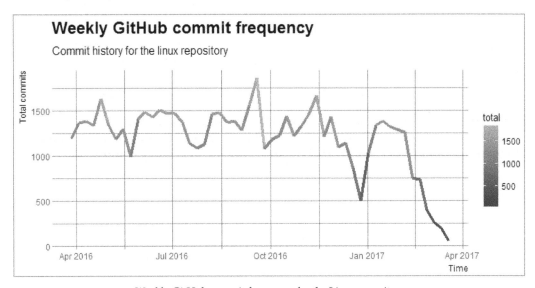

Weekly GitHub commit frequency for the Linux repository

We can clearly observe a steady flow of commits over a period of time which peaked sometime during September, 2016 and then declined from late November until the end of December, 2016, most probably due to people enjoying their winter vacation and holidays. The commit frequency seems to have picked up again since January, 2017 with a decline again after February-March, 2017.

Analyzing commit frequency distribution versus day of the week

Let's look at the distribution of commit frequencies for the `linux` repository based on the different days of a week. A week consists of five weekdays and two weekends. We will see the distribution of commit activity frequencies per day by using box plots. The idea is to see which days have the maximum or minimum commits and if there is any stark comparison between different days of the week. To achieve this, we would need to curate our data to assign the day of the week to each row in our dataset. To do this, we can use the following code:

```
# curate daily commit history
make_breaks <- function(strt, hour, minute, interval="day", length.
out=31) {
  strt <- as.POSIXlt(strt)
  strt <- ISOdatetime(strt$year+1900L, strt$mon+1L,
          strt$mday, hour=hour, min=minute, sec=0, tz="UTC")
  seq.POSIXt(strt, strt+(1+length.out)*60*60*24, by=interval)
}

daily_commits <- unlist(response$days)
days <- rep(c('Sun', 'Mon', 'Tue', 'Wed', 'Thu', 'Fri', 'Sat'), 52)
time_stamp <- make_breaks(min(response$week_conv), hour=5, minute=30,
interval="day", length.out=362)
df <- data.frame(commits=daily_commits, day=days, time=time_stamp)
```

This gives us a DataFrame of daily commits where each row consists of the number of commits, the timestamp, and the day of the week corresponding to that timestamp. We can view our curated dataset using the following command:

```
# view the daily commit history dataset
View(df)
```

This gives us a peek at the DataFrame which you can see in the following snapshot:

	commits	day	time
1	49	Sun	2016-03-27 05:30:00
2	113	Mon	2016-03-28 05:30:00
3	186	Tue	2016-03-29 05:30:00
4	278	Wed	2016-03-30 05:30:00
5	219	Thu	2016-03-31 05:30:00
6	286	Fri	2016-04-01 05:30:00
7	63	Sat	2016-04-02 05:30:00
8	71	Sun	2016-04-03 05:30:00
9	225	Mon	2016-04-04 05:30:00
10	227	Tue	2016-04-05 05:30:00

Let's now visualize this data to view the commit frequency distribution per day of the week using the following code:

```
# visualize commit frequency distribution vs. day of week
ggplot(df, aes(x=day, y=commits, color=day)) +
  geom_boxplot(position='dodge') +
  scale_fill_ipsum() +
  labs(x="Day", y="Total commits",
    title="GitHub commit frequency distribution vs. Day of Week",
    subtitle="Commit history for the linux repository") +
  theme_ipsum_rc(grid="Y")
```

This gives us the following graph depicting the distributions per day of the week for the linux repository:

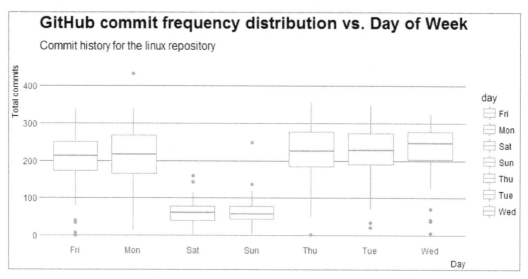

GitHub commit frequency distribution versus day of the week for the Linux repository

The distribution graph provides us with some interesting insights. We can clearly observe that the number of commits based on the median measure is highest on Wednesday, signifying more people tend to commit around mid-week and the least amount of commits usually happens around the weekends (Saturday and Sunday).

Analyzing daily commit frequency

We visualized how the commit frequency distribution looks like per day of the week. Let's now look at the daily commit frequency for the linux repository. We can reuse the curated DataFrame from the previous section and visualize the commit frequency using the following code snippet:

```
# visualize daily commit frequency
ggplot(df, aes(x=time, y=commits, color=day)) +
  geom_line(aes(color=day)) +
  geom_point(aes(shape=day)) +
  scale_fill_ipsum() +
  labs(x="Time", y="Total commits",
       title="Daily GitHub commit frequency",
       subtitle="Commit history for the linux repository") +
  theme_ipsum_rc(grid="Y")
```

This gives us the following plot showing the daily commit frequency over time per day of the week:

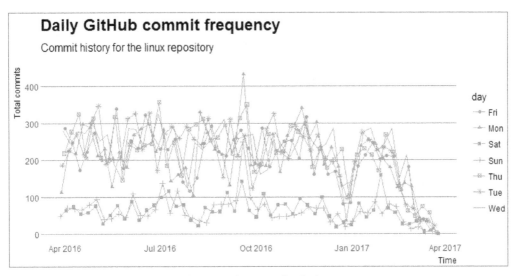

Daily GitHub commit frequency for the linux repository

The graph is basically the weekly commit frequency now broken up into daily commit frequency over time and as expected, we see a lesser number of commits over time in the weekends.

Analyzing weekly commit frequency comparison

An open source repository usually has multiple collaborators where one of them is the creator of the repository and often he/she is the owner and maintainer of the repository. Other collaborators are contributors to the repository and based on certain processes, conventions, and policies, commits are merged into the repository to add or change code. We will now do a comparative analysis of the weekly commit frequency comparing the number of commits for the owner of the repository versus all other contributors in the repository. To start with, we will retrieve the commit history for the contributors and owner of the linux repository using the following snippet:

```
# get the commit participation history
base_url <- 'https://api.github.com/repos/torvalds/linux/stats/
participation?'
repo_url <- paste0(base_url,api_id_param,arg_sep,api_pwd_param)
response <- fromJSON(repo_url)
response <- as.data.frame(response)
```

Next, we will be extracting the contributors commit frequency from the total frequency. We will also curate the dataset into a more easy-to-use format in visualizations by using the following snippet:

```
# get contributor frequency & curate dataset
response$contributors <- response$all - response$owner
response$week <- 1:52
response <- response[,c('week', 'contributors', 'owner')]
# format the dataset
df <- melt(response, id='week')
```

We are now ready to visualize the comparative weekly commit frequency for the Linux repository and the following code will help us achieve this:

```
# visualize weekly commit frequency comparison
ggplot(data=df, aes(x=week, y=value, color=variable)) +
  geom_line(aes(color=variable)) +
  geom_point(aes(shape=variable)) +
  scale_fill_ipsum() +
  labs(x="Week", y="Total commits",
      title="Weekly GitHub commit frequency comparison",
      subtitle="Commit history for the linux repository") +
  theme_ipsum_rc(grid="Y")
```

This gives us the following graph with the comparative weekly commit frequency:

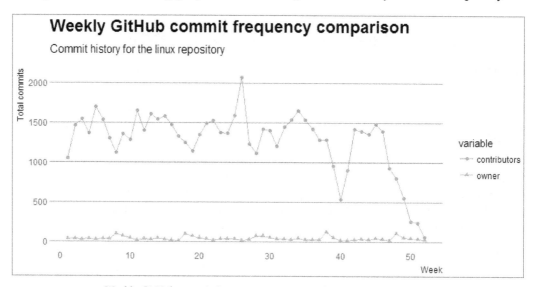

Weekly GitHub commit frequency comparison for the Linux repository

We can clearly see that over the past year, the frequency of commits made by contributors is really high as compared to that of the owner. A question might arise as to why this is the case. Well, as you might know, the Linux repository is owned by Linus Torvalds, the creator and father of the Linux operating system and also the person who created Git! Linus himself had stated in 2012 that after the initial days of intense programming and development of Linux, these days he mostly contributes by merging code written by other contributors with little programming involvement. Torvalds still has written approximately 2% of the total Linux kernel and considering the vast number of contributors, that is still one of the largest percentages of overall contribution to the Linux kernel. I hope you found this little bit of history interesting!

Analyzing weekly code modification history

Commits to any repository usually consist of additions and deletions where lines of code are usually added or deleted in various files present in the repository. In this section, we will retrieve and analyze weekly code modification history for the linux repository. The following code snippet enables us the get the code modification historical frequency data from GitHub:

```
# get the code frequency dataset
base_url <- 'https://api.github.com/repos/torvalds/linux/stats/code_
frequency?'
code_freq_url <- paste0(base_url,api_id_param,arg_sep,api_pwd_param)
response <- fromJSON(code_freq_url)
df <- as.data.frame(response)
```

We will now format this DataFrame into an easy to visualize object and also convert the number of deletions into absolute values with the following code snippet:

```
# format the dataset
colnames(df) <- c('time', 'additions', 'deletions')
df$deletions <- abs(df$deletions)
df$time <- as.Date(as.POSIXct(df$time, origin="1970-01-01"))
df <- melt(df, id='time')
```

We are now ready to visualize the total code modifications made to the linux repository over a period of time. The following snippet helps us achieve this:

```
# visualize the code frequency timeline
ggplot(df, aes(x=time, y=value, color=variable)) +
  geom_line(aes(color = variable)) +
  geom_point(aes(shape = variable)) +
  scale_x_date(date_breaks="12 month", date_labels='%Y') +
  scale_y_log10(breaks = c(10, 100, 1000, 10000,
```

```
                      100000, 1000000)) +
   labs(x="Time", y="Total code modifications (log scaled)",
     title="Weekly Github code frequency timeline",
     subtitle="Code frequency history for the linux repository") +
   theme_ipsum_rc(grid="XY")
```

This gives us the following plot showing the code modification frequency over time:

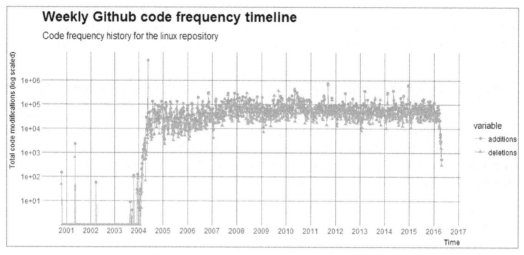

Weekly GitHub code frequency timeline for the linux repository

The plotted graph portrays an interesting picture. The obvious fact is that the total additions to the code are usually more than the total deletions. But we can see that the code additions and deletions start around 2000-01 when **GNOME** and **KNOPPIX**, two major Linux distributions, were released. We also notice a steep increase in the code modification frequency around 2004-05, which is around the time **Ubuntu**, one of the most popular Linux distributions, came into existence! A part of the Linux timeline is depicted in the following figure:

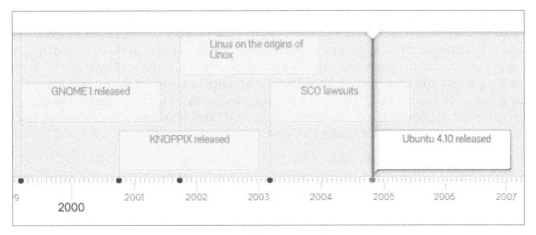

A section of the Linux timeline

You can find more information about the entire history and timeline of the Linux operating system at `http://www.linux-netbook.com/linux/timeline/`, which contains further detailed information including an interactive version of the preceding snapshot.

This brings us to the end of the repository analytics section, where we saw various statistics and ways of analyzing and visualizing repository activity.

Retrieving trending repositories

A repository is usually known as a trending repository if it's popular among the software or technical community. There are various ways to look at trending repositories on GitHub. Usually the total stargazer and fork counts are ways of measuring the popularity of repositories. In fact, you can check trending repositories on GitHub from the website itself by going to `https://github.com/trending`, where GitHub depicts the repositories which are trending in open source.

In this section, we will retrieve trending repositories based on the following conditions:

- We will use the search API
- We will retrieve trending repositories which were created over the last 3 years: 2014-2016
- The definition of trending repositories in our case will be only those repositories which have at least 500 stars or more

You can always change these conditions and experiment with conditions of your own. This is just an example to depict a way to retrieve trending repositories over time. The code used in this section is available in the file named `github_trending_repo_retrieval.R`, which you can refer to for more details. We will start by creating a function which will take a timeline of dates (a vector of dates) and the authentication tokens and retrieve the trending repositories for us. We also use a progress bar to show the retrieval progress since it takes some time to retrieve all the trending repositories over a span of 3 years:

```
source('load_packages.R')

get.trending.repositories <- function(timeline.dates, auth.id, auth.
pwd){
  # set parameters
  base_url <- 'https://api.github.com/search/repositories?'
  api_id_param <- paste0('client_id=', auth.id)
  api_pwd_param <- paste0('client_secret=', auth.pwd)
  per_page <- 100
  top.repos.df <- data.frame()
  pb <- txtProgressBar(min = 0, max = length(timeline.dates), style =
3)
  # for each pair of dates in the list get all trending repos
  for (i in seq(1,length(timeline.dates), by=2)){
    start_date <- timeline.dates[i]
    end_date <- timeline.dates[i+1]
    query <- paste0('q=created:%22', start_date, '%20..%20',
                    end_date, '%22%20stars:%3E=500')
    url <- paste0(base_url, query, arg_sep, api_id_param,arg_sep,api_
pwd_param)
    response <- fromJSON(url)
    total_repos <- min(response$total_count, 1000)
    count <- ceiling(total_repos / per_page)
    # convert data into data frame
    for (p in 1:count){
      page_number <- paste0('page=', p)
      per_page_count <- paste0('per_page=', per_page)
      page_url <- paste0(url, arg_sep, page_number, arg_sep, per_page_
count)
      response <- fromJSON(page_url)
      items <- response$items
      items <- items[, c('id', 'name', 'full_name', 'size',
          'fork', 'stargazers_count', 'watchers', 'forks',
          'open_issues', 'language', 'has_issues', 'has_downloads',
          'has_wiki', 'has_pages', 'created_at', 'updated_at',
          'pushed_at', 'url', 'description')]
```

```
    top.repos.df <- rbind(top.repos.df, items)
  }
  setTxtProgressBar(pb, i+1)
}
return (top.repos.df)
}
```

You can clearly see that we do not store all the parameters for each repository but only a handful which will be used for us in our future analyzes as depicted in the items DataFrame in the preceding snippet. The `top.repos.df` DataFrame keeps getting updated with trending repositories and contains all the trending repositories based on the timeline we give as input.

The following snippet will now help us retrieve trending repositories from 2014 to 2016 based on the rules which we talked about earlier:

```
# set timeline
dates <- c('2014-01-01', '2014-03-31',
           '2014-04-01', '2014-06-30',
           '2014-07-01', '2014-09-30',
           '2014-10-01', '2014-12-31',
           '2015-01-01', '2015-03-31',
           '2015-04-01', '2015-06-30',
           '2015-07-01', '2015-09-30',
           '2015-10-01', '2015-12-31',
           '2016-01-01', '2016-03-31',
           '2016-04-01', '2016-06-30',
           '2016-07-01', '2016-09-30',
           '2016-10-01', '2016-12-31')
> trending_repos <- get.trending.repositories(timeline.dates=dates,
+                              auth.id=auth.id,
+                              auth.pwd=auth.pwd)
  |=====================================================| 100%
```

We can now check if the retrieval worked using the following snippets:

```
# check total trending repos retrieved
> nrow(trending_repos)
[1] 9912

# take a peek at the data
> View(trending_repos)
```

This allows us to take a peek at our newly created dataset, which is depicted in the following snapshot:

	id	name	full_name	size	fork	stargazers_count	watchers	forks
1	16408992	neovim	neovim/neovim	50964	FALSE	22055	22055	1565
2	15653276	android-open-project	Trinea/android-open-project	1742	FALSE	22005	22005	10968
3	17375436	es6features	lukehoban/es6features	199	FALSE	19288	19288	1742
4	16752620	gogs	gogits/gogs	113009	FALSE	18332	18332	2088
5	18049133	slick	kenwheeler/slick	3444	FALSE	17711	17711	2856
6	18275356	pop	facebook/pop	591	FALSE	17380	17380	2744
7	15585444	Hover	ianLunn/Hover	870	FALSE	16162	16162	3467
8	18280236	gitbook	GitbookIO/gitbook	8356	FALSE	14700	14700	1849
9	16677706	awesome-sysadmin	kahun/awesome-sysadmin	2115	FALSE	14498	14498	2276
10	17165658	spark	apache/spark	270000	FALSE	12169	12169	11450

The preceding DataFrame just shows a fraction of all the columns which we had retrieved and you can check out other rows or columns by scrolling in the desired direction in the generated output. Now, we will store this dataset so we can load it up directly when we want to analyze it in the future instead of spending time again to retrieve all the necessary data points:

```
# save the dataset
save(trending_repos, file='trending_repos.RData')
```

This brings us to the end of this section on looking at a methodology to retrieve trending repositories from GitHub. In the next few sections, we will look at various ways to analyze this data. We will be focusing on analyzing trends in the following three major areas:

- Repository trends
- Language trends
- User trends

Analyzing repository trends

In this section, we will focus on various ways to analyzing different aspects of repositories, which include visualizing repository creation and updates over time, looking at various repository metrics and the various relationships among them. To start with, you can load up the necessary dependencies and the `trending_repos`. `RData` dataset which we created in the previous section in case you haven't done so already:

```
source('load_packages.R')
load('trending_repos.RData')
```

Now we are ready to analyze various trends with regard to our trending repositories and each of the following sub-sections will focus on a particular aspect of repository trends.

Analyzing trending repositories created over time

We will look at the trends with regard to our trending repositories based on their creation date over time. Basically we want to view the repository creation frequency over time and observe if there are any peaks or dips from the graph which we will be plotting. Our dataset has a field called `created_at` which depicts the timestamp when the repository was created. We will start by extracting the necessary date elements from this attribute using the following snippet:

```
# extract date elements
trending_repos$created_year <- format(as.Date(trending_repos$created_
at), "%Y")
trending_repos$created_monthyear <- format(as.Date(trending_
repos$created_at), "%b-%Y")
```

You can see that we have extracted the year and also the month and year where each repository was created. You can now aggregate on any of these fields and get repository frequencies. We will sum up the counts of all the repositories which were created in a particular month of a particular year using the following snippet:

```
# build aggregations
repos_by_created_time <- aggregate(trending_repos$created_monthyear,
by=list(trending_repos$created_monthyear), length)
colnames(repos_by_created_time) <- c("CreateTime", "Count")
```

Next, we format the `CreateTime` attribute into a date object using the following snippet:

```
# format dates
repos_by_created_time$CreateTime <- mdy(repos_by_created_
time$CreateTime)
```

This completes our aggregation and formatting operations and we can visualize our data with the following snippet:

```
# visualize data
ggplot(repos_by_created_time, aes(x=CreateTime, y=Count)) +
  geom_line(aes(color=Count), size=1.5) +
  scale_x_date(date_breaks="3 month", date_labels='%b-%Y')+
  geom_text(aes(label=Count),
```

```
                vjust=-0.3,
                position=position_dodge(.9), size=3) +
    labs(x="Creation Time", y="Trending Repository Count",
        title="Trending Repositories vs. Creation Time",
        subtitle="Total trending repositories created in GitHub over
    time") +
    theme_ipsum_rc(grid="XY") +
    theme(legend.position="right",
        axis.text.x = element_text(angle = 90, hjust = 1))
```

This gives us the following graph showing the trend of our trending repositories created over time aggregated on the basis of creation month-year:

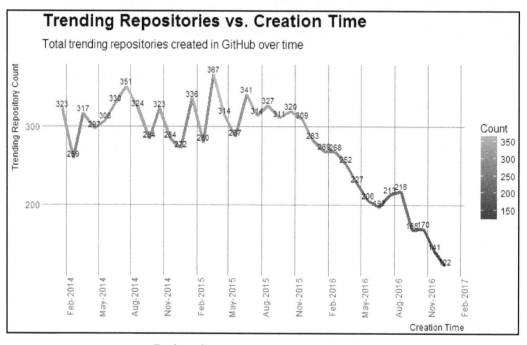

Total trending repositories versus creation time

We can see several peaks and dips with regard to the creation of our trending repositories. If we observe the patterns over 2014-2016, we can clearly see that the most repositories (over 350) were created around March, 2015 and July, 2014. The general trend of the curve slowly seems to decay and decrease over time after 2015 and that could be because we have a lesser number of trending repositories in 2016 simply because their creation date is fresher compared to the older repositories and it might take some time before more repositories get over 500 stars from the community.

Analyzing trending repositories updated over time

We have seen how to visualize the trend of our trending repositories based on their creation date over a period of time. An interesting aspect about trending repositories is that they are usually some software, product, tool, or utility which is quite popular among the software community so we usually expect it to be updated regularly for newer features, bug fixes, and release updates. In this section, we will observe whether this trend holds true for our trending repositories. The attribute, `updated_at`, in our dataset basically gives us the timestamp when the repositories were last updated in time and we can use this to find out the trend of total repositories based on when they were last updated over time. We will follow the same process we used in our previous analysis by first extracting the necessary timestamp elements using the following snippet:

```
# extract date elements
trending_repos$updated_monthyear <- format(as.Date(trending_
repos$updated_at), "%b-%Y")
```

We will now aggregate our dataset to find the total repositories which were updated over time by grouping the repositories based on the last updated month-year field we extracted:

```
# build aggregations
repos_by_updated_time <- aggregate(trending_repos$updated_monthyear,
by=list(trending_repos$updated_monthyear), length)
colnames(repos_by_updated_time) <- c("UpdateTime", "Count")
```

The `UpdateTime` attribute needs to be formatted into a date object and we do this using the following snippet:

```
# format dates
repos_by_updated_time$UpdateTime <- mdy(repos_by_updated_
time$UpdateTime)
```

Our data is now ready to be visualized and the following snippet enables us to view the repository update trends over time:

```
# visualize data
ggplot(repos_by_updated_time, aes(x=UpdateTime, y=Count)) +
  geom_line(aes(color=Count), size=1.5) +
  scale_x_date(date_breaks="2 week", date_labels='%b-%Y')+
  geom_text(aes(label=Count),
            vjust=-0.3,
            position=position_dodge(.9), size=3) +
  labs(x="Updation Time", y="Trending Repository Count",
```

```
        title="Trending Repositories vs. Updation Time",
        subtitle="Total trending repositories last updated in GitHub
over time") +
    theme_ipsum_rc(grid="XY") +
    theme(legend.position="right",
        axis.text.x = element_text(angle = 90, hjust = 1))
```

This gives us the following graph showing the trend line with regard to the repository update frequency over time:

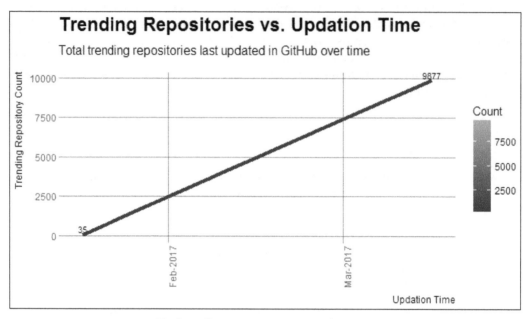

Total trending repositories versus update time

We can see there is definitely a stark difference between the trend lines with regard to the repository frequency over time versus creation and update time. In case of the last updated time, we can see all of them have in fact been last updated in 2017 and to be more precise, approximately 99% of our trending repositories have been updated very recently in April, 2017! This adheres to our hypothesis that trending and popular repositories are regularly updated over time, which we mentioned at the beginning of this section.

Analyzing repository metrics

So far, we have seen time-based frequency trends for repositories. There are other specific metrics based on various attributes in our dataset which can be computed and analyzed for trending repositories. In this section, we will be focusing on computing various repository metrics and analyzing interactions and relationships among these metrics. The general workflow we will be following here is outlined in the following steps:

1. Compute the derived metrics.
2. Aggregate all the necessary metrics by the trending repository owners.
3. Transform the aggregated dataset into an easy to consume format.
4. Analyze and visualize the metric relationships with graphs and correlations.

We will be computing various metrics from our repositories and aggregating these metrics based on the owners of these trending repositories. Even though we will be aggregating based on repository owners, analyzes pertaining to user-based metrics will be depicted in a future section on *Analyzing user trends*. Here, the focus will be more upon repository-based aggregated metrics per owner, which will cover various attributes as depicted in the following points:

- Total repository count (repo_count) which depicts total trending repositories
- Average repository size (mean_repo_size) which indicates the average size of repositories
- Total stargazers (total_stargazers) which indicates the total number of stars which the repositories have obtained from various users
- Total forks (total_forks) which indicates the total number of times repositories have been forked by other users
- Total open issues (total_open_issues) which basically is a metric portraying the total open issues or bugs in the repositories
- Average create age (mean_create_age) is an ageing attribute which indicates the average age of the repositories since they were created
- Average update age (mean_update_age) is an ageing attribute which indicates the average age of the repositories since they were last updated

Do remember that these metrics are aggregated (sum, average, and so on) per repository owner in our trending repositories dataset. The general idea is that users who have several trending repositories are usually popular users, developers, and innovators who regularly create and release software which is well received by the software community and hence leads to trending repositories on GitHub. We will be trying to analyze and see if there are any strong relationships among these metrics and visualize some of the strong relationships based on our results.

We will follow the previously mentioned workflow by first computing and getting the metric attributes which are not already present in our dataset. The following snippet helps us achieve this:

```
# create ageing variables
trending_repos$create_age <- as.integer(difftime(Sys.Date(),
trending_repos$created_at, units=c("days")))
trending_repos$update_age <- as.integer(difftime(Sys.Date(),
trending_repos$updated_at, units=c("days")))


# get repository owners
trending_repos$owner <- sapply(strsplit(trending_repos$full_name,
'/'), `[`, 1)
```

The preceding snippet helped us compute the ageing variables and get the owner for each trending repository in our dataset. We will now compute the necessary aggregations per repository owner in our dataset by using the following snippet:

```
# aggregate metrics per user
subset_df <- trending_repos[c('id', 'owner', 'size',
                'stargazers_count', 'forks', 'open_issues',
                'create_age', 'update_age')]
stats_df <- sqldf("select owner, count(*) as repo_count, avg(size)
                as mean_repo_size, sum(stargazers_count) as
                total_stargazers, sum(forks) as total_forks,
                sum(open_issues) as total_open_issues,
                avg(create_age) as mean_create_age,
                avg(update_age) as mean_update_age
                from subset_df group by owner
                order by repo_count desc")
```

You can observe that it is really easy to perform aggregations directly on DataFrames by using a SQL-like syntax with the help of the `sqldf`(...) function. Feel free to experiment and try out more aggregations. The preceding DataFrame, `stats_df`, contains the aggregated repository metrics. We will now transform the dataset into attributes and values which will be useful when we will visualize various aspects of the data:

```
# transform dataset into attributes & values
corr_df <- stats_df[c('repo_count', 'mean_repo_size', 'total_
stargazers', 'total_forks',
                      'total_open_issues', 'mean_create_age', 'mean_
update_age')]
corr_params <- melt(corr_df)
colnames(corr_params) <- c("Attribute", "Value")
```

We are now ready for the final part of our workflow: analyzing and visualizing our data. Without further ado, let's get cracking!

Visualizing repository metric distributions

Since we already have all our aggregated repository metrics in one dataset, we can now visualize their distributions with the help of box plots. The following code helps us plot multiple box plots together to visualize repository metric distributions in one graph:

```
ggplot(corr_params, aes(x=Attribute, y=Value, color=Attribute)) +
  geom_boxplot(position='dodge') +
  scale_fill_ipsum() +
  labs(x="Metric", y="Value",
       title="Comparing GitHub repository metric distributions",
       subtitle="Viewing distributions for various repository
                 metrics") +
  theme_ipsum_rc(grid="Y") +
  scale_y_log10(breaks=c(1, 10, 100, 1000, 10000, 100000)) +
  theme(legend.position="NA",
        axis.text.x=element_text(angle = 90, hjust = 1))
```

We obtain the following plot with the necessary metric distributions as expected:

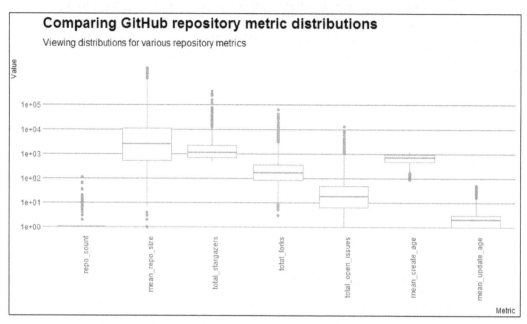

Comparing GitHub repository metric distributions

We can observe from the graph that the average creation age of repositories are much higher than the average update age and this is quite as expected based on the graphs we had generated in the previous sections. Repositories are updated more frequently, hence they have a young update age as compared to their creation age. The total count of forks is slightly lesser than the total stargazers and that is because typically more people tend to star repositories than fork them. The median number of open issues for repositories is around 50 to 60 based on the plot.

Analyzing repository metric correlations

We will now try to check for any strong relationships or associations among the various repository metrics by computing pairwise correlation coefficients and depicting the result in a plot. We can compute Pearson's correlation coefficient among the various metric attributes using the following code:

```
# compute correlation coefficients
corrs <- cor(corr_df)
```

You can directly inspect the values of the correlation coefficient matrix, `corrs`, or view the results using an easy to interpret graph using the following snippet:

```
# visualize correlation coefficient matrix
corrplot(corrs, method="number", type="lower")
```

This gives us the following graph depicting the various correlation coefficients:

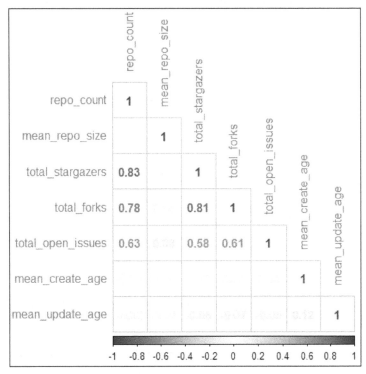

Attribute pairwise correlation coefficient matrix

Ignoring the coefficient values of the variables with themselves, we can observe very strong positive correlations between `repo_count` and `total_stargazers`, `total_forks`. We also see a very strong positive correlation between `total_stargazers` and `total_forks`. Besides this, `total_open_issues` also has strong correlations with `repo_count`, `total_forks`. We will take up some of these metrics having strong correlations amongst them and visualize the necessary data points to see if we can analyze these correlations in detail.

Analyzing relationship between stargazer and repository counts

We will look at two metric attributes here, `total_stargazers` and `repo_count`, and try to visualize the relationship between them. Basically we want to see if the total number of repositories has any strong relationship with the total stargazers based on the high correlation coefficient of **0.83** which was observed in the correlation matrix plot earlier. We will first compute the correlation coefficient between the two attributes under analysis using the following code:

```
# get correlation coefficient
corr <- format(cor(corr_df$total_stargazers, corr_df$repo_count),
digits=3)
```

We can now visualize the relationship between the attributes using the following snippet:

```
# visualize relationship
ggplot(corr_df, aes(x=total_stargazers, y=repo_count))+
  theme_ipsum_rc() +
  geom_jitter(alpha=1/2) +
  geom_smooth(method=loess) +
  labs(x="Stargazers", y="Repositories",
       title="Correlation between Stargazers & Total Repositories") +
  annotate("text", label=paste("Corr =", corr), x=+Inf, y=10,
           hjust=1)
```

This gives us the following plot along with the correlation coefficient of the two attributes:

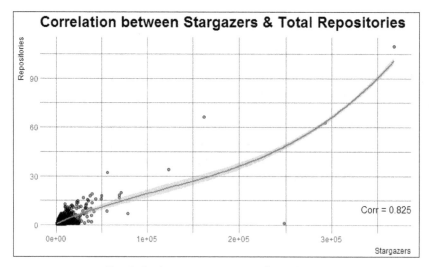

Correlation between stargazers and repositories

We can observe that we have a high correlation coefficient of **0.825** between the stargazers and repository counts. The high positive correlation score is quite evident based on the general trend and we can see from the plot that the higher the number of repositories, the more is the number of stargazers based on the majority of the data points and the polynomial loess regression line which has been fit. This is expected because the more the number of trending repositories, the more the number of people who star them based on their popularity and hence the higher count of stargazers.

Analyzing relationship between stargazer and fork counts

We will look at two metric attributes here, `total_stargazers` and `total_forks`, and try to visualize the relationship between them. Since they had a strong positive correlation coefficient of **0.81**, the idea here is to see if the trend is such that repositories with a higher number of forks should also have a higher number of stargazers. We first compute the correlation coefficient between our two attributes using the following snippet:

```
# get correlation coefficient
corr <- format(cor(corr_df$total_stargazers, corr_df$total_forks),
    digits=3)
```

Now we can visualize the relationship between the stargazer and fork counts using the following code snippet:

```
# visualize relationship
ggplot(corr_df, aes(x=total_stargazers, y=total_forks))+
  theme_ipsum_rc() +
  geom_jitter(alpha=1/2) +
  geom_smooth(method=loess) +
  labs(x="Stargazers", y="Forks",
      title="Correlation between Stargazers & Forks") +
  annotate("text", label=paste("Corr =", corr), x=+Inf, y=10,
          hjust=1)
```

This gives us the following plot showing the relationship between the stargazer and fork counts and also the correlation coefficient:

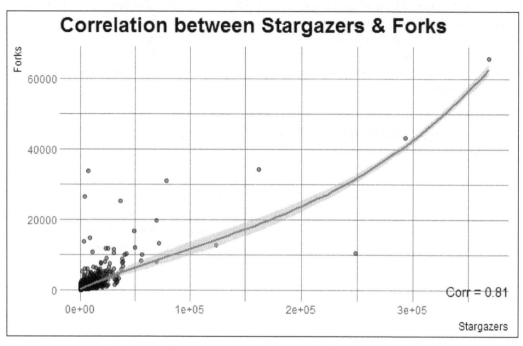

Correlation between stargazers and forks

We can observe the strong positive correlation between stargazers and forks which is **0.81** as depicted in the graph. The general trend noticed is that as the count of stargazers are more in repositories, correspondingly they have more forks. The polynomial regression loess curve shows the general growth trend.

We can in fact build a polynomial regression model to enable us to guess the total stargazers from the total fork counts based on our dataset, which will serve as the training data for the model. The following snippet can be used to build a regression model:

```
# build polynomial regression loess model
prm <- loess(total_stargazers ~ total_forks, corr_df)
```

We can now view the built model details using the following code:

```
# view model details
> summary(prm)
Call:
loess(formula = total_stargazers ~ total_forks, data = corr_df)
```

```
Number of Observations: 7011
Equivalent Number of Parameters: 5.82
Residual Standard Error: 4450
Trace of smoother matrix: 6.38   (exact)

Control settings:
  span       :  0.75
  degree     :  2
  family     :  gaussian
  surface    :  interpolate     cell = 0.2
  normalize:   TRUE
 parametric:   FALSE
drop.square:   FALSE
```

From the observed output of the model, we can see that it is a polynomial regression model of degree 2. Let's say we want to predict the number of stargazers for a new repository having 5,000 forks. We can do so using the following snippet:

```
# predict total stargazers for 5000 forks
> predict(prm, 5000)
[1] 22759.76
```

Thus we can see that our model has predicted that a repository with 5,000 forks should approximately have 22,760 stargazers approximately. Let's now check sample repositories from our training dataset which have close to 5,000 forks. We can do so using the following code:

```
# check with sample datapoints in dataset
> filter(corr_df, total_forks>=4900 & total_forks <= 5100)[, c('total_
stargazers', 'total_forks')]
  total_stargazers total_forks
1             9528        5003
2            27089        5064
3            23583        5078
4             6963        4936
5            27929        5047
```

Thus we can see that three repositories out of five having close to 5,000 forks have over 22,000 stars, which is close to our built model. Can you improve the regression model by taking into account other metric attributes? Give it a try! (You can use loess or even the lm or glm family of linear models.)

Analyzing relationship between total forks, repository count, and health

We have already seen ways to analyze association and relationships between various metric attributes by leveraging correlation and regression models. We will now compute a new metric called repository health and try to analyze the relationship of three attributes together, namely forks, repository counts, and repository health.

For computing repository health, we will leverage the `total_open_issues` attribute which indicates the total number of bugs or issues in various repositories. The logic we will be using here is such that if we have 50 or less open issues, we label that repository as healthy. If the repository has more than 50 open issues, it is labeled as unhealthy. The number 50 was basically taken from the median value of the open issue count obtained from the *Visualizing repository metric distributions* section, where we visualized the distribution box plots of the various metric attributes. The following code helps us compute the repository health for our dataset:

```
# compute repository health
corr_df$repo_health <- ifelse(corr_df$total_open_issues <= 50,
                              'Healthy',
                              'Not Healthy')
```

Now we will compute the correlation coefficient between fork and repository counts using the following code:

```
# get correlation coefficient
corr <- format(cor(corr_df$total_forks, corr_df$repo_count), digits=3)
```

We can now visualize the relationship between our attributes of interest using the following graph:

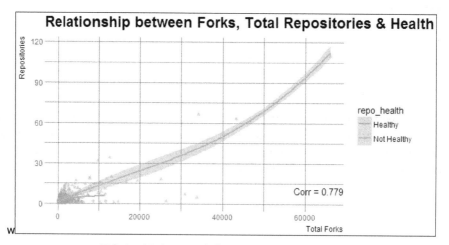

Relationship between forks, repositories, and health

Thus we can see there is definitely a strong positive correlation between forks and repository counts but we have more repositories with the *Not Healthy* status once they start crossing the 10,000+ total fork count mark. This could be because the more popular the repository, it is being developed by multiple people and hence since it is under rapid development and frequent releases, there could be multiple open issues cropping up which take substantial time to get resolved since developers are not only busy in resolving bugs and issues but also developing new content.

Analyzing language trends

Any repository on GitHub typically consists of code and other artifacts which are developed using programming languages. These can be low-level languages such as C and Assembly, or high level languages such as Python or Java. We also have languages used in web development and design such as JavaScript and HTML. The idea here is to use our trending repositories dataset and observe trends with regard to various languages used in these repositories. We will analyze trends related to the most popular languages over time, languages having the most open issues, and many more. You can find all the code used for analysis in this section in the `github_language_trend_analysis.R` file along with the code files for this chapter. Do load up the necessary dependencies and our `trending_repos` dataset if you already haven't done so using the following code snippet:

```
source('load_packages.R')
load('trending_repos.RData')
```

You are now ready to start analyzing language trends in our trending repositories dataset. Let's get started!

Visualizing top trending languages

How do we answer the question of which are the most popular languages on GitHub? We have our most trending repositories but how do we find the most popular languages which make these repositories trending? What languages do developers like to use when building software? These are some of the questions we can answer in this sub-section. We already have the `language` attribute in our trending repositories dataset which tells us which language was used for developing the majority of the code in the repositories. We will use the same field here to answer our questions.

We will begin by aggregating our dataset to get repository counts by language using the following snippet:

```
# aggregate repository counts by language
repo_languages <- aggregate(trending_repos$language,
                    by=list(trending_repos$language), length)
colnames(repo_languages) <- c('Language', 'Count')
```

Now we will filter and retrieve only the top 25 trending languages since we do not want to clutter up our visualization unnecessarily. The following code helps us filter our aggregated data easily:

```
# get top 25 languages in GitHub
top_language_counts <- arrange(repo_languages, desc(Count))[1:25,]
```

We are now ready to visualize our data and the following snippet of code helps us achieve this:

```
# visualize data
ggplot(top_language_counts, aes(x=Language, y=Count, fill=Language)) +
  geom_bar(stat="identity", position="dodge")+
  geom_text(aes(label=Count),
            vjust=-0.3,
            position=position_dodge(.9), size=3) +
  scale_color_ipsum() +
  labs(x="Language", y="Repository Count",
       title="Top Trending Languages in GitHub") +
  theme_ipsum_rc(grid="Y") +
  theme(legend.position="NA",
        axis.text.x = element_text(angle = 90, hjust = 1))
```

This gives us the following bar graph showing the top 25 most trending languages on GitHub:

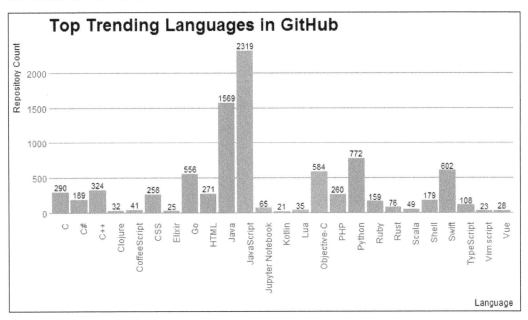

Top 25 trending languages on GitHub

From the generated plot, we can see that **JavaScript**, **Java**, and **Python** are the clear winners in the war of trending languages!

Visualizing top trending languages over time

If you remember our data retrieval process for getting trending repositories, we had retrieved repositories which were trending over the span of 3 years from 2014 to 2016. We will now try to look at the top trending languages over time and see if there is any specific change in trends with respect to languages over time for our trending repositories.

We will start by extracting the year of creation for each repository and then aggregating repository counts by language over the creation year. We will filter the data out for the top 15 trending languages based on the top trending languages we obtained in the previous section to prevent cluttering our visualization. The following snippet helps us achieve this:

```
# aggregate repository counts by language over time
trending_repos$created_year <- format(as.Date(trending_repos$created_
at), "%Y")
top_languages_by_year <- aggregate(trending_repos$language,
                              by=list(trending_repos$created_
year, trending_repos$language), length)
```

```
colnames(top_languages_by_year) <- c('Year', 'Language', 'Count')
top_languages <- arrange(repo_languages, desc(Count))
[1:15,c("Language")]
top_languages_by_year <- top_languages_by_year[top_languages_by_
year$Language %in% top_languages,]
```

We can now visualize our data to get the trending languages over time using the following snippet:

```
# visualize data
ggplot(top_languages_by_year,
       aes(x=Language, y=Count, fill=Year)) +
  geom_bar(stat="identity", position="dodge")+
  geom_text(aes(label=Count),
            vjust=-0.3,
            position=position_dodge(.9), size=2.5) +
  scale_color_ipsum() +
  labs(x="Language", y=" Repository Count",
       title="Trending Languages in GitHub over time") +
  theme_ipsum_rc(grid="Y") +
  theme(legend.position="right",
        axis.text.x = element_text(angle = 90, hjust = 1))
```

This gives us the following bar graph showing the repository counts for each trending language over the period of the last 3 years:

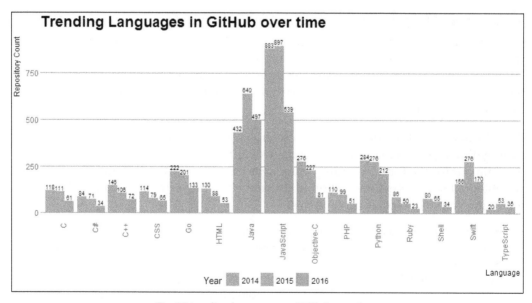

Top 15 trending languages on GitHub over time

We can clearly see that 2015 has been a good year for our top trending languages, especially **JavaScript**, **Java**, **Python**, as well as **Swift**, who had more trending repositories in 2015 on average compared to the other 2 years.

Analyzing languages with the most open issues

We have seen a couple of analyzes with regard to repository issues and health in the earlier sections of this chapter. Basically, the more the number of open issues, the more are the problems being faced by users and developers for that software product. In this section, we will try to find out which languages have the most number of open issues in GitHub repositories. For a good measure, we will select the mean or average number of open issues per language.

We will first generate the necessary aggregation of the mean open issues by each language in our trending repositories dataset. The following code helps us to achieve this:

```
# aggregate mean open issues per language
repo_issues <- aggregate(trending_repos$open_issues,
                         by=list(trending_repos$language), mean)
colnames(repo_issues) <- c('Language', 'Issues')
repo_issues$Issues <- round(repo_issues$Issues, 2)
top_issues_language_counts <- arrange(repo_issues, desc(Issues))
[1:25,]
```

We have filtered out the top 25 languages with the most open issues to prevent cluttering up the graph, which we can now generate using the following code:

```
# visualize data
ggplot(top_issues_language_counts, aes(x=Language, y=Issues,
fill=Language)) +
  geom_bar(stat="identity", position="dodge")+
  geom_text(aes(label=Issues),
            vjust=-0.3,
            position=position_dodge(.9), size=3) +
  scale_color_ipsum() +
  labs(x="Language", y="Issues",
       title="Languages with most open issues on GitHub",
       subtitle="Depicts top language repositories with highest mean
open issue count") +
  theme_ipsum_rc(grid="Y") +
  theme(legend.position="NA",
        axis.text.x = element_text(angle = 90, hjust = 1))
```

This gives us the following bar plot with the top 25 languages with the highest mean open issues count:

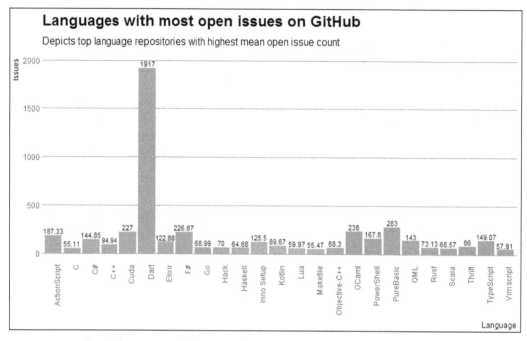

Top 25 languages with the most average open issues per repository on GitHub

We can clearly see that the **Dart** language has the highest mean open issues which are almost 5 to 10 times more than the other languages. This indicates that repositories which have software products, tools, and frameworks built with Dart must be having more issues and bugs files as compared to other languages. **PureBasic** and **OCaml** are the next two languages with the top mean open issues count. Basically, people must be facing more issues with repositories in these languages, hence they have filed issues which are yet to be resolved.

Analyzing languages with the most open issues over time

We just saw the top languages with the most open issues by using the mean statistic in the previous sub-section. We will now try to analyze the same statistic of mean open issues by languages, but we will try to visualize this over a period of the last 3 years to see when open issues started cropping up for these languages.

To start with, we will aggregate the mean open issues per language over time. For the time aspect, we will choose the year the repository was created by using the `created_year` field which we had created earlier from the `created_at` attribute. This is a fair assumption to use since any popular repository containing a software product is the most popular as soon as it gets released or within a couple of weeks from its release and users start filing issues as soon as they start using the product. The following snippet helps us perform the necessary aggregation:

```
# aggregate mean issues by language over time
top_issue_languages_by_year <- aggregate(trending_repos$open_issues,
          by=list(trending_repos$created_year,
          trending_repos$language), mean)
colnames(top_issue_languages_by_year) <- c('Year', 'Language',
'Issues')
top_languages <- arrange(repo_issues, desc(Issues))[1:10,
c("Language")]
top_issue_languages_by_year <- top_issue_languages_by_year[top_issue_
languages_by_year$Language %in% top_languages,]
top_issue_languages_by_year$Issues <- round(top_issue_languages_by_
year$Issues, 2)
```

This basically filters the mean open issues over time for the top 10 languages having open issues. We can now visualize this data using the following code:

```
# visualize data
ggplot(top_issue_languages_by_year, aes(x=Language, y=Issues,
fill=Year)) +
  geom_bar(stat="identity", position="dodge")+
  geom_text(aes(label=Issues),
            vjust=-0.3,
            position=position_dodge(.9), size=2) +
  scale_color_ipsum() +
  labs(x="Language", y="Issues",
    title="Languages with most open issues in GitHub over time",
    subtitle="Depicts top language repositories with highest mean open
issue count over time") +
  theme_ipsum_rc(grid="Y") +
  theme(legend.position="bottom",
        axis.text.x = element_text(angle = 90, hjust = 1))
```

This gives us the following bar plot showing the top 10 languages with the most mean open issues over time:

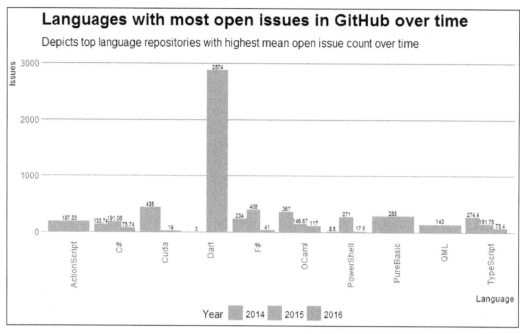

Top 10 languages with the most open issues on GitHub over time

We can clearly see that the most issues for **Dart** started cropping up in the year 2015 and it's the same with other languages including **F#**, **PowerShell**, and **PureBasic**. Can you find out any more interesting patterns? Try adding other languages too in the graph and find out!

Analyzing languages with the most helpful repositories

If you remember the features and capabilities of GitHub, besides just being a source code management platform, you can also build beautiful and descriptive wikis and pages for your repositories. Wikis enable you to describe your product in more details including installations, setup, usage, documentation, and more. Pages are just like having a personal web page for your project which helps in reaching out to more users. More documentation is always better for users since it is really helpful and easy to get started with new software by referring to it.

We will now try to analyze languages which have the most helpful repositories. We define a repository as helpful if it contains both a wiki as well as a GitHub page for it. This can be easily computed by leveraging the `has_wiki` and `has_pages` attributes using the following code:

```
# compute helpful repositories
trending_repos$helpful_repo <- (trending_repos$has_wiki & trending_
repos$has_pages)
```

We can now aggregate helpful repositories by language using the following code snippet:

```
# aggregate helpful repositories by language
helpful_repos_language <- aggregate(trending_repos$helpful_repo,
                        by=list(trending_repos$language), sum)
colnames(helpful_repos_language) <- c('Language', 'Count')
top_helpful_repos <- arrange(helpful_repos_language, desc(Count))
[1:25,]
```

When aggregating, we filter out our dataset to keep only the top 25 languages with the most helpful repositories to prevent cluttering our visualization. We use the following code snippet to finally visualize our data:

```
# visualize data
ggplot(top_helpful_repos, aes(x=Language, y=Count,
                              fill=Language)) +
  geom_bar(stat="identity", position="dodge")+
  geom_text(aes(label=Count),
            vjust=-0.3,
            position=position_dodge(.9), size=3) +
  scale_color_ipsum() +
  labs(x="Language", y="Count",
       title="Most helpful repositories in GitHub by Language") +
  theme_ipsum_rc(grid="Y") +
  theme(legend.position="NA",
        axis.text.x = element_text(angle = 90, hjust = 1))
```

This gives us the following bar plot with the top 25 languages having the most helpful repositories:

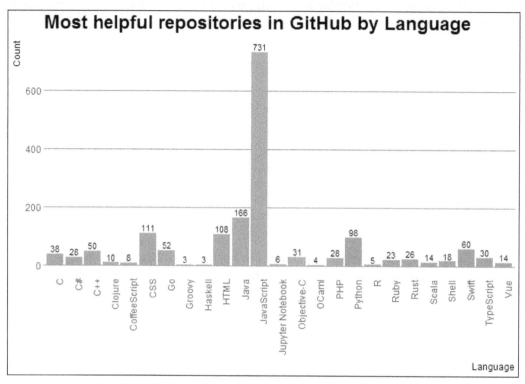

Top 25 trending languages on GitHub with the most helpful repositories

From the generated bar plot, we can see that **JavaScript**, **Java**, **CSS**, **HTML**, and **Python** occupy the top five spots. Interestingly, even **R** shows up in the top 25 helpful language-based repositories here, which shows that even if R might have less repositories on GitHub compared to other languages, its owners make sure they are well documented and provide enough help to their user community.

Analyzing languages with the highest popularity score

Trending repositories usually gain popularity once users start starring and forking them. If a user stars a repository it indicates that he/she likes it and acts as a kind of like or vote for the repository. A fork is basically when a user forks or clones a copy of the repository into his/her own account and can customize the repository and even request the original owner to add some of their own suggested changes if they make sense.

We will try to analyze languages having a high popularity score in this sub-section by building a new metric called Popularity Score by leveraging stars and forks.

To compute Popularity Score, we will basically use the following formula for each repository:

$$PS = (2 \times forks) + stars$$

Here, *PS* indicates the repository popularity score. Forks and stars can be obtained from the forks and `stargazers_count` attributes respectively from our dataset. The following code helps us compute the popularity scores:

```
# compute popularity score
trending_repos$popularity_score <- ((trending_repos$forks*2) +
trending_repos$stargazers_count)
```

Next, we will aggregate the repository popularity scores by language using the following snippet:

```
# aggregate repository popularity scores by language
popular_repos_languages <- aggregate(trending_repos$popularity_score,
          by=list(trending_repos$language), sum)
colnames(popular_repos_languages) <- c('Language', 'Popularity')
popular_repos_languages$Popularity <- round(popular_repos_
languages$Popularity, 1)
top_popular_repos <- arrange(popular_repos_languages,
desc(Popularity))[1:25,]
```

We filter and keep the top 25 languages with the highest popularity score for our visualization. We can plot our aggregated data now using the following code:

```
# visualize data
ggplot(top_popular_repos, aes(x=Language, y=Popularity)) +
  geom_bar(stat="identity", position="dodge", fill="steelblue")+
  geom_text(aes(label=Popularity),
          vjust=-0.3,
          position=position_dodge(.9), size=2.5) +
  scale_color_ipsum() +
  labs(x="Language", y="Popularity",
      title="Languages with most Popularity Score in GitHub",
      subtitle="Depicts top language repositories with highest
popularity score") +
  theme_ipsum_rc(grid="Y") +
  theme(axis.text.x = element_text(angle = 90, hjust = 1))
```

This gives us the following bar plot showing the top 25 trending languages having the highest popularity score:

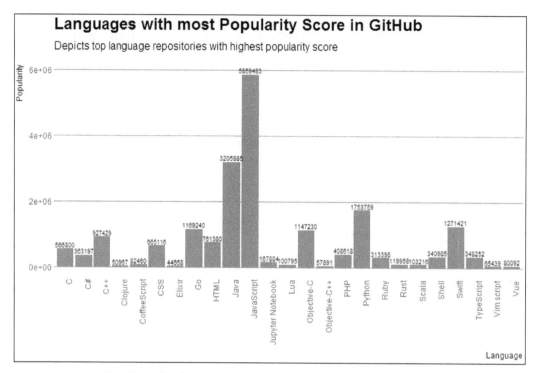

Top 25 trending languages on GitHub with the highest popularity score

The generated graph clearly shows that **JavaScript**, **Java**, and **Python** are the top three languages based on the popularity score which also indicates that software products developed in these languages get more stars and forks on GitHub.

Analyzing language correlations

Sometimes users tend to build software using a combination of languages, or they might focus on specific areas of technology such as web development, user experience, The Internet of Things, analytics, artificial intelligence, and many more! We will try to find out if any such strong correlations exist between languages, which users tend to use more from our trending repositories dataset. The idea is to find out which languages tend to be used more by the same users by making use of correlations.

We will start our analysis by trying to extract the repository owner and language for all our repositories in our trending repositories dataset. We can accomplish this by using the following code:

```
# get repository owner and languages
trending_repos$owner <- sapply(strsplit(trending_repos$full_name,
'/'), `[`, 1)
df <- trending_repos[,c('owner', 'language')]
df_pivot <- data.table(df)
```

Now that we have the repository owner and languages, we will build an owner-language usage matrix which will basically contain each owner as a row and columns will consist of all the possible languages in our dataset. A positive value in any cell would indicate the number of repositories where the owner has used a specific language. The following code helps us generate this:

```
# create owner-language usage matrix
owner_lang_matrix <- dcast.data.table(df_pivot, owner ~ language,
                    fun.aggregate=length,
                    value.var="language")
owner_lang_df <- as.data.frame(owner_lang_matrix)
```

You can view a sample of this created DataFrame from the owner-language usage matrix using the following snippet:

```
# take a peek at the owner-language data frame
> View(owner_lang_df)
```

This gives us a peek at the DataFrame showing owner-language usage statistics, a part of which can be seen in the following snapshot:

	owner	ASP	ActionScript	ApacheConf	AppleScript	Arduino	Assembly	AutoHotkey	Awk	Batchfile	C	C#	C++
1622	antirez	0	0	0	0	0	0	0	0	0	4	0	0
2195	citusdata	0	0	0	0	0	0	0	0	0	3	0	0
2859	facebook	0	0	0	0	0	0	0	0	0	3	0	9
3165	google	0	0	0	0	0	0	0	0	0	3	0	23
4950	ntop	0	0	0	0	0	0	0	0	0	3	0	0
357	EZLippi	0	0	0	0	0	0	0	0	0	2	0	0
816	Microsoft	0	0	0	0	0	0	0	0	0	2	17	15
995	Qihoo360	0	0	0	0	0	0	0	0	0	2	0	2
1652	apple	0	0	0	0	0	0	0	0	0	2	0	1
2036	c9s	0	0	0	0	0	0	0	0	0	2	0	0

We can now build our language correlation matrix which will basically be a pairwise-language correlation matrix and the following code will help to generate this:

```
# build language correlation matrix
lang_mat <- owner_lang_df[,2:length(colnames(owner_lang_df))]
lang_corr <- cor(lang_mat)
```

Next, we parse and transform this language correlation object into a more easy to use format and the following snippet helps us to achieve this:

```
# transform language correlations
diag(lang_corr) <- NA
lang_corr[upper.tri(lang_corr)] <- NA
lang_corr_final <- melt(lang_corr)
```

We can now obtain highly correlated languages by using the following code which should answer our question of which pair of languages tends to be used more on GitHub trending repositories:

```
# get highly correlated languages
filtered_corr <- lang_corr_final[which(lang_corr_final$value >= 0.7),]
View(filtered_corr)
```

This gives us the following DataFrame showing us languages which have strong positive correlations amongst themselves:

	Var1	Var2	value
403	Eagle	Arduino	0.8164772
1118	PureBasic	C++	0.6719623
3479	OCaml	Hack	0.7746188
3481	Objective-C++	Hack	0.8838914
5571	Objective-C++	OCaml	0.6844834
5865	PostScript	Objective-J	1.0000000

Top 25 trending languages on GitHub

We can observe that **PostScript** and **Objective-J** have the highest correlation. Languages such as **Objective-C++** are highly correlated with **OCaml** and **Hack**. **Eagle** and **Arduino**, which are used frequently for prototyping and building solutions in electronics, also have a high correlation coefficient as observed from our data.

Analyzing user trends

We have analyzed, visualized, and looked at various trends pertaining to both repositories and languages used to build software. Now we will take a different perspective of trying to analyze trends with regard to users who build amazing and wonderful software and open source it for the benefit of the community. We will be reusing some of the code and assets from the previous sections with regard to loading the necessary dependencies and our trending repositories dataset. The entire code which will be used in this section is also available in the github_user_trend_analysis.R file, which will be present along with all the other code files for this chapter.

In case you haven't been following along all the examples presented so far in this chapter, you can quickly load up the necessary dependencies and dataset using the following snippet:

```
source('load_packages.R')
load('trending_repos.RData')
```

This loads up the necessary packages and our trending repositories dataset in memory and we can now start analyzing specific trends which focus more on the repository owners/users.

Visualizing top contributing users

A user here is synonymous with a repository owner, which is basically a person or organization who owns a repository which is a specific software product, tool, or a framework. The idea here is to find out users who have the most contributions in our trending repositories dataset.

We will first extract the repository owner/user from our dataset by using the following code:

```
# get repository owner\user
trending_repos$user <- sapply(strsplit(trending_repos$full_name, '/'),
`[`, 1)
```

We can now easily aggregate repository counts by user with the help of the following snippet:

```
# aggregate repository counts by user
repo_users <- aggregate(trending_repos$user,
                        by=list(trending_repos$user), length)
colnames(repo_users) <- c('User', 'Count')
top_users_counts <- arrange(repo_users, desc(Count))[1:25,]
```

Besides aggregations, we also filter our aggregated dataset in the preceding snippet to get the top 25 most contributing users to build a clean visualization. We can visualize our aggregated and filtered data using the following code snippet:

```
# visualize data
ggplot(top_users_counts, aes(x=User, y=Count, fill=User)) +
  geom_bar(stat="identity", position="dodge")+
  coord_flip() +
  geom_text(aes(label=Count),
            vjust=0.3,
            hjust=-0.1,
            position=position_dodge(.9), size=3) +
  scale_color_ipsum() +
  labs(x="User", y="Count",
       title="Top contributing users on GitHub",
       subtitle="Users with the most trending repositiories") +
  theme_ipsum_rc(grid="X") +
  theme(legend.position="NA",
        axis.text.x = element_text(angle = 90, hjust = 1))
```

This gives us the following bar plot depicting the top 25 users with the most trending repositories over the last 3 years:

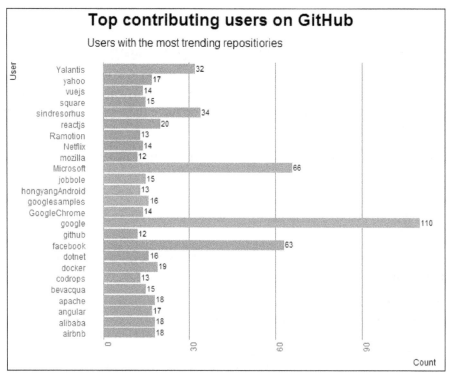

Top 25 users with the most trending repositories on GitHub over the last 3 years

We can see that organizations such as **Google**, **Microsoft**, and **Facebook** are the top three users with the most contributions towards trending repositories in open source. Among other popular users, we have organizations such as **Apache**, **Alibaba**, **Airbnb**, **Netflix**, **Mozilla**, **Yalantis**, and even **GitHub** itself! Can you find out more users who are trending in the open source community? Give it a try!

Analyzing user activity metrics

We expanded on repository metrics and ways to analyze them in an earlier section, *Analyzing repository trends*. In this section, we will focus on similar metrics with a focus on repository owners/users. We will make use of our trending repositories dataset which already has several attributes which can be used as metrics. We will follow a similar workflow which we had followed earlier when we had analyzed repository metrics. The major steps are as follows:

1. Compute the derived metrics from the dataset attributes

2. Aggregate the desired metrics by the repository owner/users

3. Transform and scale the metrics if needed for visualizations

4. Analyze and visualize the data

The following snippet will help us calculate the necessary derived metrics for our data:

```
# compute derived metrics
trending_repos$user <- sapply(strsplit(trending_repos$full_name, '/'),
    `[`, 1)
trending_repos$create_age <- as.integer(difftime(Sys.Date(),
                                 trending_repos$created_at,
                                         units=c("days")))
trending_repos$update_age <- as.integer(difftime(Sys.Date(),
                                 trending_repos$updated_at,
                                         units=c("days")))
```

create_age and update_age are basically ageing attribute metrics that indicate the age of repositories since their creation and the age of the repositories since they were last updated, respectively. We can now generate the necessary aggregations on our metrics by users using the following code:

```
# build aggregations
subset_df <- trending_repos[c('id', 'user', 'size',
                               'stargazers_count', 'forks',
                               'open_issues', 'create_age',
                               'update_age')]
stats_df <- sqldf("select user, count(*) as repo_count,
                   avg(size) as mean_repo_size,
                   sum(stargazers_count) as total_stargazers,
```

```
      sum(forks) as total_forks,
      sum(open_issues) as total_open_issues,
      avg(create_age) as mean_create_age,
      avg(update_age) as mean_update_age
      from subset_df group by user
      order by repo_count desc")
```

Just like we aggregated the repository metrics, we also leverage the sqldf (...) function here to aggregate the metrics directly from the DataFrame itself. Next, we will filter the aggregated stats_df DataFrame to keep the top 20 popular users with the most trending repositories and view the result using the following code:

```
# filter and view stats
top_user_stats <- stats_df[1:20, ]
colnames(top_user_stats) <- c("User", "Total Repos",
                      "Avg. Repo Size", "Total Stargazers",
                      "Total Forks", "Total Open Issues",
                "Avg. Repo Create Age", "Avg. Repo Update Age"
)
View(top_user_stats)
```

This gives us the desired DataFrame with user activity metrics as depicted in the following snapshot:

	User	Total Repos	Avg. Repo Size	Total Stargazers	Total Forks	Total Open Issues	Avg. Repo Create Age	Avg. Repo Update Age
1	google	110	51002.0818	367855	65872	8436	734.5909	4.200000
2	Microsoft	66	73480.2121	162025	34115	13092	597.4697	4.363636
3	facebook	63	12748.3333	293052	43315	5726	763.7619	3.666667
4	sindresorhus	34	823.3529	123868	12599	503	724.4412	3.852941
5	Yalantis	32	7917.0000	56388	9857	214	562.6875	4.031250
6	reactjs	20	1197.3000	71494	13115	568	799.7500	3.600000
7	docker	19	21335.0526	39221	7939	2421	658.4737	3.736842
8	airbnb	18	14871.2222	69384	7895	1570	455.4444	3.444444
9	alibaba	18	57282.1111	49804	11902	1050	493.7222	3.555556
10	apache	18	129155.3889	36920	25123	1824	778.0556	3.222222
11	angular	17	19852.4118	69383	19591	3598	726.8235	5.294118
12	yahoo	17	11650.5882	30052	4598	482	655.2353	5.647059
13	dotnet	16	53718.1250	42736	10253	7883	647.5000	3.812500
14	googlesamples	16	17200.3125	49216	16752	576	690.1875	3.937500
15	bevacqua	15	3281.6667	34193	2112	232	791.9333	5.933333
16	jobbole	15	73.0000	23737	8977	23	472.4000	3.400000
17	square	15	5528.5333	34912	4371	278	707.2667	4.200000
18	GoogleChrome	14	12635.2143	23522	2718	483	648.2143	5.428571
19	Netflix	14	8709.0714	22415	1826	334	665.7857	4.428571
20	vuejs	14	4304.5714	38985	6766	378	713.9286	3.428571

The DataFrame is sorted by users having the most trending repositories and you can also look at other metrics such as stargazers, forks, open issues, and the create and update age. Google seems to be the clear winner in the popularity section having the most stargazers, forks, as well as trending repositories.

There is a better way of visualizing this data in the form of a heatmap to look at these user activity metrics and interpret them in a better way. Heatmaps are an intuitive way to represent data in the form of a color or gradient map where the data values can be represented by different intensities or shades of colors. For example, if Google is having the most trending repositories, it would have a darker shade of color for that metric. To build a heatmap, we will first scale or normalize the values of each metric attribute since they are of different scales. The following code helps us scale the dataset to relative proportions or percentages and assign values in the range of 0 to 1, with 0 being the lowest and 1 being the highest:

```
# scale metric attributes
scale_col <- function(x){
  round(((x-min(x))/(max(x)-min(x))), 2)
}

scaled_stats <- cbind(top_user_stats[,1],
                      as.data.frame(apply(top_user_stats[2:8],
                                          2, scale_col)))
colnames(scaled_stats)[1] <- 'User'
scaled_stats_tf <- melt(scaled_stats, id='User')
colnames(scaled_stats_tf) <- c('User', 'Metric', 'Value')
```

Now that we have scaled all our metrics to the relative proportions, we can visualize our user activity metrics in the form of a heatmap using the following code:

```
# visualize data as a heatmap
ggplot(data=scaled_stats_tf, aes(x=Metric, y=User)) +
  geom_tile(aes(fill=Value)) +
  geom_text(aes(label=Value),
            size=3) +
  scale_fill_gradient(low="#FFB607", high="#DB3D00") +
  theme_ipsum_rc() +
  labs(x="User", y="Metric",
       title="User Activity Metrics Heatmap",
       subtitle="Analyzing trending user activity metrics on GitHub")
+
  theme(legend.position="NA",
        axis.text.x = element_text(angle = 45, hjust = 1))
```

This generates the following heatmap for the top 20 most popular users with the most trending repositories depicting various user activity metrics:

User Activity Metrics Heatmap
Analyzing trending user activity metrics on GitHub

Metric	Total Repos	Avg. Repo Size	Total Stargazers	Total Forks	Total Open Issues	Avg. Repo Create Age	Avg. Repo Update Age
Yalantis	0.19	0.06	0.1	0.13	0.01	0.31	0.3
yahoo	0.03	0.09	0.02	0.04	0.05	0.58	0.89
vuejs	0	0.03	0.05	0.08	0.05	0.75	0.08
square	0.01	0.04	0.04	0.04	0.03	0.73	0.36
sindresorhus	0.21	0.01	0.29	0.17	0.03	0.78	0.23
reactjs	0.06	0.01	0.14	0.18	0.05	1	0.14
Netflix	0	0.07	0	0	0.05	0.61	0.44
Microsoft	0.54	0.57	0.4	0.5	0.4	0.41	0.42
jobbole	0.01	0	0	0.11	0	0.05	0.07
googlesamples	0.02	0.13	0.08	0.23	0.07	0.68	0.26
GoogleChrome	0	0.1	0	0.01	0.07	0.56	0.81
google	1	0.39	1	1	0.15	0.81	0.36
facebook	0.51	0.1	0.78	0.65	0.18	0.9	0.16
dotnet	0.02	0.42	0.06	0.13	1	0.56	0.22
docker	0.05	0.16	0.05	0.1	0.26	0.59	0.19
bevacqua	0.01	0.02	0.03	0	0.03	0.98	1
apache	0.04	1	0.04	0.36	0.2	0.94	0
angular	0.03	0.15	0.14	0.28	0.43	0.79	0.76
alibaba	0.04	0.44	0.08	0.16	0.12	0.11	0.12
airbnb	0.04	0.11	0.14	0.09	0.17	0	0.08

User

User activity metrics heatmap for the top 20 trending users on GitHub

I have also added the relative proportional values for each metric along with the color intensities to make things more clear. From the metrics visualized in the heatmap, we can easily interpret the following insights:

- It is evident that Google has the highest proportion of trending repositories, stargazers, and forks which we had discussed earlier
- Facebook and Microsoft are second and third respectively in total stargazers and forks
- Apache has the highest repository size on average followed by Microsoft
- The users dotnet and angular seem to have repositories with the most open issues

- The users reactjs, bevacqua, and apache seem to have repositories which have been created quite some time back since their average create age is the highest

- Yahoo! seems to have not updated its repositories in some time compared to other users such as Facebook or Apache

These are just a few insights. There are tons of other valuable insights which can be uncovered by using the power of analysis as well as visualizations on software collaboration from GitHub, so get cracking!

Summary

The main intent of this chapter was to give you exposure to a completely different domain in social media by taking a journey through the world of software collaboration and social coding. GitHub has truly been one of the success stories in both the technology and software collaboration landscape with over 19 million developers, 52 million repositories, and 100 K teams worldwide! We followed a step-by-step approach in this chapter by getting to know more about our domain in detail before diving into analysis. By now, you should know all the necessary concepts and methodologies which are followed in collaborative development and distributed source code management. Detailed steps and description, of all the necessary packages and datasets which were used in this chapter have also been explained for everyone's benefit to get started with the hands-on examples effortlessly.

We covered detailed steps on how to retrieve, parse, and transform data from GitHub using its REST APIs and also how to build reusable functions to retrieve trending repositories from GitHub. We focused on four main areas of analyzing GitHub: repository activity, repository trends, language trends, and user trends. The vast and diverse examples along with detailed code snippets are just stepping stones and tools to help you learn the concepts, syntax, and analyzes, and adopt them for your own analysis needs.

This concludes part I of the two chapters focusing on software collaboration trends and we will continue with a fresh perspective on analyzing data from StackExchange in the next chapter. Hope to see you there!

6

Analyzing Software Collaboration Trends II - Answering Your Questions with StackExchange

The previous chapter introduced the collaborative development landscape through the perspective of GitHub. Collaboration has another facet to it which emulates our usual curiosity cycle of questions and answers. Internet has time and again seen some very popular **Question and Answer** (**Q&A**) platforms such as Yahoo Answers, Wiki Answers, and so on, which provide users with the ability to ask questions and utilize their collective might to find answers. Yet they all lacked the quality and discipline to stand the test of time. This second chapter on a similar theme introduces you to the world of **StackExchange** which is, in certain ways, a gold mine of information. It caters to topics from mathematics to programming languages, and even spirituality, all available at the click of a button!

A Q&A platform such as StackExchange doesn't just assist users to find answers but also acts as a perfect partner to a collaborative development platform such as GitHub. Both of these platforms are very popular amongst developers in particular and the whole of Internet in general. Through this chapter, we will cover:

- The basics of the StackExchange platform, its origins and popularity
- Understand its data access patterns through APIs, data dumps, and so on
- Work upon specific use cases to uncover interesting insights related to the platform, demographics, user base, and so on
- Challenges faced while working with data from a platform such as StackExchange

This chapter builds and complements the previous one in terms of overall theme yet readers can focus on this as a complete chapter of its own.

Understanding StackExchange

What started as a single website in 2008 by the name of StackOverflow for developers/programmers has now outgrown its humble beginnings to become a full-fledged Q&A platform catering to topics as varied as mathematics, biology, music, and many more.

Stated simply, StackExchange is a platform consisting of various Q&A websites under its umbrella (one for each topic) where questions, answers, and users are subject to a reward/award process. The platform gamifies the Q&A process and rewards its users with increasing privileges as their reputation scores improve based upon their activity on the network. The reputation scores in turn have been really successful in moderating the content on the network and thus providing useful high quality answers to the majority of the questions unlike other Q&A platforms.

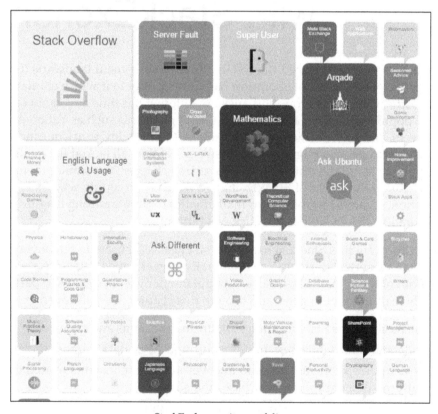

StackExchange site portfolio

In terms of numbers, StackExchange has over 150+ sites for as many topics and growing, it handles about 1.3 billion page views per month catering to over 4 million+ registered users.

 More statistics related to StackExchange can be accessed at `http://stackexchange.com/performance`

The sites under the StackExchange umbrella contain tons of data which is available through various methods under the Creative Commons license. Amazing, isn't it?

 Creative Commons is an American non-profit organization which handles and releases copyright licenses free of cost to promote and protect creative work. The licenses are crafted in an easy to understand manner and allow users to reserve certain rights and waive off others for the benefit of users or other creators. You can read more on this here: `https://creativecommons.org/`

Let us now understand the various methods of getting this wealth of data to play with.

Data access

Most social networks/platforms provide certain predefined ways of accessing their data. Across previous chapters, we have seen and utilized **Application Programming Interfaces (APIs)** in general. Unlike other platforms we have covered so far, StackExchange provides a slightly different way to access its data. Since the data on the platform is under the Creative Commons license, the StackExchange team takes it seriously and has opened up most of its data for the public. The following are popular methods of getting data related to any StackExchange website:

- **Data dump**: StackExchange regularly releases a data dump of all of its user generated public data. This data is available in the form of separate XML files for each of the sites in the platform. Each site's archive includes data for posts, users, votes, comments, post history, links, and tags.

- **Data explorer**: This is a tool based on SQL. It allows users to execute arbitrary queries on the user generated public content of the platform. The queries are publicly available for reuse/modification along with the ability to write new ones. The base data is similar to what is available in the data dumps. More details at: `https://data.stackexchange.com/help`:

One of the popular queries on the data explorer

- **APIs**: StackExchange exposes data through its APIs as well. The APIs utilize OAuth for authentication and respond with JSON data. The APIs have restrictions in terms of request counts and hence should be utilized with care. Though most of the data can be extracted through APIs as well, usually these are utilized by developers of apps based on the StackExchange platform rather than for data science projects. More details at: `https://api.stackexchange.com/docs`

The StackExchange data dump

As discussed in the previous section, StackExchange provides multiple ways of getting data from the platform. Depending upon the use case, one method may be preferred over the other. We as users can be sure of the fact that the same data is available across the methods. For the use cases in this chapter, we will be utilizing the data dumps from the platform.

StackExchange's data dumps are fairly extensive in information they contain and granular enough to work with. These also free us of the query rate limitations imposed upon APIs or row count limitations set on the data explorer methods. This method may be limited from the perspective that the data is not real-time. This should not be much of a barrier given the fact that the data is not too old (usually lags by a month or so) and we can work on most behaviors with a little data lag unless we have a real-time analytics use case to work with. Before we dive into the use cases, let us get familiarized with the data dumps themselves.

Accessing data dumps

Unlike APIs (we have seen plenty of those in the previous chapters) which require us to create an app to get keys/tokens and then use certain packages to request the data, data dumps are plain, simple downloads. Anybody familiar with Internet knows how to download stuff and getting StackExchange data dumps is as simple as that. No registrations or apps are required.

The data dumps are available at `https://archive.org/details/stackexchange`. These are available under CC-by-SA license for anyone to use with attribution. Readers may download the complete dump from the website as a direct dump or through a torrent file. Both methods are listed on the website mentioned.

The full data dump, consisting of data from all StackExchange websites is more than 40 GBs in size. Each website's data is available in the form of XML files. Users can also choose to work with a subset of this data based upon the use case and thus limit the amount of data to be downloaded. For the use cases in the upcoming section, we will be relying on a subset but readers can easily extend the same to the complete data dump as well.

Contents of data dumps

The data is available in the form of eight separate XML files for each of the sites under the StackExchange umbrella. The different XML files are as follows:

- `Badges.xml`: This file consists of data related to badges earned/associated with each user on the respective site. This data is keyed on the user's ID itself.

- `Comments.xml`: As the name suggests, this file contains comments for each of the questions or answers on the website. It contains the text, date and timestamp, and user identification fields for each comment.

- `Posts.xml`: This is the main data file for each site. This file contains data related to the questions and answers themselves. Each of the posts is keyed on an ID and its type identifies whether it is a question post or an answer post. Each row in this XML file is associated with a post and contains a multitude of attributes which we will see in the coming sections.

- `PostHistory.xml`: StackExchange websites are one of the best examples of collaborative/crowd sourcing efforts. The website is magically self-moderated. This self-moderation is seen through posts (questions and answers) being edited/revised for the sake of clarity and details. Posts are even marked duplicate or closed down altogether for a variety of reasons (such as being off topic). Such changes are tracked in this file which contains data associated with every change a post goes through, including the user's information associated with the same.

- `PostLinks.xml`: This file acts more like a look-up of sorts. It helps in maintaining links between similar/associated posts as well as duplicate ones for easy traversal/analysis.

- `Users.xml`: As the name suggests, this file contains public information associated with each user registered with the site under consideration

- `Votes.xml`: As briefly discussed in the introduction to StackExchange, gamification is the key to this platform. Posts are voted up and down based on their relevance. StackExchange even allows users to attach bounties with questions as an added incentive. This information is available through this file for analysis.

- `Tags.xml`: Each StackExchange website caters to millions of users asking and answering thousands of different things. Tags are unique markers to each such post for better reach and searching. This file contains a summary of tags associated with posts on the site under consideration. Unlike `Posts.xml` wherein all tags associated with a post are listed as a list, this file contains frequencies and other information at a per tag level.

Quick overview of the data in data dumps

StackExchange exposes quite an extensive set of data from the platform which is neatly segregated based on sites and entity levels. To get a complete picture of the data landscape, let us visually understand how the different files are associated:

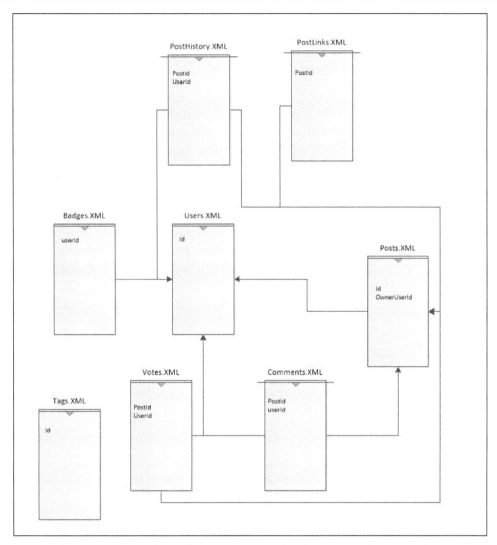

StackExchange sample site wise entity relationships (diagram only shows key fields)

 This is not an ER diagram per se, it is a visual representation of relationships between different entities available as part of a StackExchange data dump. We have taken the liberty of using ER concepts and digressing wherever required for clarity and brevity purposes.

The preceding visual representation not just helps us understand the relationships between different data elements available, it also helps us during our analysis of the data to think critically and try and find potential spots for deriving insights. This will be clearer when we dive into the use cases.

As is evident from the preceding diagram, posts and users are the most important and central entities to the whole landscape. This shouldn't be surprising at all since posts (Q&A) are the site's bread and butter and it is the users who drive the whole platform.

Let us have a brief look at post and user files for a better understanding.

Posts

We discussed in the previous section about `Posts.xml` in brief. Now let us have a look at the contents of this file to see what we have at hand and prepare a strategy to utilize the contents to uncover insights. The `Posts.xml` file looks like the following snapshot:

```xml
<?xml version="1.0" encoding="utf-8" ?>
<posts>
    <row Id="5" PostTypeId="1" CreationDate="2014-05-13T23:58:30.457"
    Score="7" ViewCount="315" Body="&lt;p&gt;I've always been interested in machine learning, but I can't figure out one thing about
    OwnerUserId="5" LastActivityDate="2014-05-14T00:36:31.077"
    Title="How can I do simple machine learning without hard-coding behavior?"
    Tags="&lt;machine-learning&gt;" AnswerCount="1"
    CommentCount="1" FavoriteCount="1" ClosedDate="2014-05-14T14:40:25.950"
    />
    <row Id="7" PostTypeId="1" AcceptedAnswerId="10"
    CreationDate="2014-05-14T00:11:06.457"
    Score="2" ViewCount="297" Body="&lt;p&gt;As a researcher and instructor, I'm looking for open-source books (or similar materials)
    OwnerUserId="36" LastEditorUserId="97"
    LastEditDate="2014-05-16T13:45:00.237"
    LastActivityDate="2014-05-16T13:45:00.237"
    Title="What open-source books (or other materials) provide a relatively thorough overview of data science?"
    Tags="&lt;education&gt;&lt;open-source&gt;"
    AnswerCount="3" CommentCount="4" FavoriteCount="1"
    ClosedDate="2014-05-14T08:40:54.950"
    />
</posts>
```

Sample Posts.xml

The file consists of multiple `<row>` tags, one for each post (where a post can be a question or answer). Each row element consists of various attributes. Each post is uniquely identified by its `Id` field. It has attributes such as:

- `PostTypeId`: This signifies if a post is a question or an answer
- `CreationDate`: This creates a date and timestamp of the post
- `Title`: This is the question header we get on the website
- `Body`: This is the post's actual text

There are many more attributes. Each row consists of about 20 such attributes. The attributes are a mix of numeric, string, and categorical data types. The following is a snapshot of the data in tabular form at:

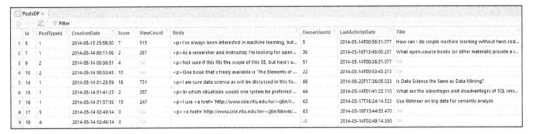

Posts data in tabular format

Users

It is the users who drive any social network and StackExchange is no exception. The Users.xml file contains public information associated with each registered user. Users on the platform are characterized by the following attributes:

- CreationDate: The date and timestamp when the user registered on the platform

- DisplayName: The identifiable string used by the user while interacting with the platform

- UpVotes/DownVotes: The count of votes this user has contributed to

There are many more attributes associated with demographic information such as age, location, and so on. We can utilize this information to get user-centric insights from the data. The following is a snapshot of this data in tabular format:

Users data in tabular format

Getting started with data dumps

Now that we have a basic understanding of what is available as part of the StackExchange data dumps, let us get our hands dirty and work upon a few use cases.

As discussed in the previous sections, the data is available on a per site basis and each site's data is segregated into separate XML files. For the purpose of the use cases to be discussed in the coming sections, we will be loading these XML files as required into R for analysis (mostly in the form of R DataFrames).

 For the remainder of this chapter, we will be referring to the data associated with `https://datascience.stackexchange.com/` obtained through the official data dump from `https://archive.org/details/stackexchange`.

The following is a quick utility function we will be utilizing to load the XML files into R as DataFrames:

```
# load XML data
loadXMLToDataFrame<- function(xmlFilePath){
  doc <- xmlParse(xmlFilePath)
  xmlList<- xmlToList(doc)
  total<-length(xmlList)
  data<-data.frame()

  for(i in 1: total){
    data <- rbind.fill(data,as.data.frame(as.list( xmlList[[i]])))
  }
    return(data)
}
```

The functions `xmlParse()` and `xmlToList()` are available through the package `XML`. This package contains many such utility functions. The rest of the code is pretty straightforward and returns a `dataframe` object from the XML input.

XML files can be huge in size. The preceding utility function performs a full load of XML data in memory. This method may not work beyond certain file sizes due to system memory limitations. For analysis of files which are bigger in size (StackOverflow's data is close to 30 GB as compared to `http://datascience.stackechange.com/` which is a few MBs), a better solution would be to load data into a database and extract into R, a subset of it based on the requirements. Using data through a database is also straightforward but is beyond the scope of this chapter. Readers are encouraged to explore the same.

Now that we have the utility to get data into R, let us load the `Posts.xml` into R. The following snippet will return a DataFrame consisting of rows from `Posts.xml`:

```
> PostsDF <- loadXMLToDataFrame(paste0(path,"Posts.xml"))
```

Similarly, we can load other XML files as required. Let us now get started with our use cases.

Data Science and StackExchange

Data science is not just an industry buzzword but an actual field of study which encompasses a whole lot of academic research and industry level application of these concepts. The `https://datascience.stackexchange.com/` is one of those sites where users from different backgrounds and levels of expertise ask questions and discuss a whole lot of interesting concepts and things related to the field of data science, machine learning, advanced analytics, and so on.

As part of this use case, we will be making use of the `Posts.xml` file primarily from the said site for the analysis and uncovering of insights. Introduced in the previous section, we will utilize the same utility to load the XML and perform a couple of pre-processing steps, such as date-time cleanup to get our dataset in useable form. The following snippet performs the cleanup as well as brings the `Tags` attribute into useable form:

```
PostsDF <- loadXMLToDataFrame(paste0(path,"Posts.xml"))

# change data type
PostsDF$CreationDate <- strptime(PostsDF$CreationDate,
                                 "%Y-%m-%dT%H:%M:%OS")
```

```
# cleanup the tag column
PostsDF$tag_list <- lapply(str_split(PostsDF$Tags,"<|>"),
                            function(x){x%>%unlist()}) %>%
                lapply(.,function(x){x[x!=""]})
```

Now that we have the DataFrame with fields in the required formats, let us first begin with something basic yet interesting. The StackExchange platform allows sites on different topics, these begin with a public beta and become mainstream after achieving certain critical mass. Let us begin with some basic metrics related to the site such as total questions, answer count, number of answers to questions asked, and so on. The following snippet provides us with answers to these queries:

```
# number of Posts
> dim(PostsDF)
[1] 9879    23

# number of questions
> sum(na.omit(PostsDF$PostTypeId) == 1)
[1] 4228

# number of answers per question
> dim(PostsDF[(PostsDF$PostTypeId==2),])[1]/
  dim(PostsDF[(PostsDF$PostTypeId==1),])[1]
[1] 1.285005
```

These simple metrics along with a few more are utilized by StackExchange admins to determine the health/critical mass of a site on the platform.

Information related to critical mass and metrics for each StackExchange site are available at `http://area51.stackexchange.com`. For numbers specific to data science, check out `http://area51.stackexchange.com/proposals/55053/data-science`

Let us now see how the post frequencies have been since the site came into public beta. The following code snippet generates this:

```
# Posts by date
ggplot(data = PostsDF, aes(x = CreationDate)) +
  geom_histogram(aes(fill = ..count..)) +
  theme(legend.position = "none") +
  xlab("Time") + ylab("Number of Posts")
```

The following plot shows that since inception, the site has consistently seen an upward trend in the number of posts. This coincides with the increase in the amount of buzz data science has been getting recently:

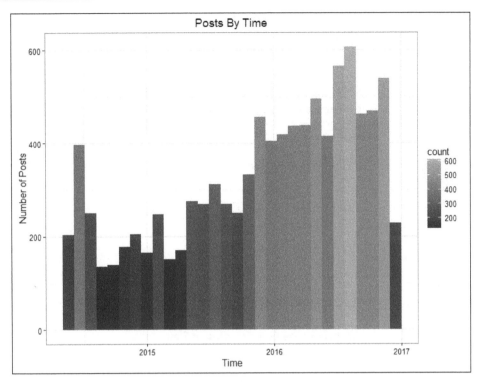

Posts trends over time

 As an additional exercise, readers may try to calculate the number of posts/questions asked on a daily basis. This can be taken a step further by calculating the same on a per language basis and see these numbers point to something interesting.

Let us now see how this distribution looks at a per language level. We have created a derived field in our DataFrame called `prog_lang`. This field is derived from the `Tags` attribute itself wherein we are assuming that the questions are appropriately tagged. Also, we are assuming each question is tagged with at most one programming language tag (this is mostly true but not always). These assumptions are not 100% accurate yet help us get a decent enough idea of the overall trends.

The following snippet plots post counts over time on a per language basis. We have used the `aggregate()` function to aggregate the posts at a per month level from the original daily level:

```
# posts by language over time
langDF <- PostsDF[,c('CreationDate', 'prog_lang')]
langDF$date <- format(langDF$CreationDate, '%b-%Y')
```

```
langDF <- langDF[langDF$prog_lang != 'rest_of_the_world',]
aggLangDF <- aggregate(langDF$prog_lang,
                 by=list(langDF$date, langDF$prog_lang),
                 length)
colnames(aggLangDF) <- c('date', 'tag', 'count')
aggLangDF$date <- as.Date(paste("01",
                 aggLangDF$date,
                 sep = "-"),
              "%d-%b-%Y")
```

We again use `ggplot` to visualize the preceding aggregated data using the following snippet:

```
# language posts over time
ggplot(aggLangDF, aes(x=date, y=count, group=tag)) +
  geom_point(aes(shape=tag)) +
  geom_line(aes(color=tag)) +
  theme_bw()
```

The following is the plot generated by the snippet:

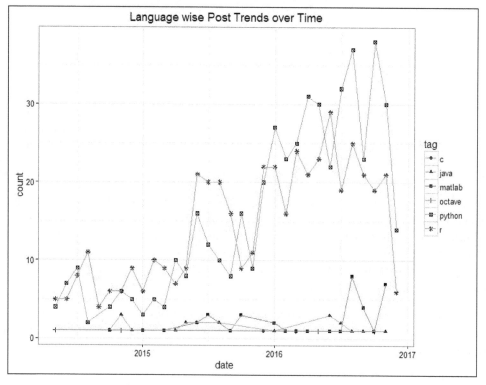

Posts trends per programming language over time

The plot clearly marks out that R and Python are favorites on the platform or, we take the liberty to say that R and Python are the major languages preferred and discussed by the data science community in general. This plot also clearly shows how the popularity of these two languages has grown over time.

Before we move on to other attributes, let us quickly also see how the overall post distribution looks on a per language basis. The following snippet does the same using `ggplot`:

```
# Posts by language
ggplot(PostsDF[PostsDF$prog_lang !="rest_of_the_world",], aes(reorder_
size(prog_lang))) +
  geom_bar(aes(fill = prog_lang)) +
  theme(legend.position="none", axis.title.x = element_blank()) +
  ylab("Number of Posts") +
  ggtitle("Posts By Language")
```

The plot generated shows high frequencies for R and Python with Python leading the pack and traditional programming languages such as C and Java lagging:

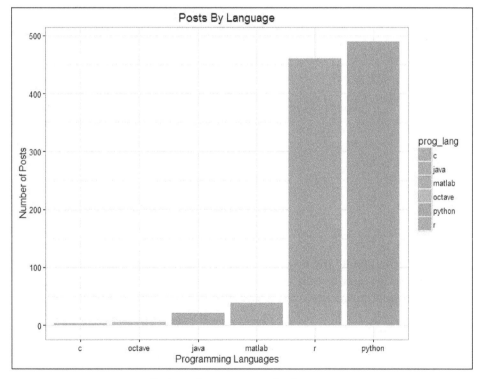

Post counts per programming language

Now that we have some good understanding of the distribution of posts across multiple dimensions, let us see how long it takes to get answers on this site. We have already seen that there are multiple answers per question (see the code snippet for the number of answers per question asked). To get the average time for a question, we first need to do some wrangling.

We will make a smart use of some of the fields in the posts DataFrame itself. Each post contains a field called `PostTypeId`, a value of 1 refers to questions while 2 refers to answers (there are other IDs as well but these two suffice our use case). Also, each post contains a field called `AcceptedAnswerId`. There may be multiple answers to a question but we are interested in finding out when the actual answer (post marked as accepted answer) came up. Once we have identified the fields, we do a self-join of the posts DataFrame with keys being `AcceptedAnswerId` and `Id`. The following snippet gets us the self-joined DataFrame:

```
# Language wise avg time to get answers
mergeddf <-merge(PostsDF[,c('Id',
                            'CreationDate',
                            'PostTypeId',
                            'Score',
                            'ViewCount',
                            'OwnerUserId',
                            'ParentId',
                            'AcceptedAnswerId',
                            'prog_lang')],
               PostsDF[,c('Id',
                          'CreationDate',
                          'PostTypeId',
                          'Score',
                          'ViewCount',
                          'OwnerUserId',
                          'ParentId',
                          'AcceptedAnswerId',
  'prog_lang')],by.x='AcceptedAnswerId',by.y='Id')
```

The next step is to calculate the time it took from the moment a question was posted to the point where an answer to it was accepted. We use the `difftime` function in the following snippet to calculate the time difference:

```
mergeddf$time_to_answer <- difftime(mergeddf$CreationDate.y,
                                    mergeddf$CreationDate.x,
                                    units = "mins")
```

The next step is to use the `aggregate()` function to calculate the average time to get an accepted answer on a per language per year basis. The following snippet plots the results achieved using the aggregation function:

```
# average time to get answers by language per year
ggplot(data=agg_time[agg_time$language!='rest_of_the_world',],
        aes(x=language, y=as.numeric(avg_time_to_answer)/60,
            fill=as.factor(year))) +
    geom_bar(stat="identity",
            position=position_dodge())+
    theme(legend.position="right",
        axis.title.x = element_blank()) +
    ylab("Avg Minutes to Answer") +
    ggtitle("Avg Time to get answers by Language")
```

The plot generated is as follows:

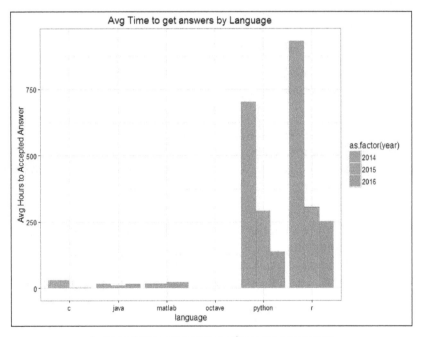

Average time to get answer per language across years

The preceding plot clearly points out that over the years, the time taken to get an accepted answer has reduced dramatically for Python and R. This can be attributed to the fact the number of users and their sophistication levels have gone up over the years. This also can be correlated to increase in the activity/number of posts across years. Reader may take this as an exercise and calculate the actual correlation if any. This also brings forth a clear insight that it takes slightly less time to get accepted answers for Python as compared to R.

So far, we have dealt with numerical, date, and categorical attributes of this DataFrame. It has two free text fields called the `Title` and `Body`. The `Title` refers to the short and crisp title of the post while the `Body` contains the actual complete text related to the post. These fields contain the actual data related to the posts (the others act more like metadata) and can be potentially used for use cases such as:

- Identifying the quality of tags based on post content using text analytics
- Sentiment analysis upon comments
- Clustering questions or suggesting tags based on post content
- Identifying duplicate posts, and many more

We leave these use cases for readers to explore further utilizing some of the concepts shared in earlier chapters related to text analytics, sentiment analysis, clustering, and so on.

But before we move on to use cases related to other files from the data dump, let us try our hands at correlation. There are a lot of attributes in this DataFrame and usually it is a good practice to check if there are any correlations between attributes. For the sake of completeness, we will utilize the `Title` and `Body` attributes for this check.

We simply calculate the length of the `Title` and the `Body` for each post in our DataFrame. We then utilize the `corrplot` package to visually check if there are any correlations. We perform data type conversions and handle missing rows before checking the correlations. The following snippet generates the required plot:

```
M <- cor(mergedLangDf[mergedLangDf$prog_lang.x!='rest_of_the_world',
                      corr_lang_list],
         method = "pearson")

corrplot(M, method="number",type = "lower")
```

The generated plot is as follows:

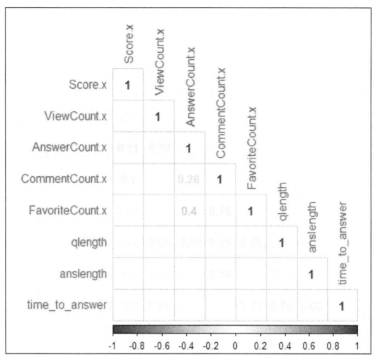

Correlation between post attributes

The preceding plot uses a lower triangular matrix to color code the correlations, blue being highest while red being the opposite. As is apparent from this plot, the highest correlation (if any) is 0.4 between the favorite count of the questions and number of answers for the same question.

Not very encouraging results but the motive of this quick activity was to show how to use `corrplots` to quickly check for correlations. Readers may try checking correlations at a per language or a per year basis to see if that brings out some insights. Similar analysis was also performed on the GitHub data in the previous chapter.

Demographics and data science

Social networks exist for and by its user base. StackExchange rides upon its wide
user base which has a diverse set of skills. In this use case, let us try and understand
the demographic related dynamics of `https://datascience.stackexchange.com/`.

We first begin with loading the user related data from the dumps. As discussed
earlier, this information is available in the `Users.XML` file. We utilize the same
`loadXMLToDataFrame` utility function to get the required DataFrame. We then
get some quick details from the DataFrame such as number of users, average age,
average reputation, and so on. The following snippet gets us started on the same:

```
# Total Users
> dim(UsersDF)
[1] 19237    14

# Average Reputation Score
> max(as.numeric(UsersDF[!is.na(UsersDF$Reputation),'Reputation']))
[1] 5305

# Average age of user on data.stack exchange
> mean(as.numeric(UsersDF[!is.na(UsersDF$Age),'Age']))
[1] 30.83677
```

> Readers should check data types for each of the attributes before
> performing processing/analysis. For example, if the attributes `Age`,
> `Reputation`, and `Views` were loaded as a factor then calculating the
> mean or min/max on a factor data type without first converting to the
> numeric would have resulted in incorrect outcomes.

The logical next step is to combine the user details with the posts they are generating
and see if we can find some interesting insights from it. For this purpose, we join
our posts DataFrame with the user DataFrame on the `OwnerUserId` and `Id` fields
respectively. The following snippet creates a combined DataFrame where each post
contains user details as well:

```
# join post and user details
PostUserDF <-merge(PostsDF[,c('Id',
                              'CreationDate',
                              'PostTypeId',
                              'Score',
                              'ViewCount',
                              'OwnerUserId',
                              'ParentId',
```

```
                              'AcceptedAnswerId',
                              'prog_lang')],
             UsersDF[,c('Id',
                              'CreationDate',
                              'Reputation',
                              'DisplayName',
                              'Location',
                              'Views',
                              'UpVotes',
                              'DownVotes',
                              'Age')],by.x='OwnerUserId',by.y='Id')
```

We checked for the average age of users on the site, now let us see how it differs from the average age of users answering the questions. This can be easily extended to a per-language basis as well. Remember a `PostTypeID` value of 2 denotes an answer post. The following snippet gets us the average age of users answering a question:

```
> mean(as.numeric(PostUserDF[!is.na(PostUserDF$Age) &
               (PostUserDF$PostTypeId==2),
                                                'Age']))

[1] 32.32324
```

This shows that there is little difference between the average age of a user on the site and the average age of a user answering the queries. Compare this with a population specific to R and see if the results change.

> It will be an interesting exercise to see how the population age differs across different sites on the StackExchange platform and which platform has the youngest and the oldest population answering the questions. We can then leverage such information to understand interest trends and other interesting aspects of social networks like StackExchange.

There are a lot of posts generated by a community account for which the `OwnerUserId` is -1. Also, we have performed a very naïve programming language tagging for each post which leaves quite a few posts marked as `rest_of_the_world`. We will filter out all rows which meet the preceding criteria for the rest of the analysis.

Let us now understand the distribution of this user base and posts related to particular programming languages across geographical boundaries. For this very purpose, we make use of a couple of utility functions and R packages called `ggmap` and `rworldmap`.

In our combined DataFrame, we have details of both posts and users. For each user on the site, we have his/her location in the form of the place name. The user may have entered his/her city, state, country, or nothing at all. To get understandable aggregations, we plan to map everything to the country of the user. To perform this transformation, we utilize Google's map APIs exposed through the ggmap package to get the latitude and longitude for each location. We then map these coordinates to the country level using the rworldmap package. The following snippet shows the utility functions:

```
# reverse geocoding
coords2country = function(points)
{
  countriesSP <- getMap(resolution='low')

  # converting points to a SpatialPoints object
  # setting CRS directly to that from rworldmap
  pointsSP = SpatialPoints(points, proj4string=CRS(proj4string(countr
iesSP)))


  # use 'over' to get indices of the Polygons object containing each
point
  indices = over(pointsSP, countriesSP)

  as.character(indices$ADMIN)   #returns country name
}

# set country for given location
postLocation <- function(locationName){
  if(!is.na(locationName)){
    tryCatch(coords2country(geocode(locationName)),
             warning = function(w)  {
               print("warning");
               # handle warning here
             },
             error = function(e)  {
               print("error");
               # handle error here
             })
  }
}
```

The function `coords2country()` is a tweak suggested by @Andy on `http://stackoverflow.com/`, details can be found at: `http://stackoverflow.com/a/21727515/218745`

Now, that we have the utilities, let us geocode our posts and see the distribution. The following snippet helps us get the country for each post where location information is available followed by an aggregation for the number of posts by country and programming language:

```
# get country
filteredPostUserDf$Country <- sapply(as.character(filteredPostUserDf$L
ocation),postLocation)
filteredPostUserDf$Country <- as.character(filteredPostUserDf$Country)
filteredPostUserDf$Counter <- 1

CountryLangDF <- aggregate(filteredPostUserDf$Counter,
                           by=list(filteredPostUserDf$Country,
                                   filteredPostUserDf$prog_lang),
                       sum)

colnames(CountryLangDF) <- c('country','language', 'num_posts')
```

The following snippet then generates a plot for visualizing the distribution.

```
# question tags by country
ggplot(data=CountryLangDF[(CountryLangDF$country!='NULL') &
                          (CountryLangDF$country!='warning') &
                          (CountryLangDF$num_posts>2),],
      aes(x=reorder(country,num_posts),
          y=as.numeric(num_posts),
          fill=as.factor(language))) +
  geom_bar(stat="identity",
           position=position_dodge()) +
  coord_flip()+
  theme(legend.position="right",
        axis.title.x = element_blank()) +
  ylab("Country") +
  ggtitle("Posts by Country and Language")+theme_bw()
```

The generated plot is as follows:

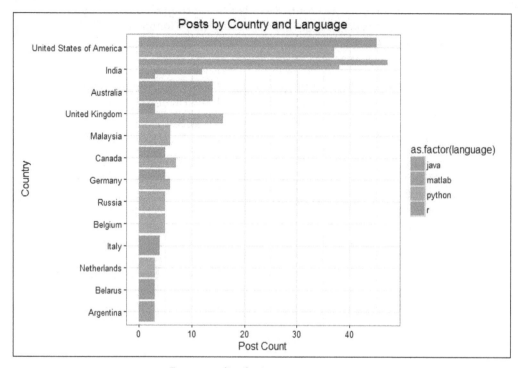

Post count distribution across countries

The plot points towards maximum posts coming from **United States of America**, **India**, and **Australia** wherein R-related posts are the maximum. Such information can be utilized by recruiters for example to understand the dynamics and target locations where required skillsets are available! Such a use case might require further drill down and deeper analysis but this is certainly a nice starting point. An interesting insight is the lack of contributions from China! It might be the case that like other services, China has its own version of StackExchange and hence no posts come up here. Yet another interesting insight is that even though United States has highest number of posts, it is India which has posts from a lot of programming languages which are missing from other countries.

Let us now extend the same discussion with geographically mapped posts from the site. We are now interested in identifying the age distribution of posts across countries. The following snippet aggregates the posts across country and programming languages and helps us get the average age in each case:

```
CountryLangAgeDF <- aggregate(filteredPostUserDf[!is.na(as.numeric(fil
teredPostUserDf$Age)),'Age'],
```

```
                              by=list(filteredPostUserDf[!is.na(filteredP
ostUserDf$Age),'Country'],

                                  filteredPostUserDf[!is.na(filteredP
ostUserDf$Age),'prog_lang']),
                              mean)


colnames(CountryLangAgeDF) <- c('country','language', 'avg_age')
```

The plot from this aggregation looks like the following visualization:

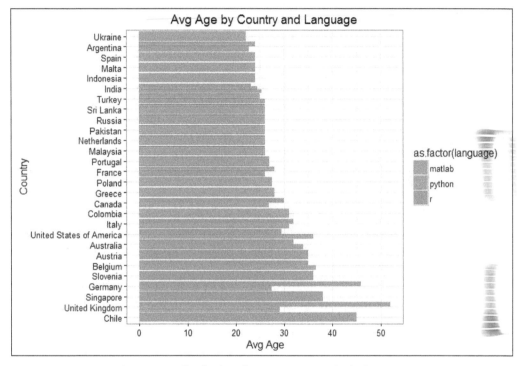

Average age distribution of users across countries by language

The plot points out the R-related posts are from an aging population while python is popular amongst the younger generation. **India** again features in the top 10 list as a country with an average population of less than 30 across all 3 programming languages while **United States of America** slips to the bottom 10! We can also clearly see that a lot more countries have posts with Python tags as compared to R while MATLAB has very few posts overall. It would be interesting to see a similar visualization of questions and answers separately to see how experience is distributed across the globe when it comes to data science. We leave this as an exercise for the readers to explore.

Challenges

Data is the main asset for any social network. Yet StackExchange does a wonderful job of exposing its data for exploration and analysis. Unlike other social networks, which expose their data through APIs mostly and restrict many details, StackExchange not only provides multiple channels like data dumps and data explorer apart from APIs, but it also provides access to an almost complete set of public information.

That being said, there are challenges while working with a platform such as StackExchange. The following are a few of them:

- Data dumps expose the data in the form of XML files. Though there are parsers available in R for using XML data, there is an inherent limit imposed if the XML files are huge (StackOverflow's XML files amount to 30 GB). This limitation can be overcome by first loading the data into a local database such as MySQL and then working upon the required subset of data.

- Data explorer has row limits imposed upon the data extracted through the explorer (current limits are set to 50,000 rows per query). Also, frequent querying may not be feasible due to heavy network load if the query results are huge.

- The data, once extracted, requires multiple steps of preprocessing to bring it into the required shape. Since most of the information on StackExchange is transactional in nature, certain nested attributes complicate this process even further.

- StackExchange is a user-driven platform which usually has high quality posts. Yet data quality can be a challenge and requires additional diligence from the end users analyzing the data. For instance, optional attributes like age and location may contain weird values or be missing altogether. Similarly, even though moderators do a great job, tag quality can still be a cause of worry while analyzing the data.

Summary

The virtual world of the Internet is evolving at breakneck speeds and it is the developers/programmers/innovators that are driving it in the background. GitHub and StackExchange are the two most popular social networks leveraged by this community to share, help and expand their knowledge.

As discussed in the previous chapter on GitHub, there are some strong trends and insights clearly visible from the data available. Building upon the same, this chapter dealt with data related to StackExchange.

We started off with understanding the humble beginnings of this platform followed by ways of getting our hands upon its data. This was followed by utilizing the data dumps as our primary source of data from the StackExchange platform. The next step was to understand what data is available to us and how it is organized into separate files. We then utilized the power of R to use this data and extract some interesting insights related to programming languages, demographics, and so on from the data itself. This chapter also leveraged our learnings from the previous chapters to preprocess, visualize, and analyze the data.

This chapter, in conjunction with the previous one, brings about an interesting point wherein we see somewhat similar trends and practices when it comes to a population with similar skill sets. It will be interesting to see how and if data from both GitHub and StackExchange together can be utilized to uncover even more interesting information.

The next set of chapters raise the bar and provide even more challenging exercises for readers to explore through two completely different, yet long standing, social media platforms. Stay tuned!

Summary

7
Believe What You See – Flickr Data Analysis

Through the chapters of this book, we have travelled a journey encompassing different social networks, covering varied aspects of our digital lives, and we've utilized the tools from the data science toolbox to understand them better. This penultimate chapter is about a social network which has stood the test of time and is still widely used: Flickr. Once one of the most popular kids on the block, it still stands strong with a huge user base and some interesting features. In this chapter, we will learn about this visually driven social network through the lens of a data scientist. We will leverage what we learned from previous chapters to first understand the platform followed by ways of getting data from it, and then discuss different use cases. We will also touch upon some photography basics on the way to utilize domain knowledge for better results. Let's get start; say cheese!

A Flickr-ing world

In the age of ephemeral messaging and disappearing photos, square instant clicks with amazing filters and AI rendered art pieces from phone cameras, platforms that come to mind are Snapchat, Instagram, Prisma, and so on. While these young platforms hog the limelight and have become mainstream, **Flickr** stands at the other extreme of this *instant* spectrum.

Flickr started in 2004 as a side project, but it quickly became a mammoth project loved and used by millions of users across the world. It has gone through multiple iterations of interface changes, feature enhancements, and owners (the last one being Yahoo! Inc.); and yet it has stayed consistent with its theme as a photo sharing platform. It caters to, not only the instant generation, but also amateur and professional photographers to share, discuss, and appreciate photography from across the world.

Flickr is one of the oldest social networks to cater to photography enthusiasts, and it has features related to uploading, commenting, liking, exploring and so on that are now common across all major social networks. Apart from these, it provides copyright related features, and more, which are extensively used and liked by professional photographers from across the world. Yet, there has to be something which makes Flickr interesting as a platform.

Since its inception, Flickr has been at the forefront of community build up and using its vast data assets to understand and improve user behavior, computer vision, object identification, and so on. With over 100 million+ active users, an average of a million photo uploads every day, and a total of 10 billion photos, Flickr has formidable data assets to do and assist research in various fields including data science and machine learning.

Flickr has another trick up its sleeve and it's called the *interestingness* feature. It is a proprietary algorithm which looks at many attributes/parameters of each photograph uploaded onto the site to select and present them to users when they log in to the platform on the Explore page. The exact details of this algorithm have been kept secret, though researchers and photographers across the world have tried to understand and uncover its mysteries to find interesting photos. As part of this chapter, we will also try to make use of this feature and uncover interesting insights as well.

More details on interestingness: https://www.flickr.com/ explore/interesting/. Flickr also upped the ante with another take on interestingness by introducing Flickr Pandas: check it out here: http://code.flickr.net/2009/03/03/panda-tuesday-the-history-of-the-panda-new-apis-explore-and-you/

Accessing Flickr's data

Now that we have a brief overview of Flickr, let's get started with our ritual of getting access to a platform's data. Pretty much as we have already seen across different social networks, Flickr exposes its data through a set of APIs for which we would need to create an app. For the use cases to be discussed further in this chapter, we will be relying on the latest API endpoints exposed by Flickr through direct calls, instead of R packages to do so. Flickr datasets, similar to StackExchange data dumps, though not official in certain cases, are also available on the Internet but are beyond the scope of this chapter.

Flickr exposes its data through APIs which accept and respond in formats such as JSON, XML, SOAP, and so on. It also supports developer API kits in various programming languages such as C, Java, Python, and so on, but unfortunately not in R. Though R has certain packages to connect and work with Flickr APIs, most of them are not updated with the latest changes and so pose a problem.

 A complete list of Flickr APIs and documentation related to them is available here: `https://www.flickr.com/services/api/`

Flickr API methods are cleanly segregated into various categories based on their purpose, such as activity, auth, interestingness, groups, favorites and so on. We will be using API methods under some of these categories for our use cases.

Creating the Flickr app

The process of creating a Flickr app is pretty straightforward. We will go through a step-by-step process to create one for this chapter to be used across the use cases.

To begin with, we assume you have a Flickr or a Yahoo! account. Once you have one, go to the following URL: `https://www.flickr.com/services/apps/create/`. Then click on the **Request an API Key** link:

Creating a Flickr app

On the next screen, select the appropriate option related to commercial use or non-commercial use of the APIs.

The next screen is where you enter details related to the app. The following image shows the brief form you need to fill out:

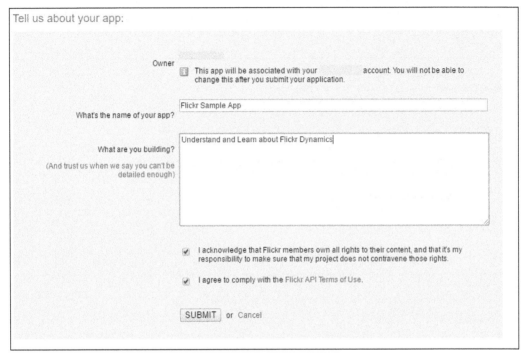

Providing app details

Once submitted, the final screen presents the app details with an API key and secret for use. It also adds your app to what Flickr calls **The App Garden**. **The App Garden** is a repository of all Flickr apps and is a good place to draw inspiration on what can be done using Flickr data and APIs. The following is a screenshot of our newly created app:

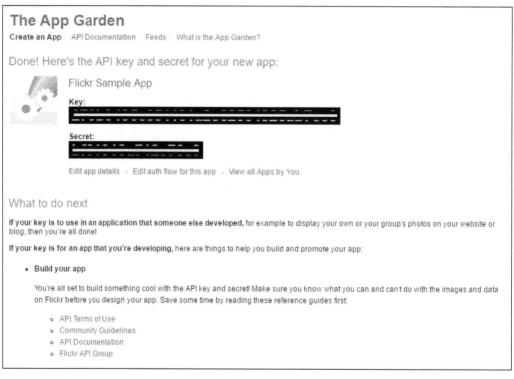

App is ready

This page also outlines resources and links related to **API Terms of Use**, **Community Documentation**, **Flickr API Group**, and **Community Guidelines**. We ask readers to go through them before proceeding with the use cases.

Connecting to R

Now that we have an app on Flickr with the required credentials, our next step is to test the connection to its APIs.

As mentioned earlier, we will be directly interacting with Flickr APIs instead of using outdated R packages. Using an API directly also gives us an opportunity to learn how to extract data in cases where helper methods/abstractions through packages are not available. Also, in cases where APIs are undergoing constant change, it is hard to keep the packages relevant and updated unless there is strong demand.

For interacting directly with the APIs, we will be utilizing the `oauth_app()` function from the `httr` package to connect and extract information. The following code snippet sets up the required variables and connects to our Flickr app using R:

```r
library(httr)

api_key <- "XXXXXXXXXXXXXXXXXXXXXXXXXXXXXXXXX"
secret <- "XXXXXXXXXXXXXXXX"


flickr.app <- oauth_app("Flickr Sample App",api_key,secret)


flickr.endpoint <- oauth_endpoint(
  request = "https://www.flickr.com/services/oauth/request_token"
  , authorize = "https://www.flickr.com/services/oauth/authorize"
  , access = "https://www.flickr.com/services/oauth/access_token"
)

tok <- oauth1.0_token(
  flickr.endpoint
  , flickr.app
  , cache = F
)
```

Upon execution, the code snippet takes us to Flickr's authorization page to allow this session to be authenticated and to proceed with using its API methods, as shown in the following screenshot:

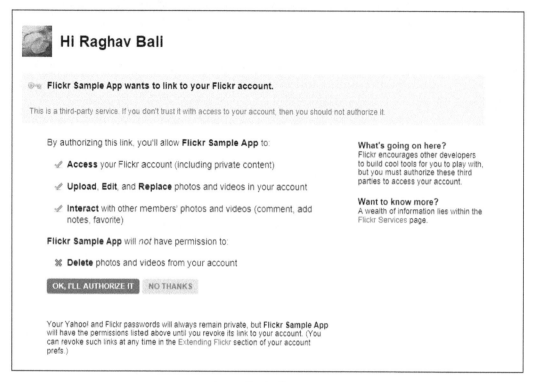

App authorization page

Once you select the **OK, I'LL AUTHORIZE IT** button, your credentials are verified and the following screen is presented:

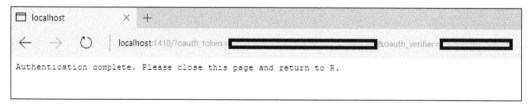

Authorization complete

This completes our connection to Flickr using R and now we can proceed to extract data and uncover interesting insights.

Getting started with Flickr data

Before we get into the actual use cases, let's spend some time extracting sample data from the APIs and see what it looks like. The following code snippet uses the `interestingess` method to fetch interesting photos from yesterday. We use the `GET()` method from the `httr` package to use the API as follows:

```
raw_sample_data <- GET(url=sprintf(
"https://api.flickr.com/services/rest/?method=flickr.interestingness.
getList&api_key=%s&date=%s&format=json&nojsoncallback=1"
  , api_key
  , format( Sys.Date()-1, "%Y-%m-%d")
  , tok$credentials$oauth_token
)
)
```

The returned data structure is a list with multiple attributes, the most important ones being $status_code and $content. A status code of 200 refers to OK and that server has indeed returned a response with some data. Since we mentioned the format as JSON in the URL, $content needs to be parsed as a JSON to make sense out of it.

Since our `response` object needs to go through multiple preprocessing steps, we make use of an R library called `pipeR`. This package helps in chaining function calls using the `%>>%` and `.` operators. We use it to extract the data retrieved from the Flickr API under the $content attribute. We also chain helper methods from the `jsonlite` package to handle JSON.

> For more details on pipeR, refer to this tutorial: https://renkun.me/
> pipeR-tutorial/

The following snippet transforms the raw `response` object into a DataFrame by extracting photo related information from $photos attribute under $content:

```
# extract relevant photo data
processed_sample_data <- raw_sample_data %>>%
                         content(as="text") %>>%
                         jsonlite::fromJSON ()%>>%
                         ( data.frame(
                          date = format( Sys.Date() - i, "%Y-%m-%d")
                          , .
                          ,stringsAsFactors=F
)
)
```

The output from this snippet generates a DataFrame as shown in the following screenshot:

	date	photos.page	photos.pages	photos.perpage	photos.total	photos.photo.id	photos.photo.owner
1	2017-04-13	1	5	100	500	33889334161	70992083@N07
2	2017-04-13	1	5	100	500	34008897645	28306652@N03
3	2017-04-13	1	5	100	500	34004112525	136761463@N05
4	2017-04-13	1	5	100	500	33964817906	88576252@N00
5	2017-04-13	1	5	100	500	33631068610	55032983@N07
6	2017-04-13	1	5	100	500	33633604560	10641418@N00
7	2017-04-13	1	5	100	500	34014561785	89187987@N03
8	2017-04-13	1	5	100	500	33964869026	34368269@N04
9	2017-04-13	1	5	100	500	33846511952	100360106@N04

Sample data from Flickr

The preceding exercise helped us extract a day's worth of raw interestingness data from the Flickr API and convert it into an R DataFrame. We create a utility function so as to reuse the code for the upcoming use cases. The following snippet is a quick example to showcase extraction of three days' worth of data using our utility method: `getInterestingData()`:

```
# extract multiple days worth of data

#use this to specify how many days to analyze
daysAnalyze = 3

raw_sample_data <- lapply(1:daysAnalyze,getInterestingData) %>>%
                    # combine all the days into a data frame
                    ( do.call(rbind, .) )
```

Understanding Flickr data

Now that we have created a sample app and extracted data using it in the previous section, let us move ahead and understand more about the data we get from Flickr. We will leverage packages such as `httr`, `plyr`, `piper`, and so on and build on our code base, as in previous chapters.

To begin with, let's use our utility function to extract ten days' worth of data. The following snippet extracts the data using the interestingness API end point:

```
# Mention day count
daysAnalyze = 10
```

```
interestingDF <- lapply(1:daysAnalyze,getInterestingData) %>>%
                    ( do.call(rbind, .) )
```

Now, if we look at the attributes of the DataFrame generated using the previous snippet, we have details like, `data`, `photo.id`, `photo.owner`, `photo.title` and so on. Though this DataFrame is useful in terms of identifying what photographs qualify as interesting on certain days, it does little to tell us much about the photographs themselves.

So the logical next step is to find, extract, process, and leverage image-related attributes of these interesting photos from the past ten days. However, before we get to image specific attributes, let us take a detour and understand a bit about EXIF!

Understanding more about EXIF

Exchangeable Image File Format (**EXIF**) is a format used by digital cameras, smartphones, and other devices to handle and store information related to images, sounds, videos, and so on. It is a long-standing standard, first released in the mid-1990s, and now widely used by digital devices with photographic capabilities. Without going into too much detail, EXIF defines how and what all metadata related to images, sounds and videos is stored by these devices and/or editing software such as Adobe Photoshop, Gimp and the likes.

Some of the most commonly found metadata attributes in image files are:

- Date and time information
- Camera settings, such as focal length, aperture, ISO, and so on
- Device information, such as model, make, lens type, lens model, and so on
- Copyright and descriptions

EXIF metadata or EXIF for short is not just used for the handling of digital images by software and hardware but is used in common lingo by professional photographers as well. Photographers use EXIF to discuss and convey details about how a particular image was taken, using what camera and lens, in a concise and standard format, which is consistent across images taken using cameras from different manufacturers.

The following is a snapshot showcasing a particular image's EXIF information:

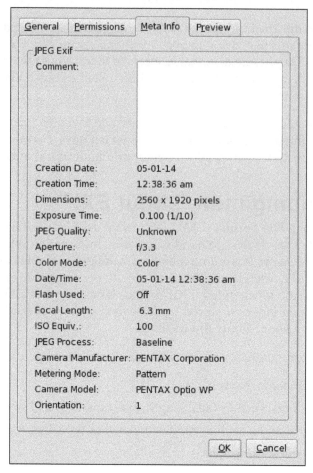

EXIF Sample [source: By Sysy~commonswiki - Own work, Public Domain,
https://commons.wikimedia.org/w/index.php?curid=1468710]

Getting a bit of a background about the domain certainly helps. Now that we have a brief understanding of EXIF, let us proceed and extract EXIF information for the interesting photos we have extracted.

 Readers are encouraged to go a step further and learn about image specific attributes like ISO, aperture, focal length and so on to better appreciate the insights. This will also enable readers to go deeper into Flickr data to uncover more insights.

Similar to interestingness, Flickr has a separate API endpoint to extract EXIF information. To get to the EXIF information, this API endpoint requires an image's corresponding `photo.id` and `photo.secret` which is available to us in our base DataFrame. We write another small utility function to use this API endpoint as follows:

```
# utility function to get EXIF for an image.
getEXIF<- function(image){
exif <- GET(url=sprintf(
"https://api.flickr.com/services/rest/?method=flickr.photos.
getExif&api_key=%s&photo_id=%s&secret=%s&format=json&nojsoncallback=1"
          , api_key
     , interestingDF[image,"id"]
     , interestingDF[image,"secret"]
     )
) %>>%
content( as = "text" ) %>>%
jsonlite::fromJSON ()
}
```

Using the preceding utility function, we simply iterate over our base DataFrame `interestingDF` to get each image's EXIF data.

 Please note that EXIF information is optional, which may result in no data for any attribute or partially populated information.

The following snippet performs the previously mentioned action:

```
# get exif information for each image
exifData <- lapply(1:nrow(interestingDF),
                   getEXIF)
```

We now proceed towards extracting and preprocessing individual EXIF attributes from `exifData` object. As we saw previously with interestingness data, the EXIF `response` object is also a complex nested structure. We make use of `pipeR`, `plyr` and `dplyr` to get to relevant attributes. The following code snippet extracts ISO and camera make information from `exifData` object:

```
# Use EXIF Data to get specific attributes
# ISO
iso_list <- as.numeric(exifData %>>%
                       list.map(as.numeric(
```

```
                              as.data.frame(.$photo$exif)[
                                which(.$photo$exif["label"]=="ISO,
                                Speed"),"raw"])
    )
    )


    # Manufacturer/Make
    make_list <- exifData %>>%
                    list.map(unlist(
                      as.data.frame(
                        .$photo$exif)[
                          which(.$photo$exif["label"]=="Make"),
                          "raw"] )[1] %>>% as.character
                    )%>>% as.character


    # handle missing make information
    make_list <- ifelse(make_list=="character(0)",
                    NA,
                    make_list)
```

In a similar manner, we extract details related to focal length, white balance, metering mode, and so on with pre/post processing as required for the particular attribute.

Readers may find the preceding snippet a bit complex and convoluted but it is similar to how we achieved our interestingness DataFrame in the initial sections of this chapter. Reading more about pipeR, plyr, and similar packages will help get more clarity. Also, it should be noted that there may be other concise and faster ways of achieving equivalent results, but the point of this section and chapter in general is to showcase simple and easy to understand snippets. Readers should feel free to experiment.

We now merge these individual attributes of EXIF metadata to our main DataFrame as follows:

```
    # Add attributes to main data frame
    interestingDF$iso <- iso_list
    interestingDF$make <- make_list
    interestingDF$focal_length <- focal_list
    interestingDF$white_balance <- whiteBalance_list
    interestingDF$metering_mode <- meteringMode_list
```

The additional attributes of the updated DataFrame are shown in the following snapshot. It has all the additional EXIF attributes we extracted in the preceding steps:

iso	make	focal_length	white_balance	metering_mode
160	NIKON CORPORATION	24.0	Manual	Multi-segment
100	Canon	100.0	Manual	Spot
100	Canon	17.0	Auto	Multi-segment
100	Canon	50.0	Auto	Multi-segment
3200	Canon	NA	Manual	Multi-segment
100	SONY	85.0	Manual	Spot
NA	NA	NA	NA	NA
50	SONY	130.0	Manual	Multi-segment
NA	NA	NA	NA	NA
160	Canon	182.0	Auto	Multi-segment
100	Canon	58.0	Auto	NA

InterestingnessDF with EXIF attributes

Flickr also provides view counts for each of the images available on the platform. To get to the view count information, we write another utility function using the `getInfo` API end point. This endpoint returns tags and view counts on a per image basis. We use the following snippet to extract view counts for images in our base DataFrame:

```
# get tag and view count data
tagData <- lapply(1:nrow(interestingDF),
                  getInfo)

# Image View Count
views_list <- as.numeric(tagData %>>%
                    list.map(
                        unlist(.$photo$views)) %>>%
                    as.character)
```

We merge this additional attribute as well with our main DataFrame `interestingDF`.

Now that we have our base DataFrame enhanced with additional information in the form of EXIF attributes and view counts, we should wear our data science hats and get started with some initial exploratory analysis of this dataset.

The following is a quick summary of the DataFrame using the function `summary()` to begin with:

```
> summary(interestingDF[,c('iso','make','focal_length','white_balance','metering_mode','views')])
      iso              make          focal_length      white_balance      metering_mode          views
 Min.   :   20.0  Length:994      Min.   :  0.00   Length:994       Length:994       Min.   :   843
 1st Qu.:  100.0  Class :character 1st Qu.: 19.25   Class :character Class :character 1st Qu.: 13543
 Median :  200.0  Mode  :character Median : 50.00   Mode  :character Mode  :character Median : 25423
 Mean   :  588.5                   Mean   :135.45                                     Mean   : 37464
 3rd Qu.:  400.0                   3rd Qu.:129.10                                     3rd Qu.: 61411
 Max.   :25600.0                   Max.   :850.00                                     Max.   :151069
 NA's   :316                       NA's   :335
```

Summary of InterestingnessDF

The summary of the DataFrame gives us a nice overview of the quality of the data. Apart from information related to min/max and other statistical attributes, we get to know that about 65-70% of the data is populated across all available attributes. We may have to work out a strategy to handle this missing information by using our domain knowledge and other methods learned in previous chapters. We may also choose to ignore rows with missing information if we can work with a reduced dataset.

Let us make use of `ggplot` to visualize some of these attributes to get a better understanding of the data. The following snippet plots the frequency distribution of images based on different makes/manufacturers:

```
# Plot images counts by make
ggplot(interestingDF[!is.na(interestingDF$make),],
        aes(make)) +
  geom_bar() +
  coord_flip() +
  labs(x="Make", y="Image Counts",
        title="Make wise Image distribution"
        ) +
  theme_ipsum_rc(grid="XY")
```

The output plot is as follows:

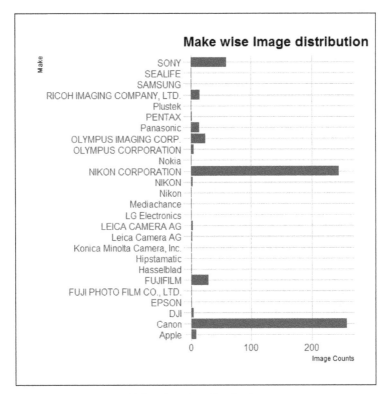

Make wise photo distribution

The preceding plot clearly shows that the most interesting photos are being clicked using Canon and Nikon cameras. These two are followed by other DSLR manufacturers, with a minor presence from smartphones such as the Apple iPhone.

This plot also points towards two interesting insights. Firstly, it seems that Flickr's set of interesting images for this brief 10-day period seems to have a lot more DSLR clicked images as compared to other image sharing websites/platforms like Instagram, which primarily cater to the smartphone audience. Secondly, it points us towards a potential data issue which would require some further preprocessing to achieve better results. If we look closely, there are a few manufacturers, such as Nikon, Olympus, and others, that have multiple entries in the plot due to different names available as part of the EXIF data. This may be due to different models, post-processing software, or other reasons.

Along the same lines, let's see how the distribution related to the metering mode is spread. We again make use of our friendly `ggplot()` as shown in the following snippet:

```
ggplot(interestingDF[!is.na(interestingDF$metering_mode),],
       aes(metering_mode)) +
  geom_bar()+
  coord_flip() +
  labs(x="Metering Mode", y="Image Counts",
       title="Metering Mode wise Image distribution"
  ) +
  theme_ipsum_rc(grid="XY")
```

The metering mode distribution is as follows:

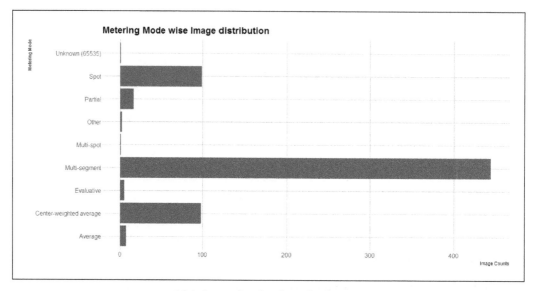

Metering mode-wise photo distribution

Multi-segment seems to be the favorite here, followed by spot and center-weighted average metering modes. The high counts for spot and center-weighted average may point towards quite a sizeable number of images being portraits, or to images with subjects in the middle. Further analysis would require a deeper understanding of these metering modes which is beyond the scope of this chapter.

Understanding interestingness – similarities

We started off this chapter discussing Flickr and its interestingness algorithm: the enigma of an algorithm which brings forth some amazing photos for us to explore and enjoy from millions uploaded every day. The Explore page presents a pretty diverse set of photos showcasing different photography styles, clicked using different photography equipment by photographers of varied skills. Yet the interestingness algorithm picks them all!

Through this use case we will try to find out what type of photos are being picked up by the algorithm and understand/uncover if there are certain patterns or similarities between such interesting photos.

Since we do not know much about the algorithm other than the fact that it presents excellent photos to explore, we'll take the unsupervised approach to see what we have here.

Under the unsupervised umbrella of machine-learning algorithms, one of the simplest and most widely used algorithms to get started with is the k-means clustering algorithm. It is not just the simplest, it is also a fairly easy to understand algorithm that can be used in a variety of domains, and it handles different data types with ease.

Let's get started with preparing the dataset for this use case. We will use the same `interestingDF` DataFrame we built in the previous section and tweak it to our requirements for this use case. To begin with, we will subset the DataFrame by working only with rows that do not have missing information and with a subset of attributes. We will use `iso`, `focal_length` and `views` as the only set of attributes. Readers can easily expand it to other attributes as well. The following snippet gives us the base DataFrame to get started:

```
# remove NA data
nomissing_interesting <- na.omit(interestingDF[,c('iso','focal_
length','views')])
```

Finding K

The K-means clustering algorithm is a fairly simple algorithm which is easy to use. However, this simplicity comes at a cost: The *k* in k-means is a user defined parameter. Since this is an unsupervised problem, we do not know how many clusters will actually be there. The situation though is not as hopeless as it sounds. We have a couple of tricks up our sleeves to narrow down our search in pursuit of the optimal value of k.

There are multiple methods to identify the optimal value of k, the simplest being hit and trial. We will be making use of the Elbow and Silhouette methods to help us get the right answers. Before we proceed with the use case, let us take a quick detour and review some details about these two methods.

Elbow method

For any clustering algorithm, the cohesiveness of clusters is an indicator of quality, that is, the closer the data points within a cluster are to its centroid the better it is. To quantify the same, we use a metric called **Within the cluster distance to centroid** or withiness or WCSS for short. We use this metric as a function of k (the k in k-means) to help us find the optimal value of it for the given dataset. Notice that, as the value of k increases, the value of WCSS decreases and approaches a minima.

In other words, we look at the variance explained by the clusters as a function of k. If we plot WCSS versus K, this variance sees an inflection; that is, there comes a point when any more clusters do not help in providing significant gains in terms of cluster quality. Hence, this point of inflection is what points towards optimal k.

It should be noted that the Elbow criteria gives us a ball-park value of k that may or may not be optimal. Yet it is a good enough criterion to narrow down the search for optimal k. The following sample plot shows how WCSS changes with the value of k and it also clearly shows the elbow or point of inflection at 5:

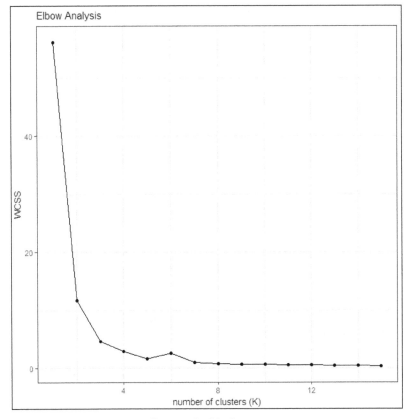

Elbow method for k-means

Silhouette method

The Elbow method helps us narrow down the search space for k and, more often than not, provides us with a meaningful value as well. To further improve and use the correct value of k, there is another method called the Silhouette method.

The Elbow method works with WCSS as a function of k but does not take into account other factors. With the Silhouette method, we work with dissimilarities.

A Silhouette is defined as a measure of how close a data point is to its cluster and how far off it is from other clusters. Thus, the Silhouette method checks for both cohesiveness and separation between clusters. A value of 1 signifies a nice match while -1 points towards an incorrect cluster for a given data point.

To put it formally:

$$s(i) = \frac{o(i) - c(i)}{\max\{o(i), c(i)\}}$$

Here:

- $s(i)$: Silhouette value of a data point i
- $o(i)$: Lowest average dissimilarity of i with any cluster that it is not part of
- $c(i)$: Average dissimilarity of i with other data points in its cluster

The average of $s(i)$ for all data points in a cluster is a measure of how tightly its data points are grouped. The following is a sample silhouette plot. In the plot, each of the colored silhouettes represents a cluster with their average $s(i)$ value and overall average silhouette value mentioned at the bottom of the plot. As we can see from the plot, some clusters are wider than others along with a difference in the number of members in each.

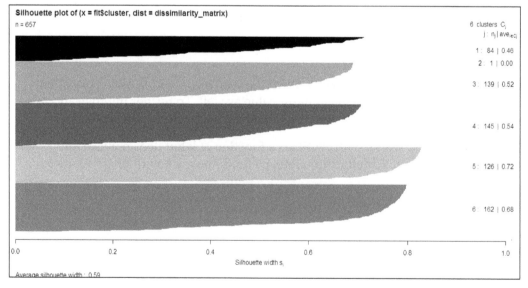

Silhouette plot for k-means

Now that we have details on how to find k for our k-means algorithm, let us apply this knowledge to our use case. The `kmeans()` function from the `stats` package provides an easy to use function. This function takes the DataFrame and number of clusters as input to generate a fit for our dataset.

Since we do not know the optimal value of k, let us employ the Elbow criterion to find it. The following snippet uses `kmeans()` in a loop with k varying from 1 to 15 clusters and collecting the withiness or WCSS value for each value of k in a vector `withiness_vector`:

```
# elbow analysis for kmeans
withiness_vector <- 0.0
for (i in 1:15){
   withiness_vector[i] <- sum(kmeans(nomissing_interesting,
                                     centers=i)$withinss)/(10^10)
}

# prepare dataframe for plotting
eblowDF <-data.frame(withiness_vector,1:15)
colnames(eblowDF)<-c("withiness",
                     "cluster_num")
```

Now that we have WCSS for different values of k, let us find our elbow point. The following snippet uses `ggplot` to generate the required plot:

```
# plot clusters with regions marked out
ggplot(data = eblowDF,
       aes(x = cluster_num,
           y = withiness)) +
geom_point() +
geom_line() +
labs(x = "number of clusters",
     y = "scaled withiness",
     title="Elbow Analysis") +
theme_ipsum_rc()
```

The generated plot points towards an optimal value of k as 4, after which the value of WCSS remains fairly constant:

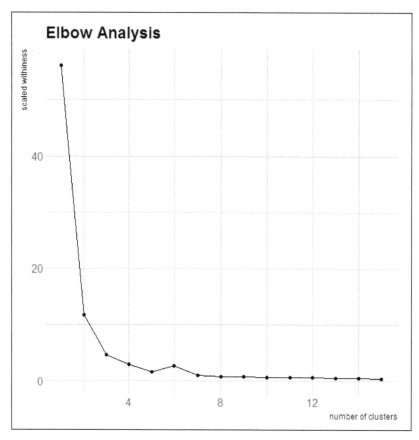

Elbow plot for interesting photos

To validate our findings related to value of k, we apply the silhouette method for values of k, such as 3, 4, 5 and 6.

The following snippet uses the `daisy()` method from the `cluster` package to generate a dissimilarity matrix which we then use to plot and analyze the quality of clusters at *k=4*:

```
# silhouette analysis for kmeans
dissimilarity_matrix <- daisy(nomissing_interesting)
plot(silhouette(fit$cluster,
                dissimilarity_matrix),
     col=1:length(unique(fit$cluster)),
     border=NA)
```

The silhouette plot shows an average of 0.65 for *k=4*, which is maximum as compared to values observed at *k=5* or *6*.

The following is the plot in consideration. The plot also outlines similar Silhouette widths as well:

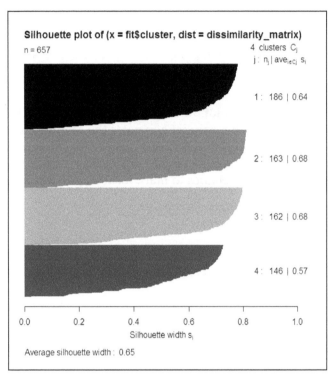

Silhouette plot for k=4

Once we have identified the value of k to work with, we regenerate the clustering output for our dataset on the `interestingDF` DataFrame.

The logical next step is to visualize how the clusters look. Using the output of our clustering step, we assign each data point its corresponding cluster number using the attribute `$cluster` from the `fit` object. Since the focal lengths are very thinly spread across our DataFrame, we aggregate the results, using `ddply()`, by taking the max of focal length as an indicator for each cluster. We also add a derived attribute called `fl_bin`. This attribute is a categorical value which describes focal length in one of seven bins we have decided upon. The following snippet gets us the required summary object:

```
# aggregate results
cluster_summary <- ddply(
```

```
                    nomissing_interesting,
                    .(iso, views,cluster_num),
                    summarize,
                    focal_length=max(focal_length)
                    )
```

```
    # bin focal_lengths for plotting
    cluster_summary$fl_bin <- sapply(cluster_summary$focal_
    length,binFocalLengths)
    cluster_summary$fl_bin<- as.factor(cluster_summary$fl_bin)
```

The final step in this puzzle is to plot the clustered data points. For this we again rely on ggplot as usual. The following snippet generates the required plot with each of the cluster regions clearly marked out. To visualize all three dimensions (iso, views and focal length): the plot uses colors to identify clusters, x and y axis to denote views and iso respectively, and shapes to mark focal length bins:

```
    # plot clusters with regions marked out
    ggplot(data = cluster_summary,
           aes(x = views,
               y = iso ,
               color=factor(cluster_num))) +
      geom_point(aes(shape=fl_bin)) +
      scale_shape_manual(values=1:nlevels(cluster_summary$fl_bin)) +
      geom_polygon(data = hulls[hulls$cluster_num==1,],
                   alpha = 0.1,show.legend = FALSE) +
      geom_polygon(data = hulls[hulls$cluster_num==2,],
                   alpha = 0.1,show.legend = FALSE) +
      geom_polygon(data = hulls[hulls$cluster_num==3,],
                   alpha = 0.1,show.legend = FALSE) +
      geom_polygon(data = hulls[hulls$cluster_num==4,],
                   alpha = 0.1,show.legend = FALSE) +
      labs(x = "views", y = "iso",title="Clustered Images") +
      theme_ipsum_rc()
```

The following is the generated plot:

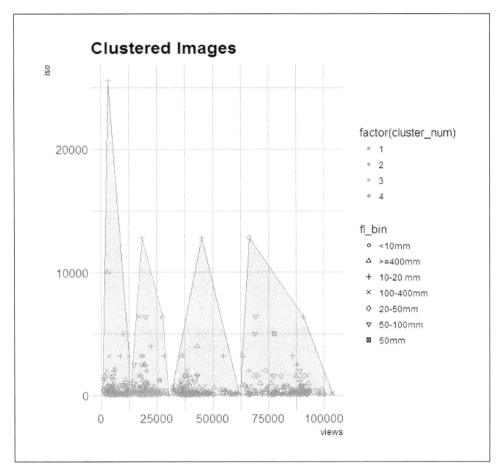

Metering mode wise photo distribution

As we can see with the preceding plot, the clusters are nicely defined across the attributes of our dataset. Focal lengths are more or less distributed across clusters, with each cluster visually being limited by view count. Also, it is interesting to see that clusters 2, 3 and 4 all have images clicked with a lens of focal length between 10-20mm have maximum iso values.

Further investigation of individual clusters may help uncover further insights. We'll leave this as an exercise for the readers to explore.

Are your photos interesting?

We have dedicated a lot of effort to extracting, processing, and understanding the data from Flickr. We have also tried to analyze and use unsupervised learning methods to see if there are any patterns in the data. Luckily enough, the previous section helped us understand that there are intrinsic patterns in the data which are being used by Flickr to identify interesting photos of the day.

It would be interesting to see if we can answer the question, *Will a given photo end up on the Explore page or not*, by just using the metadata attributes we have been using so far in this chapter.

Preparing the data

Before we get started with building a classifier to answer the preceding question, we need some more data. Apart from the data we have collected so far (corresponding to interesting images only), we need to collect data related to photos which have never made it to the Explore page. Employing techniques similar to those we have used for collecting data for interesting photos, we'll use the getpublicphotos API to get the other set of photos.

The following snippet uses that API to build a utility function called getPhotosFromFlickr based on the user_id provided:

```
# extract photos of given user_id
# use flickr.people.getpublicphotos
getPhotosFromFlickr <- function(api_key,
                                token,
                                user_id){
  GET(url=sprintf(
 "https://api.flickr.com/services/rest/?method=flickr.people.
getpublicphotos&api_key=%s&user_id=%s&format=json&nojsoncallback=1"
    , api_key
    , user_id
    , token$credentials$oauth_token
  )
 ) %>>%
    content( as = "text" ) %>>%
    jsonlite::fromJSON () %>>%
    ( .$photos$photo ) %>>%
    ( data.frame(
      .
      ,stringsAsFactors=F
    ))
}
```

We reuse the utilities for extracting EXIF and view counts for each of the images we extract for user_ids. The following snippet shows the utility function which returns a DataFrame of photos for a given user_id using the utilities developed so far:

```
# Get Photos for given user_id
getUserPhotos <- function(api_key,
                          token,
                          user_id){

  #get user's photos in a dataframe
  photosDF <- getPhotosFromFlickr(api_key,token,user_id)

  # get exif for each photo in dataframe
  photos.exifData <- getEXIF(api_key,photosDF)


  # Image ISO
  iso_list <- extractISO(photos.exifData)

  # Image Manufacturer/Make
  make_list <- extractMakes(photos.exifData)

  # Image Focal Length
  focal_list <- extractFocalLength(photos.exifData)

  # Image White Balance
  whiteBalance_list<-extractWB(photos.exifData)

  # Image Metering Mode
  meteringMode_list <- extractMeteringMode(photos.exifData)


  # Add attributes to main data frame
  photosDF$iso <- iso_list
  photosDF$make <- make_list
  photosDF$focal_length <- focal_list
  photosDF$white_balance <- whiteBalance_list
  photosDF$metering_mode <- meteringMode_list

  # get view counts
  photosDF$views <-   getViewCounts(api_key,photosDF)

  as.data.frame(photosDF)
}
```

The output DataFrame consists of all the attributes we have in the `interestingDF` DataFrame with the attributes correctly type-casted.

Most classification algorithms expect the features to be numeric in nature. In our dataset, attributes such as `iso`, `focal_length`, and `views` are already numeric. Since the make of the camera used to take the photo, along with settings like white balance and metering mode, have a significant impact on the outcome, we'll convert these attributes to factors.

The following snippet typecasts the attributes to be used by the classification algorithm:

```
# typecast dataframes for use by classifier
prepareClassifierDF <- function(classifyDF){

  # convert white balance to factor and then encode numeric
  classifyDF$white_balance <- as.factor(classifyDF$white_balance)

  # convert metering mode to factor
  classifyDF$metering_mode <- as.factor(classifyDF$metering_mode)

  # convert make_clean to factor
  classifyDF$make_clean <- as.factor(classifyDF$make_clean)

  as.data.frame(classifyDF)
}
```

We use the utility `getUserPhotos` to extract photos from a randomly chosen set of Flickr accounts and prepare a DataFrame consisting of negative examples, that is, photos which have never made it to the Explore page. The following snippet iterates through a list of `user_ids` listed in the list `mortal_userIDs` and assigns a classification label of 0 to each entry. We similarly assign a class label 1 to all our photos in the DataFrame `interestingDF`:

```
neg_interesting_df <- lapply(mortal_userIDS,
                        getUserPhotos,
                        api_key=api_key,token=tok) %>>%
                    ( do.call(rbind, .) )


neg_interesting_df <- na.omit(neg_interesting_df)
neg_interesting_df$is_interesting <- 0

# Photos from Explore page
pos_interesting_df <- na.omit(interesting)
pos_interesting_df$is_interesting <- 1
```

We use `rbind()` to concatenate both positive and negative examples in a common DataFrame and then restrict the set of attributes to only `iso`, `focal_length`, `views`, `white_balance`, `metering_mode`, and `make_clean`. The following snippet performs these actions:

```
# prepare overall dataset
classifyDF <- rbind(pos_interesting_df[,colnames(neg_interesting_df)],
                    neg_interesting_df)

# restrict columns
req_cols <- c('is_interesting',
              'iso',
              'focal_length',
              'white_balance',
              'metering_mode',
              'views',
              'make_clean')

classifyDF <- classifyDF[,req_cols]
```

Now that we have our dataset ready, we have one last step before we learn from the data to build a classifier: we need to split our data in training and testing samples. Without going into much detail, a supervised learning algorithm is provided with a set of data points with actual class labels to learn from. This dataset is called the training dataset. The algorithm is then tested for performance using another set of data points whose labels are not known to the algorithm. This is called the test dataset. Usually, there is another dataset called the validation dataset which is used to fine tune the algorithm and check for issues such as overfitting and so on.

> For an in depth understanding on machine learning and further details with examples, refer to *Chapter 2, Let's Help Machines* from *R Machine Learning by Example* [https://www.packtpub.com/big-data-and-business-intelligence/r-machine-learning-example]

The following snippet samples the `classifyDF` DataFrame into `train` and `test` datasets in 60:40 ratio:

```
# train - test split
set.seed(42)
samp <- sample(nrow(classifyDF), 0.6 * nrow(classifyDF))
train <- classifyDF[samp, ]
test <- classifyDF[-samp, ]
```

Building the classifier

Now that we have our features in the required shape and the data split into training and testing sets, we can proceed towards building our classifier. For the current use case, we will build a classifier based on the random forest classification algorithm, which is available from the `caret` package. We'll pass the train DataFrame with formula denoting `is_interesting` as the class label based on all other attributes to `train()`. This function also takes input to preprocess the data, and we use scaling since our attributes are measures of different qualities of a photo. We'll use the attribute `trControl` to cross validate our training model and improve performance against overfitting. The following snippet helps us learn a random forest classifier.

Random forests are a class of ensemble classifiers. Ensemble classifiers in machine learning refer to set of algorithms which make use of multiple learners/learning algorithms to obtain performance improvements. Random forests work by creating multiple decision trees (hence the word forest) each of which works by randomizing the features used at each decision point during the learning phase. Random forests are especially useful in scenarios where feature space is large. Ensembling helps in controlling the overfitting as well. More details can be found here:

`http://ect.bell-labs.com/who/tkh/publications/papers/odt.pdf`,

`https://www.stat.berkeley.edu/~breiman/randomforest2001.pdf` and

Chapter 6, Credit Risk Detection and Prediction – Predictive Analytics from R Machine Learning by Example.

```
# train model
rfModel <- train(is_interesting ~ ., train,
                 preProcess = c("scale"),
                 tuneLength = 8,
                 trControl = trainControl(method = "cv"))
```

Now that we have our classifier ready, let's test its performance by generating some class predictions. For this we use our `test` dataset. The `predict` function takes the classifier model as input followed by the test dataset without the class labels. We use `type= "prob"` to generate output probabilities for each class label. Remember class label 0 refers to photos not making to the Explore page, while class label 1 refers to photos which have been listed on the Explore page. The following snippet generates the required predictions:

```
# Prediction
predictedProb <- predict(rfModel, test[,-1], type="prob")
```

To test the performance of our classifier, we use the **Receiver Operating Characteristic (ROC)** measure. ROC is available from the pROC package. The following snippet plots the ROC curve for our classifier:

```
# Draw ROC curve.
resultROC <- roc(test$is_interesting, predictedProb$"1")
plot(resultROC,
     print.thres="best",
     print.thres.best.method="closest.topleft")

#to get threshold and accuracy
resultCoords <- coords(resultROC,
                       "best",
                       best.method="closest.topleft",
                       ret=c("threshold", "accuracy"))
```

The generated plot is shown in the following diagram. It clearly points towards a very nicely learned classifier, with an ROC curve lying well above the random guess and the highest accuracy of 98% approx at a threshold value of 0.68:

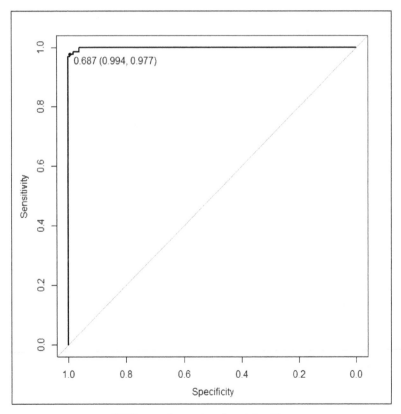

ROC curve for random forest classifier

The confusion matrix based on the test data also shows the classifier working correctly in the majority of the cases. The following is a snapshot of the confusion matrix:

```
Confusion Matrix and Statistics

             Reference
Prediction    0    1
         0  151    6
         1    2  258

              Accuracy : 0.9808
                95% CI : (0.9625, 0.9917)
```

Confusion matrix for random forest classifier

Now that we have a classifier which has learned to classify between interesting and non-interesting images, let us put this classifier to the test. We use this random forest based classifier to classify images for another random set of user(s). You may try to test the classifier on your own images as well. For our current use case, we extracted public photos from one of our own accounts and then allowed the classifier to work and suggest labels. Note that we use the same `predict` function with `type="prob"`. The following is the output generated by our classifier:

```
        0      1
63  0.584  0.416
64  0.864  0.136
65  0.582  0.418
66  0.580  0.420
67  0.560  0.440
68  0.832  0.168
74  0.666  0.334
75  0.686  0.314
96  0.368  0.632
```

Class output probabilities by random forest classifier

In the preceding snapshot, the first column is the image identifier, while column 0 denotes probabilities for a photo not making it to the Explore page, and column 1 points to the probability of making it to the Explore page. Please note that each row's probabilities add up to 1 (as they should).

Since the images used for this test were from one of our own Flickr accounts, we already know that none of these photos have ever made it to the Explore page. Interestingly, the classifier works correctly for eight out of the nine photos while generating a wrong result for the last one!

Of course, far more sophisticated methods can also be employed, such as deep learning, convolutional neural networks, and so on, to improve the results. However, the results achieved in this section are still impressive and point towards the fact that we can answer questions related to them with a certain level of confidence. These topics are beyond the scope of this chapter but you are encouraged to learn more about them.

> Note that the interestingness algorithm pits photos from each day against each other to determine the most interesting ones. Also, it's believed that the algorithm goes through changes so building a perfect classifier may be very difficult.

Challenges

Flickr is one of the longest-standing social networks and it has evolved over the years. Pretty much like Flickr, we have progressed through this book and evolved our methods and techniques across chapters. Flickr presented its own set of challenges and the following is a quick summary of these:

- **API response objects**: Flickr has a nicely documented and updated set of APIs which provide access to most of its publicly usable content. The challenge comes from the design and response of these APIs. While the design of the APIs is something for which Flickr engineers must have put in a lot of thought, they pose difficulties for analytical use cases. It is difficult to use multiple API methods to extract data related to a single entity and so on. On the same lines, the response objects are deeply nested and require some thought and creativity before one can preprocess and use the data for any analysis. Moreover, any changes to the APIs may require extensive rework with regards to extraction and preprocessing.

- **Lack of standard packages/libraries**: The presence of packages/libraries from a social network platform or a third party doesn't just make life easy, it also helps in keeping things modular and to maintain a separation of concern. As a person working on data science related use cases, playing around with APIs is a basic requirement, yet the existence of standard packages helps in speeding up the overall use case development and helps us to stay focused on solving business problems. Flickr provides a standard set of libraries for a variety of languages, though R is missing from the list. There are a couple of third-party R packages but most of them are outdated or provide limited functionality. You can take this up as a challenge and come up with you own solutions using the learnings from this chapter itself and give back to the community.

- **Data quality**: Data quality is a common pain point for any analytical/ machine-learning/data science related use case. In the case of Flickr, apart from user-related information, a lot of information (read EXIF) is extracted by the platform from the photos uploaded. Since EXIF is a standard with recommended fields, many attributes are missing or the values are not standardized. One should be careful before using such data.

Apart from these, the few minor challenges are mostly logic/programming or use case related which can be solved with a bit of creativity and of course the Internet.

Summary

This chapter presented an opportunity to learn about a social network which has so far passed the test of time. Flickr has evolved with the Internet and has been, for a long time now, a popular site for professional and amateur photographers alike. Since its very inception, Flickr has been part of numerous research studies and their APIs have provided analysts/researchers access to their data. With about 10 billion photos, Flickr is a goldmine of sorts. In this chapter, we covered ways of interacting with Flickr using its APIs, and prepared some useful utilities to extract and preprocess the deeply nested response objects. We learnt a few basics related to photography, in particular EXIF, and used this domain knowledge to cluster our set of extracted photos using the K-means clustering algorithm. We also utilized photo attributes such as `iso`, `focal_length`, `views`, and so on, to build a random forest based classifier to help us identify whether a photo will land on the Explore page or not. Through these use cases and our discussions across the chapter, we attempted to understand Flickr's interestingness algorithm. A lot more insights can be extracted, and Flickr data can be used to answer a whole lot of questions.

This chapter also brings out the point that there is a lot happening in the background on platforms such as Flickr that is waiting to be explored!

8
News – The Collective Social Media!

News is ubiquitous in nature, be it a breaking news flash, an opinion piece about the latest issues, or just a gossip-monger column on page 3 of your favorite daily. In the new age world of media such as Twitter, Facebook, and so on there is an indistinguishable line between what constitutes news and what constitutes social media content. We share the notion that the unique position news shares in today's electronic world makes it eligible to be termed social media. News can be described as a collective social media outlet, although each individual does not produce the news articles directly, but they collectively represent the beliefs, hopes, and dreams of the society.

In this chapter, we will try to go through the various steps that are involved in analyzing news from different sources. We will deal with the process of using news data and build use cases that will serve as an introduction for the complex analyzes that can be done on that data. We will be going through these broad topics as we progress through the chapter:

- Identifying news sources that can be used for data collection
- Gaining API access to the aforementioned news sources to facilitate large-scale data collection
- Scraping article pages to extract information provided by APIs
- Sentiment analysis of news articles to extract collective sentiments from a news database
- Topic modeling for news articles to make sense of the vast amount of textual data in an easily palatable way

News data mostly comprises large bundles of text, and text mining/analytics is a whole area of study in itself. This chapter will serve as an introduction to that broad area of analyzes. An important takeaway from this chapter is the process of data collection from normal web pages. This procedure, called scraping, is a highly coveted skill for any data professional as it allows him/her to access data in the public domain, which is not often exposed through neat APIs.

News data – news is everywhere

A single search of the term "news" yields around 10,43,00,00,000 results, which clearly proves that there is no dearth of news data. A few credible news sources, such as **The Guardian** and **The New York Times,** have excellent APIs for data access:

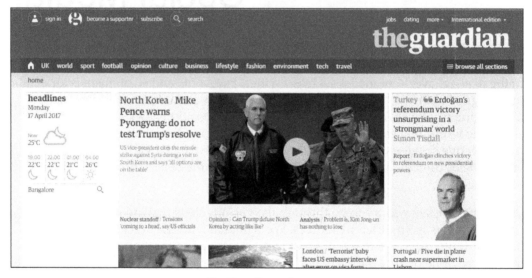

The Guardian main page
Image source: https://www.theguardian.com/international

All the major print newspapers have a very strong online presence. Most allow free access to their data, while some will typically charge you for accessing their news feed. But there are few that not only provide news data for free but also ensure easy access to that data through their APIs.

In addition to the individual newspaper websites, an excellent source of news data is a news aggregator. A news aggregator will keep track of news from different sources and will give you access to collective news sources instead of a single one. One such news aggregator is Metanews.

The metanews main page. Image source: `http://metanews.com/`

Accessing news data

The introduction to this section highlighted the abundance of news data, but the sad truth is that all that data is not easily available. News data is often commercial in nature and a lot of data providers don't open up access to their data to maintain a commercial edge. It becomes a huge problem for the data professional to access the data of interest. In theory, as the news data is in the public domain, that is, on the Internet, you can extract it and use it, but the complex process of web scraping alone makes it a tough ask.

This is where news providers such as The Guardian (`https://www.theguardian.com/international`) and The New York Times (`https://www.nytimes.com/`) stand out. They maintain an excellent set of APIs, which helps to ease access to their news data. For this chapter, we will use The Guardian's APIs and a little web scraping to get the required data. The APIs have an extensive set of documentation, which the reader can read through to get comfortable with it. The documentation is available at `http://open-platform.theguardian.com/documentation/`. We encourage the reader to go through it and, especially, to get acquainted with the terms of usage.

Creating applications for data access

The first step for securing access to any APIs is the creation of the developer account. We will do the same to get access credentials for our news access APIs. We will use The Guardian's APIs to get the required news data for our analysis.

The step-by-step process for creating a The Guardian developer account is illustrated as follows:

1. Go to The Guardian open platform web page located at `http://open-platform.theguardian.com/`.

2. Click on the **Get Started** link and then on the **Register developer key** page.

3. This will get you to the following page, which needs you to fill in the required details and then click on **Register**. This will complete the registration process. Please see the following image for more details:

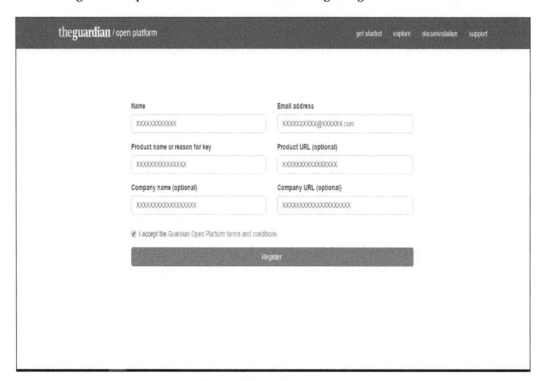

The Guardian registration page

Once the registration process is complete, you will get your API key through an e-mail to the e-mail address that you gave on the registration page:

E-mail with API key

This key will be required for each of your API calls. Please keep the key secret, as it is used for accounting purposes by the data provider.

Important reminder for API access

One important aspect of API-driven data access is the applicable fair-use policy. Please get acquainted with the limits that apply to you, otherwise you risk restrictive actions against your account, including restrictions or even blocking of the account.

Data extraction – not just an API call

The data access procedure in our earlier excursions was relatively simple when compared to the access process required for extracting the news data. The procedure involves a two-step process (we will detail both of them later):

1. In the first step, we will get the necessary data from the API call. Normally, this data will give us the URL of the news article.

2. In the next step, we will use the URL to extract the textual data of the article.

The API call and JSON monster

The Guardian's APIs have an R wrapper around them, but it doesn't seem to work properly. So, we will borrow the API access mechanism that we developed in *Chapter 4, Foursquare – Are You Checked in Yet?*

To jog your memory about the steps involved in the process, here is a recap of them:

1. Find the required end points for the required data.
2. Construct the required URL for data access using the API key.
3. Get the JSON response by querying the URL.
4. Parse the JSON response into a tabular format.

The Guardian's API has a very friendly resource here, which will allow us to skip the process of tediously going through the documentation to arrive at the required URL. Go to the address `http://open-platform.theguardian.com/explore/`. You will be greeted with the following page:

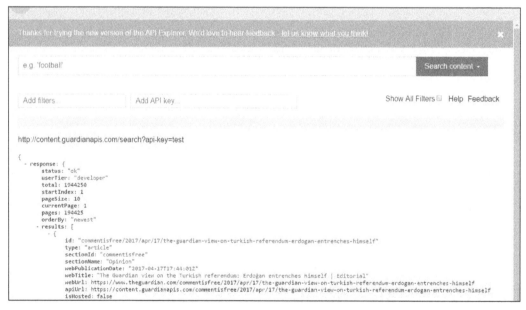

Exploring The Guardian's API

This useful web page allows you to construct your access URL by inputting the various filters available. The available filters can be accessed by selecting them from the **Add filters...** option box. Adding a filter adds a corresponding text box to the page, which can be used to specify the value for the filter.

For an example, suppose we want to search for articles mentioning `brexit` in the Opinion section of The Guardian between **01-06-2016** and **25-06-2016** (please note the British date format of dd-mm-yyyy as this is a UK website). The required API end point URL can be constructed from the preceding page by selecting the filters and then specifying the values. Take a look at the following completed web page to get the hang of the process:

Interactively creating API URL

We can directly use the URL generated to make our API call. This interface makes the URL creation a very simple process. The next step is to query it and then parse the JSON response to extract the required information.

Once we have generated the URL, we make the API call and then use the JSON returned by the call to extract the data. Let's use the same example as previously to extract the required data:

```
# The uri extracted from the online page

URI = "http://content.guardianapis.com/search?from-date=1016-06-01&to-
date=2016-06-25&section=commentisfree&q=brexit&api-key=xxxxxxxxxxxxx"

# Making the API call

json_res <- getURL(URI, .mapUnicode=TRUE)
```

Once we have the response from the API call, we again have to parse the JSON result to get the data. To parse a JSON, it is very important to know the structure of the object. Here we are in luck, as the same web page that helped us in creating the URL will also give a sample of results that we can use to find out the structure of the JSON response. The image shown here gives the structure of the API call we have just executed:

```
{
- response: {
    status: "ok"
    userTier: "developer"
    total: 587
    startIndex: 1
    pageSize: 10
    currentPage: 1
    pages: 59
    orderBy: "relevance"
  - results: [
    - {
        id: "commentisfree/2016/jun/21/brexit-damage-health-drug-research-funding-free-treatment-europe"
        type: "article"
        sectionId: "commentisfree"
        sectionName: "Opinion"
        webPublicationDate: "2016-06-21T17:31:19Z"
        webTitle: "How Brexit could damage our health | Christopher Birt"
        webUrl: https://www.theguardian.com/commentisfree/2016/jun/21/brexit-damage-health-drug-research-funding-free-treatment-europe
        apiUrl: https://content.guardianapis.com/commentisfree/2016/jun/21/brexit-damage-health-drug-research-funding-free-treatment-europe
        isHosted: false
      }
    - {
        id: "commentisfree/2016/jun/25/why-leaving-brexit-britain"
        type: "article"
        sectionId: "commentisfree"
        sectionName: "Opinion"
        webPublicationDate: "2016-06-25T07:29:08Z"
```

JSON structure for parsing

The structure of result is a very simple one, which is good news for us as it simplifies our data extraction logic. Please revisit the parsing process explained in an earlier chapter to find out how this JSON can be parsed.

To parse this JSON we need to enter the `results` object, gather all its elements as an array, and then extract all the fields as string fields. The code that will do this is quite straightforward and can be easily written based on our earlier excursions. But there is an extra complexity here. Typically, for an article search, you will get multiple results and not all of those results will be returned in a single API call. We would need to solve this problem if we want to extract all our news articles' information.

To do this we need to pay attention to the other fields in the JSON response; we have two parameters called `pagesize` and `pages`. The `pagesize` parameter tells us the number of responses in a page and `pages` parameter gives us the total number of pages. We can combine these two pieces of information and write code so that we iterate the required number of pages, making multiple calls, and combine all that information in to a resultant DataFrame, which will be our final output. Here is the code that will complete this process:

```
# Find out the number of pages

num_pages = json_res %>%
    enter_object("response") %>%
    spread_values(num_pages = jnumber("pages"))
num_pages = num_pages$num_pages

# Initialize an empty data frame

out_df = data.frame()
for (num in 1:num_pages){
    uriTemplate <- "http://content.guardianapis.com/search?from-
date=1016-06-01&to-date=2016-06-25&section=commentisfree&q=brexit&api-
key=xxxxxxxxxxxxxxxxxxxxxxxx&page=%s"
    apiurl<- sprintf(uriTemplate,num)
    json_res <- getURL(apiurl, .mapUnicode=TRUE)
    urls <- as.data.frame(json_res %>%
enter_object("response") %>%
enter_object("results")  %>%
            gather_array() %>%
                spread_values(url = jstring("webUrl"),
                type =   jstring("type"),
                sectionName = jstring("sectionName"),
```

```
                        webTitle = jstring("webTitle"),
                        sectionId = jstring("sectionId")
                                     ))
    urls$document.id <- NULL
    urls$array.index <- NULL
    out_df = rbind(out_df, urls)
    Sys.sleep(10)
}
```

An important part of the preceding code is the `Sys.sleep(10)`; this code instruction makes the execution of our code pause for specified time period, here `10` seconds, which is important when we are querying a data provider repeatedly and want to avoid hitting their ceiling API call rate.

The preceding code will compile a DataFrame; a part of which is shown here:

	url	type	sectionName	webTitle	sectionId
1	https://www.theguardian.com/commentisfree/2016...	article	Opinion	How Brexit could damage our health	Christopher Birt	commentisfree
2	https://www.theguardian.com/commentisfree/2016...	article	Opinion	Why I will be leaving Brexit Britain	Oliver Imhof	commentisfree
3	https://www.theguardian.com/commentisfree/2016...	article	Opinion	Brexit stands as a warning to American conservatives	commentisfree
4	https://www.theguardian.com/commentisfree/2016...	article	Opinion	The dispossessed voted for Brexit. Jeremy Corbyn of...	commentisfree
5	https://www.theguardian.com/commentisfree/2016...	article	Opinion	The leftwing case for Brexit (one day)	commentisfree
6	https://www.theguardian.com/commentisfree/2016...	article	Opinion	A Brexit won't stop cheap labour coming to Britain	L...	commentisfree
7	https://www.theguardian.com/commentisfree/2016...	article	Opinion	Brexit supporters have unleashed furies even they c...	commentisfree
8	https://www.theguardian.com/commentisfree/2016...	article	Opinion	Brexit could start a disastrous EU drift to the east	An...	commentisfree
9	https://www.theguardian.com/commentisfree/2016...	article	Opinion	My advice to Brexit battlers: forget Hitler, think Welli...	commentisfree

DataFrame with the links data

HTML scraping from the links – the bigger monster

Even after the elaborate first step, we are still not close to extracting the textual data. The procedure for extracting text is easy to explain: iterate through the DataFrame, visit each URL, and extract the text data. Those who are familiar with the complexities of web page scraping will understand the sarcasm of the previous lines. We will be using the `rvest`, `tidyjson`, `magrittr`, and `RCurl` libraries for our scraping process, which we assume are installed on your system.

The general steps involved in any web scraping task are as follows:

1. Extract the HTML source of the web page.
2. Analyze the HTML source of the web page.
3. Find tags of interest that contain the information.
4. Extract the data for those tags programmatically and repeat the whole process.

The first step is extracting the HTML source of the page. If you look at the DataFrame of results that we extracted in the last step, it contains a column that will give us the URL of the news story. After that, we can read the `read_html` function to extract the HTML tree of the URL.

```
# Extracting the HTML data

b <- read_html(curl(url, handle = curl::new_handle("useragent" =
"Mozilla/5.0")))
```

It is important to add the `handle` argument, as it identifies our system as a legitimate client and we avoid being timed out by the server.

The next step is the toughest part of the process. Every web page is unique and yet similar in some sense. As we are looking at web pages only from a single source, the web pages will be similar, but even with that information we will have to analyze the source to find out how we can extract the textual data. Take a look at the HTML source of one of the URLs that we extracted:

Web source of a sample URL

You can observe that the HTML source of our URL is a scary sight, and it runs for some 2,000 lines. How can we ever get the required information from this huge garbled text?

This is the part of scraping where you go through the source looking for some clues, which can be used for the parsing. In our case, the clue is the text of the article. We also have access to the web page that is generated by this source. The web page will give us the text that we are looking for in our source. See the next image in which we have searched for some of the text snippets on the web page; it will reveal a very repeatable structure that we can use:

```
Last modified on Friday 17 February 2017 <span class="content__dateline-time">11.53 GMT</span>
</time>
</p>
<meta itemprop="dateModified" content="2017-02-17T11:53:44+0000">
</div>
<div class="content__article-body from-content-api js-article__body" itemprop="articleBody" data-test-id="article-review-body">
<p><span class="drop-cap"><span class="drop-cap__inner">Mu</span></span>ch of the EU debate is conducted at the level of insults and unsupported claims and assertions. But, if we
care to look, there are many areas where it is not difficult to identify the effects of Brexit. <a href="https://www.theguardian.com/society/health" data-link-name="auto-linked-tag"
data-component="auto-linked-tag" class="u-underline">Health</a> and health services are one such area - and Brexit could be devastating.</p>
<p>European health insurance cards, which have for many years guaranteed emergency treatment for Britons wherever they are in the EU would of course disappear in case of Brexit -
leaving the UK government to negotiate new arrangements with each individual country. While this is widely known, the right of EU citizens to undergo any kind of healthcare anywhere
in the EU is perhaps less familiar - possibly because it is the result of much more recent EU legislation. It is now not unusual for UK residents to choose to have hip replacements in
France, or to travel to Belgium for spectacles, or to Budapest for dental treatment, all paid for (as according to EU legislation) by the local UK "purchaser".</p>
<p>Of course the <a href="http://www.bbc.co.uk/news/uk-politics-eu-referendum-36046900" title="" data-link-name="in body link" class="u-underline">1.2 million Brits</a> living in
other EU countries - including around 300,000 in Spain - rely on these facilities. And we should not forget this freedom of movement works both ways - to our benefit. It is thanks to
an <a href="https://www.theguardian.com/society/2016/jun/14/brexit-nhs-health-social-care-disabled-people-eu-referendum" title="" data-link-name="in body link" class="u-
underline">influx of medical professionals from around the EU</a> that the NHS and care services are able to continue to operate at such a high standard. Would all these vital health
care workers suddenly no longer be welcome?</p>
<aside class="element element-rich-link element--thumbnail element-rich-link--not-upgraded" data-component="rich-link" data-link-name="rich-link-1 | 1">
<div class="rich-link">
<div class="rich-link__container">
<div class="rich-link__header">
<h1 class="rich-link__title">What would Brexit mean for the NHS, social care and disabled people? | Denis Campbell, David Brindle and Patrick Butler</h1>
</div>
<div class="rich-link__read-more">
<div class="rich-link__arrow">
<span class="inline-arrow-in-circle inline-icon ">
```

Web source of a sample URL (continued)

If you look closely at the image, you will observe that all the textual data is contained within <p> (paragraph tag of HTML) tags. This is interesting information as this will make our parsing process a breeze.

 Please keep in mind that the HTML structures of web pages are not only unique but they are very dynamic in nature. A simple change to the structure can break our nicely written scraping routine. To fix any such changes, the process is same as before. You go fishing in the source and find out information that can be used for parsing.

Now that we know the tags of interest, we can easily find them out using the `html_nodes` function from the library:

```
# Find the nodes for paragraph tags

paragraph_nodes = html_nodes(b, xpath = ".//p")
```

The preceding line of code will search for all paragraph nodes in the tree structure of the HTML source and extract them for processing. Once you have the nodes extracted, the next step is super simple:

```
# Tidy up by removing whitespaces, newlines and collapsing all nodes
into a single node

nodes<-trimws(html_text(paragraph_nodes))
nodes<-gsub("\n", "", nodes)
nodes<-gsub("  ", "", nodes)
content = paste(nodes, collapse = " ")
```

Now we have the textual content of the web page extracted. The following image gives the extracted textual content:

> content
[1] "Tuesday 21 June 2016 18.31 BSTLast modified on Friday 17 February 2017 11.53 GMT Much of the EU debate is conducted at the level of insults and unsupported claims and assertions. But, if we care to look, there are many areas where it is not difficult to identify the effects of Brexit. Health and health services are one such area - and Brexit could be devastating. European health insurance cards, which have for many years guaranteed emergency treatment for Britons wherever they are in the EU would of course disappear in case of Brexit - leaving the UK government to negotiate new arrangements with each individual country. While this is widely known, the right of EU citizens to undergo any kind of healthcare anywhere in the EU is perhaps less familiar - possibly because it is the result of much more recent EU legislation. It is now not unusual for UK residents to choose to have hip replacements in France, or to travel to Belgium for spectacles, or to Budapest for dental treatment, al... <truncated>

Extracted textual content

We can iterate the whole process for all of the DataFrame to end up with the content for each of our URLs.

Sentiment trend analysis

You may wonder why we are doing a sentiment-based analysis again, and the reason is a simple one: it is obvious analysis to do when the data is a large corpus of text. In our case, it is even more important as news and sentiment are closely related. If you can deduce the sentiment-based theme of a large corpus of news data, then it means that you have gained an important insight into what might be a long and tedious process of classifying each document manually. Simple at it may seem, it is one of the most coveted tools of any text data miner.

For our use case, we will do an interesting analysis. We will go through The Guardian's articles with a mention of Indian Prime Minister Narendra Modi and try to see how the sentiment trends about him have changed over the years.

Getting the data – not again

In the last section, we came to understand the building blocks of data gathering from normal web pages. We will build a strategy around that procedure to extract the necessary data for our analysis. Please note, we will skip the usual step of building the URL and making the API call as they must be very familiar to the reader by now.

Based on the discussion in the previous section, we have built three utility functions, which will do most of the data extraction:

- `extract_all_links`: This function will get all the links for any given query that we construct. Here, our query will be an exact search for the name `narendra modi`.

- `extract_url_data`: This is a wrapper function that will complete the whole process that we described in the last section.

- `extract_all_data`: This is the function that will take the links generated by the first function and then extract content from all of those links. As we are doing a good amount of scraping, we have built in some simple error handling to ensure smooth data extraction.

The data required can be easily extracted using these utility functions, with the code given here:

```
# Extract all links data frame
links_df <- extract_all_links()

# Seperate the links from the data frame
links <- links_df[,"url"]

# Get me all the data
data_df <- extract_all_data(links)
```

This DataFrame will be the starting point of all our analyzes. Before we start our analysis, we note that we don't have any field that will give us the data about the publication of the article. So, we will create the publishing date by finding it out from the article text. We will use a regular expression, which will extract the first occurrence of a date from the article text and append it to the DataFrame. The following code snippet will achieve this task:

```
for (i in 1: nrow(articles_df)){
    m <- regexpr("\\d{1,2} \\w{3,9} \\d{4}", articles_df[i,
"content"], perl=TRUE)
    if(m !=-1){
        articles_df[i,"article_date"] <- regmatches(articles_df[i,
"content"],m)
    }
}
```

The following image shows how our DataFrame will look once all the pre-processing steps are done:

type	sectionName	webTitle	sectionId	content	article_date
gallery	Art and design	Photo highlights of the day	artanddesign	The Guardianâ€™s picture editors bring you a select...	8 May 2014
gallery	Art and design	The 20 photographs of the week	artanddesign	Jim Powell Saturday 24 May 2014 13.27Â BSTFirst pu...	24 May 2014
article	Art and design	Sydney Biennale 2016: Belgiorno-Nettis family may b...	artanddesign	Chairman Phillip Keir is hopeful Belgiorno-Nettis famil...	2 December 2014
article	Art and design	Buddha statue found to have been stolen will be ret...	artanddesign	Kushan Buddha statue, dating from second century, ...	4 January 2015
article	Australia news	Australian coalmining is entering â€" structural decli...	australia-news	Demand from India and China predicted to falter due ...	5 May 2014
article	Australia news	David Cameron, Narendra Modi and Xi jinping to addr...	australia-news	Leaders of Britain, China and India will speak to parlia...	14 October 2014
liveblog	Australia news	Clashes over education, GST and petrol â€" as it hap...	australia-news	Senate to consider second tranche of national secur...	28 October 2014
liveblog	Australia news	G20: David Cameron addresses Australian parliament ...	australia-news	British prime minister outlines plans to counter extre...	14 November 2014

Final DataFrame

Basic descriptive statistics – the usual

In the previous chapters we have learned the importance of doing a through descriptive exploration of the data. We will continue with this trend in this chapter also. We will start by looking at the distribution of the sections in which the name Narendra Modi appears. The following code snippet finds the distribution of articles across the sections:

```
section_summary <- articles_df %>%
                group_by(sectionName) %>%
                summarise(num_articles = n())

ggplot(data = section_summary, aes(x = sectionName, y = num_articles))
+
    geom_bar(aes(fill = sectionName), stat = "identity") +
    xlab("Section") + ylab("Total Articles Count") + ggtitle("Articles
distribution by Section") + theme_bw()+
    theme(axis.text.x = element_text(size = 20,angle = 90, hjust =
1,vjust=0.5))
```

The following image shows the different sections in which the articles about Mr. Modi tend to end up. By looking at the image, you can find a few anomalies; for example, the mention of Mr. Modi in the football section is not particularly useful for our analysis. So we will prune our data to include only the sections in which we have a minimum of 20 articles:

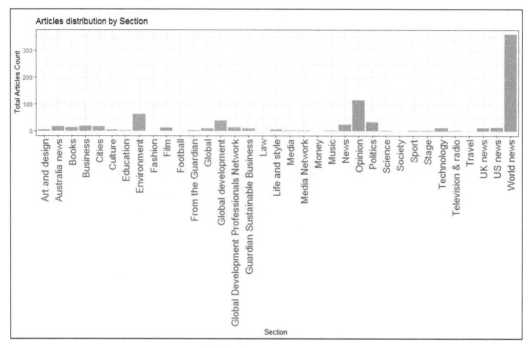

Distribution across sections

The following code snippet will do the filtering based on the number of articles:

```
section_names <- as.data.frame(articles_df %>% group_by(sectionName)
%>% summarise(num_articles = n()) %>%
                                filter(num_articles>20) %>%
select(sectionName))
selected_section_articles <- articles_df[articles_df$sectionName %in%
section_names[,"sectionName"],]
articles_df <- selected_section_articles
```

Next, we want to see how the articles are distributed across the time period. Please note that we have selected a 15-year time period for our data collection. We expect the article count to be low in the time period before Mr. Modi became the prime minister of India and then to steadily rise afterward. As we don't directly have the year of publication, we will also generate that data from the date field. The following code snippet will generate the year-wise distribution of the article counts for us:

```
articles_df[,"article_date_formatted"] <- as.Date(articles_
df[,"article_date"],"%d %B %Y")
articles_df[,"article_year"]<- format(as.Date(articles_df[,"article_
date_formatted"]),"%Y")
year_article_summary <- articles_df %>% group_by(article_year) %>%
summarise(num_articles = n())
ggplot(data = year_article_summary, aes(x = article_year, y = num_
articles)) + guides(fill=FALSE) +
    geom_bar(aes(fill = article_year), stat = "identity") +
    theme(legend.position = "none") +
    xlab("Year") + ylab("Total Articles Count") + ggtitle("Articles
distribution by Year") +
    theme(axis.text.x=element_text(angle=90,hjust=1,vjust=0.5)) +
theme_bw()
```

The image generated by the code snippet is as follows. It confirms our prediction of having a higher article count after the year 2014, which was the year when Mr. Modi was elected:

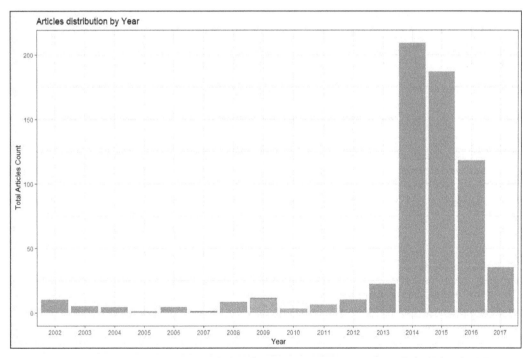

Article distribution across years

Numerical sentiment trends

In the previous chapters we have touched upon sentiment analysis and we know that we can interpret sentiment in multiple ways. First, we will try to look at the numerical sentiment trends that our data exhibits. Before we proceed to the actual code and inference part, let us have a very brief refresher about numerical sentiments. (Please refer to *Chapter 2, Twitter – What's Happening with 140 Characters,* for a detailed discussion).

Every text composition will have words of polarity. The polarity of a word can be either negative or positive. To find out the overall polarity of a text we can gather the numerical count of positive and negative polarity words. Subtracting the negative count from the positive count will give us an approximate measure of the overall polarity. We have to keep in mind that the subtleties of language are tough to capture with such a simple scheme, but this method is surprisingly effective in practice.

Coming back to our use case, we want to find out how the aggregated numerical sentiments have varied for Mr. Modi. We can do this easily by determining the sentiments for each article we have in the corpus and then finding out the mean sentiment score for all the years. The following code snippet will perform the task for us:

```
sentiments_df <- get_nrc_sentiment(articles_df[,"content"])

articles_sentiment_df <- cbind(articles_df,sentiments_df)

articles_sentiment_df$sentiment <- articles_sentiment_df$positive -
articles_sentiment_df$negative

sentiments_year_summary_df <- articles_sentiment_df %>%
                          select(-c(positive,negative)) %>%
                          group_by(article_year) %>%
                          summarise(mean_sentiment =
mean(sentiment))
```

This generates a DataFrame for us in which we have the mean sentiment score for all the articles in a year. We can plot this data so that we can visually interpret how the trends have varied:

```
ggplot(data=sentiments_year_summary_df, aes(x=article_year, y=mean_
sentiment, group=1)) +
    geom_line(colour="red", linetype="dashed", size=1.5) +
    geom_point(colour="red", size=2, shape=21, fill="white")+
    ylab("Sentiment score") +
    ggtitle("Numeric Sentiment across years")+ theme_bw()
```

The plot generated by the code snippet is given here. It gives an interesting implication, as the sentiment scores have increased sharply from the lows of 2002 and they seem to settle in a median range:

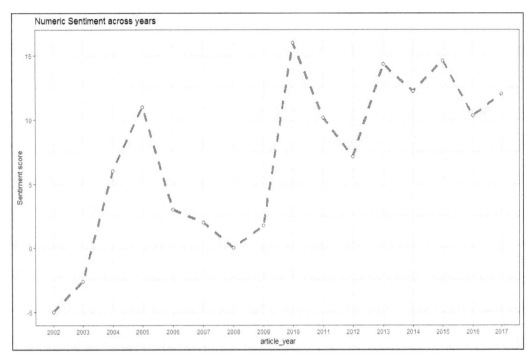

Numerical sentiment across years

This may seem like too much of an aggregate analysis. Let's try to zoom in on this aggregate chart and see if we can determine the sentiment scores as they vary across each month of the time period. Such a graph will allow us to clearly see if there was a specific month in which there was a sharp increase in the overall sentiments. To do that, we have to make two adjustments to the data: we have to group by the combined `Year-Month` instead of just the year. We can generate that data easily by using a function from `zoo` library, which will take an input date and convert it into a `Year-mon` format. Once we have done that conversion, the rest of the code is quite similar. The following code snippet will generate the summary DataFrame for us:

```
articles_sentiment_df[,"date_year_month"] = as.yearmon(articles_
sentiment_df[,"article_date_formatted"])
yearmon_num_sentiment <- articles_sentiment_df
yearmon_summary_df <- yearmon_num_sentiment %>%
                select(-c(positive,negative)) %>%
                group_by(date_year_month) %>%
```

```
                    summarise(mean_sentiment = mean(sentiment))

ggplot(data=yearmon_summary_df, aes(x=as.Date(date_year_month),
y=mean_sentiment, group=1)) +
    geom_line(colour="black", size=1.5) +
    geom_point(colour="red", size=1.5, shape=21, fill="white")+
    ylab("Sentiment score") + xlab("Year-Month") +
    scale_x_date(labels = function(x) format(x, "%Y-%b"), date_breaks
= "1 year") +
    theme(axis.text.x=element_text(angle=90,hjust=1,vjust=0.5))+
    ggtitle("Numeric Sentiment across years broken by months")+ theme_
bw()
```

The resultant chart generated by the preceding code snippet is given here:

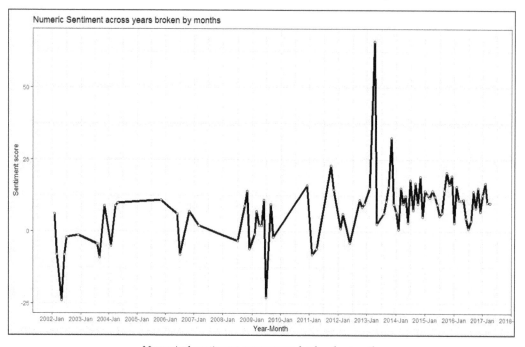

Numerical sentiment across years broken by month

This is a very interesting plot. If you look closely, you will find a sharp increase in the overall sentiment around the time period of January 2013. This increase is significant as this was about the time when the PM candidacy of Mr. Modi was announced. Before this the sentiment score is a mixed bag and revolves around a median figure. The graph can be interpreted as a gradual build-up of positive sentiments starting from the candidacy announcement. Another interesting point is the shift in range of the sentiments after the election of Mr. Modi as prime minister; before that, the sentiments vary a lot but since then they tend to cluster in a very narrow range and rarely venture into negative territory.

An interesting analysis for the reader to perform would be the distribution of sentiments across the different types of article. Based on that analysis, we could see if there is a particular class of news that is contributing a large chunk of positive or negative values to the overall figure.

Emotion-based sentiment trends

The other form of sentiment analysis that we have explored is based on the classification of words into different sentiments. By first classifying words into categories, such as `fear`, `joy`, `disgust`, and so on, and then creating a sum across all of those categories, we can find out the approximate composition of a text. This gives an interesting insight into the different, sometimes opposing, emotions exhibited by the same article.

We will begin our analysis by starting from the initial DataFrame and aggregating the values of all the emotions across all the articles. This gives us the most prevalent emotion among our corpus. The code for producing this analysis is as follows:

```
sentiments_summary_df <-articles_sentiment_df %>%
                        select(-c(positive,negative)) %>%
                        summarise(anger = sum(anger),anticipation =
sum(anticipation),disgust = sum(disgust), fear= sum(fear) , joy =
sum(joy) , sadness = sum(sadness), surprise = sum(surprise), trust
=sum(trust))

sentiments_summary_df <- as.data.frame(t(sentiments_summary_df))
sentiments_summary_df <- cbind(row.names(sentiments_summary_df),
sentiments_summary_df)

colnames(sentiments_summary_df)<- c("sentiment", "count")

ggplot(data = sentiments_summary_df, aes(x = reorder(sentiment,
count), y = count)) +
    geom_bar(aes(fill = sentiment), stat = "identity") +
    theme(legend.position = "none") + guides(fill=FALSE)+ coord_flip()
+
    xlab("Sentiment") + ylab("Total Sentiment Count") +
    ggtitle("Overall sentiment across all articles") +
    theme(axis.text.x=element_text(angle=90,hjust=1,vjust=0.5)) +
theme_bw()
```

The image generated by the code snippet is given here:

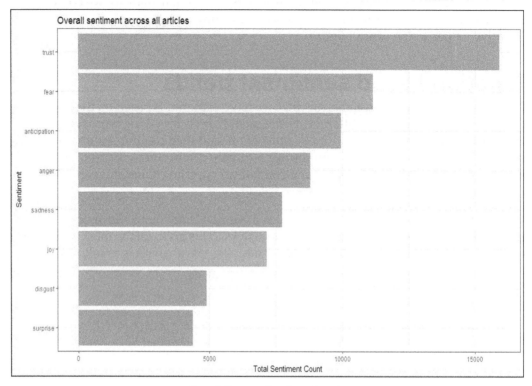

Cumulative emotional sentiments

The most prevalent emotion among all our articles is `trust`, followed by `fear`. This looks a little contradictory, but may happen if we have a skewed distribution of these emotions during the time period. Next, we want to check if such a skewed distribution exists in the data or not. We can do this analysis by breaking down the emotion counts grouped by year instead of aggregating it across all our data.

The following code snippet will break down our data into yearly buckets and plot the yearly sentiments over time. This will allow us to take a look at the distribution of each emotion across the years:

```
sentiments_year_summary_df <- articles_sentiment_df %>%
                        select(-c(positive,negative)) %>%
                        group_by(article_year) %>%
                        summarise(anger =
mean(anger),anticipation = mean(anticipation),disgust = mean(disgust),
fear= mean(fear) , joy = mean(joy) , sadness = mean(sadness), surprise
= mean(surprise), trust =mean(trust)) %>%
                        melt
```

```
names(sentiments_year_summary_df) <- c("Year", "sentiment", "Sum_
value")
ggplot(data = sentiments_year_summary_df, aes(x = Year, y = Sum_value,
group = sentiment)) +
    geom_line(size = 2.5, alpha = 0.7, aes(color = sentiment)) +
    geom_point(size = 0.5) +
    ylim(0, NA) +
    ylab("Mean sentiment score") +
    ggtitle("Sentiment across years")+ theme_bw()
```

The chart generated by the code snippet is given here. It confirms the doubt that we had about the skewed distribution of emotions across the time period:

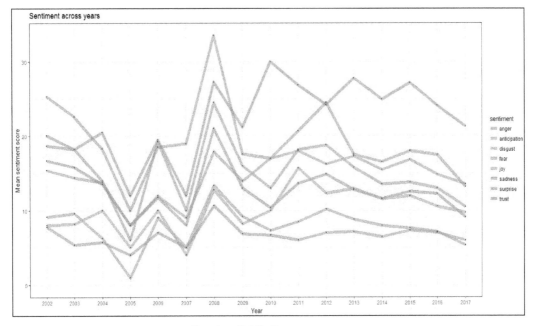

Emotion distribution across years

We see that, initially, the emotion of fear was dominant, but it has been steadily decreasing in the subsequent years. Whereas, the emotion of trust was initially low, but it displays steep ascent in the past few years. Together, these two are the reason that we end up with a contradicting overall emotion count. This analysis underlines the important point of digging deeper when the data seems to display such anomalies.

We will end this section with an analysis of the emotions that are displayed across different sections. We will see if there is a particular section of news that is contributing the bulk of a particular emotion:

```
sentiments_year_summary_df <- articles_sentiment_df %>%
                            select(-c(positive,negative)) %>%
                            group_by(sectionName) %>%
                            summarise(anger =
mean(anger),anticipation = mean(anticipation),disgust = mean(disgust),
fear= mean(fear) , joy = mean(joy) , sadness = mean(sadness), surprise
= mean(surprise), trust =mean(trust))%>%melt
p <- ggplot(data=sentiments_year_summary_df, mapping=aes(x=variable,
y=value)) + geom_bar(aes(fill = variable), stat = "identity")
p <- p + facet_grid(facets = sectionName ~ ., margins = FALSE) +
theme_bw()
print(p)
```

The chart generated by the code snippet is given here. It provides some information, but we don't see a very distinctive trend that we can call out:

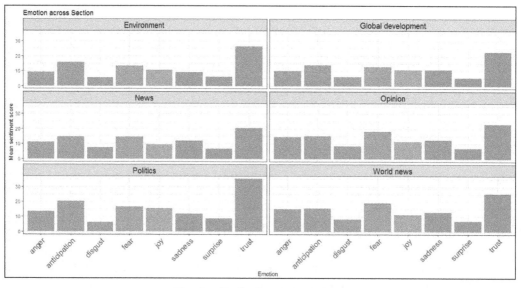

Emotion distribution across sections

We see that a lot of the trust score is generated by **Politics**, while **Opinion** and **World news** are a major contributor to the emotion of fear. This is not very conclusive, but we encourage the reader to dig deeper and find out if we can determine the percentage contribution of each emotion per section. This analysis will put a numerical value to each of the emotion-generating sections.

Topic modeling

In the most basic words, topic modeling is the process of finding out the hidden topics that exist in any document. We will try to explain the basic concept of topic modeling by using an analogy of a lavish buffet spread.

Suppose you go to a wedding that features a large number of items from various cuisines. You, being an absolute foodie, go to all the counters and collect a very large number of items at your table (with the obvious disapproving looks of other guests). Now one of your other friends arrives at the table and takes a look at the large number of food items at your table. He tries to guess the various cuisines on offer from the snapshot of items you have collected. He is able to do so because there is an association between the food item and the cuisine it comes from. For example, if you have various types of pasta and sea foods on your table, he could guess that a major cuisine at the buffet was Italian. This is very much similar to the thought process of exploring topic modeling.

We assume that, while the content was being developed, a news article in our case, the writer had some major themes in his mind. Each of these themes can be linked to a collection of words. The process of writing then becomes deciding on the themes, selecting words from those themes, and composing those using rules of grammar and language. The end result of this process is our article.

Topic modeling assumes that there is a hidden structure in the data, which is a direct result of the various themes the writer had selected at the time of its writing (as explained previously). Then, we assume that every topic is identified by a distribution over a collection of words. Topics have different words with associated probabilities, and these probabilities can be used to distinguish topics. For example, a topic about cricket will have higher probabilities for words such as "bat", "ball", etc., whereas a topic about finance will have higher probabilities for words such as "money", "stocks", and so on.

For the process to find out these topics, along with the words associated with each topic, we will follow the following set of steps:

1. We assign topics with a random set of words for the initiation.

2. We go through the collection word by word and reassign them to topics in which similar words occur. This reassignment is the most mathematical and tough to understand part of the algorithm. We can demonstrate this with an example. Suppose we assign a topic randomly and then encounter the word "stock". Now, in the random collection of topics we will have some document in which the word "stock" already appears. So, initially, we can assign the word "stock" to a similar topic to that of the other document containing "stock".

3. We reiterate the process and keep reassigning words using similar logic. The actual logic is a bit of advanced math and is hence excluded from this book.

4. Once we reach a point where the reassignment of words to different topics doesn't change our overall topic model distribution, we break our process.

So, this completes our basic introduction to *topic modeling*. Please bear in mind that this is as vanilla as it gets. The interested reader can refer to the many excellent papers on the topic, including the one introducing **Latent Dirichlet Allocation (LDA)** by *David Blei, Andrew Ng* and *Michael Jordan*.

In our second use case for textual data, we plan to perform topic modeling on an interesting collection of news articles. We all know that in the last US presidential election the victory of Donald Trump was a surprising event for almost all of the world. There were three major events in his election campaign:

- **Official announcement of his candidacy**: June 16, 2015
- **Confirmation of Mr. Trump as the republican candidate**: July 16, 2016
- **Election date**: November 8, 2016

We want to collect news articles written about Mr. Trump in the opinion section of The Guardian in two phases:

- **Phase 1**: June 16, 2015–July 16, 2016
- **Phase 2**: July 17, 2016–November 8, 2016

Once we have collected the data for these two periods, we will try to build topic models on both. This will help us to investigate whether the major topics of discussion changed or not in the course of Mr. Trump's campaign.

Getting to the data

For the topic modeling exercise we have planned, we will extract news articles in the different time periods. For once in our journey, the data extraction part is a little more straightforward, mostly due to the extensive work we have done on developing the data extraction pipeline in the previous section. The only part of the process that we have to adapt for this section is the `query` and the `date range` part of the query. Once we have made the necessary changes to the API endpoint, we can use the same three functions we developed in the last section for the data extraction. We will give the changed API end point and then the function calls that are required for the data extraction:

```
endpoint_url = http://content.guardianapis.com/search?from-
date=2016-04-01&to-date=2016-07-01&section=commentisfree&page=1&page-
size=200&q=brexit&api-key=xxxxxxxx
```

```
# Extract all links data frame
links_df <- extract_all_links()

# Seperate the links from the data frame
links <- links_df[,"url"]

# Get me all the data
data_df <- extract_all_data(links)
```

This will get us all the data for a particular date range. As our analysis will deal with finding topics in different time periods, we will have to execute the same code with appropriate values for the `from-date` and `to-date` sections. Once we have extracted all the textual data for all time intervals we can start with our analysis.

Basic descriptive analysis

As always, we will start with some basic descriptive analysis because we know that starting simple is the right start for all analytics use cases. The first article of interest is usually the distribution of articles. Our first time interval starts from the point where Mr. Trump officially announced his candidacy for the post of president and ends when he was officially selected by the Republican Party as its candidate. Our second time interval starts from his official selection as their candidate and ends just before when the results were announced. We are interested to see if there is a stark difference in the average number of total articles in these two time periods.

The following code snippet will do the task of creating this summarization for the two phases and plot the result for us. We will also create some date-type columns as we did in the last section:

```
trump_phase1[,'time_interval'] <- 'Phase 1'
trump_phase2[,'time_interval'] <- 'Phase 2'

trump_df <- rbind(trump_phase1,trump_phase2)

articles_df <- trump_df

for (i in 1: nrow(articles_df)){
  m <- regexpr("\\d{1,2} \\w{3,9} \\d{4}", articles_df[i, "content"],
perl=TRUE)
  if(m !=-1){
    articles_df[i,"article_date"] <- regmatches(articles_df[i,
"content"],m)
  }
}

articles_df[,"article_date_formatted"] <- as.Date(articles_
df[,"article_date"],"%d %B %Y")
```

```
articles_df[,"date_year_month"] = as.yearmon(articles_df[,"article_
date_formatted"])


articles_across_phases <- articles_df %>%
                          group_by(time_interval) %>%
                          summarise(average_article_count = n()/n_
distinct(date_year_month))

p <- ggplot(data=articles_across_phases, mapping=aes(x=time_interval,
y=average_article_count)) + geom_bar(aes(fill = time_interval), stat =
"identity")
p <- p + theme_bw() + guides(fill = FALSE) +
   theme(axis.text.x = element_text(size = 15)) +
   ylab("Mean number of articles") + xlab("Phase") +
   ggtitle("Average article count across phases") + theme(strip.text =
(element_text(size = 15)))
print(p)
```

The graph generated by the code snippet is given here. The result is as we would
expect: the average number of articles goes way up when Mr. Trump is confirmed
by the Republican Party as their official candidate:

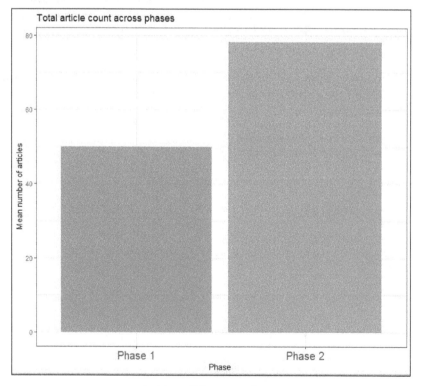

Average articles across phases

Another interesting descriptive analysis is to take a look at the average number of words per article and see how that has changed as we go along the timeline. This will give us a feel of how much coverage was given to Mr. Trump by the writers of the Opinion section of The Guardian. The following code will generate the chart that we want to observe:

```
trump_wc <- Corpus(VectorSource(articles_df[,"content"]))
temp_articles <-tm_map(trump_wc,content_transformer(tolower))
dtm <- DocumentTermMatrix(temp_articles)
word_count <- rowSums(as.matrix(dtm))
articles_df[,"word_count"] <- word_count

wordcount_across_time <- articles_df %>%
  group_by(date_year_month) %>%
  summarise(average_article_count = mean(word_count))


ggplot(data=wordcount_across_time, aes(x=as.Date(date_year_month),
y=average_article_count)) +
  geom_line(colour="orange", size=1.5) +
  ylab("Average word count") + xlab("Month - Year") +
  ggtitle("Word count across the time line")+ theme_bw() +
  scale_x_date(date_labels = "%b %Y",date_breaks = "2 month") +
  geom_vline(xintercept = as.numeric(as.Date("2016-07-01")),
linetype=4)
```

The image generated by the preceding code snippet is given here. We have marked the month of the confirmation of Mr. Trump's candidacy with a vertical line so that we are able to clearly differentiate the average word count before and after that event:

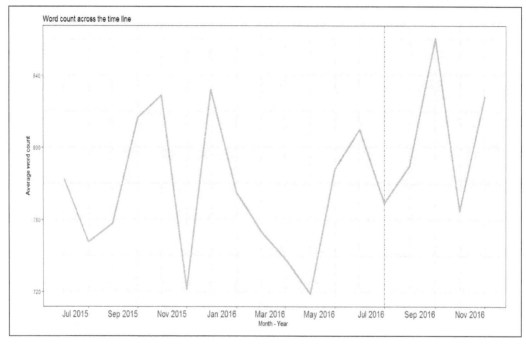

Time variation of article word count

We observe that once the candidacy was confirmed the word count has a slight upward swing. Immediately after the confirmation there is a stark rise in the average word count, which probably reflects the in-depth discussion of Mr. Trump once it was confirmed that he was officially in the running for the title of *Most Powerful Person in the World*. This is quite expected and we assume this pattern to be consistent across other news sources too.

Topic modeling for Mr. Trump's phases

We will separate our data into the appropriate phases, and perform the cleaning and pre-processing tasks for both of those DataFrames. Once we have cleaned and pre-processed the data for both the phases, we will fit topic models to both of them and try to analyze the results of those models.

Cleaning the data

The first step in any data-mining task is to perform some data-cleaning tasks. The specific methods selected for cleaning will often depend on the nature of the data. We will perform a few very basic steps to achieve the required sanity of our data. The following code will perform the basic cleaning tasks for us. The code is commented to give the function that we are performing. We have already explained the logic of these functions in *Chapter 2, Twitter – What's Happening with 140 Characters,* and the user can refer to it for more details:

```
articles_phase1 <- articles_df %>% filter(time_interval == "Phase 1")
articles_phase1 <- Corpus(VectorSource(articles_phase1[,"content"]))

# Convert all text to lower case
articles_phase1 <-tm_map(articles_phase1,content_transformer(tolower))

# Remove all punctuations from the text
articles_phase1 <- tm_map(articles_phase1, removePunctuation)

# Remove all numbers from the text
articles_phase1 <- tm_map(articles_phase1, removeNumbers)

# Remove all english stopwords from the text
articles_phase1 <- tm_map(articles_phase1, removeWords,
stopwords("english"))

# Remove all whitespaces from the text
articles_phase1 <- tm_map(articles_phase1, stripWhitespace)
```

Pre-processing the data

The most important decision to be taken at this stage is the representation of the documents we want to use. This numerical representation is used by text-mining algorithms. The simplest representation is the bag-of-words representation. In this representation, we find out the total words in the corpus, and each document is represented as the numerical vector of its constituent words.

Here is a very simple example of a term matrix. Suppose we have two documents in the corpus, as given here:

- **Document 1**: Red roses
- **Document 2**: Black cloud

For this simple document corpus, the document term matrix will be as given here:

	Red	Roses	Black	Cloud
Document 1	1	1	0	0
Document 2	0	0	1	1

Before we convert our text data into such a representation, we will also stem the data; that is, we will reduce all the words to their base forms. Once we have completed these two steps, we will have a representation of our document, which we can then use for topic modeling. The following code will perform these two actions:

```
# Stem all word in the text
articles_phase1 <- tm_map(articles_phase1, stemDocument)

# Creating a Document term Matrix
dtm_trump_phase2 <- DocumentTermMatrix(articles_phase1)
```

Please note that we will not include the code for cleaning and processing the second phase of articles. The reader can easily do this themself using the preceding sequence of code.

The modeling part

Once we are done with both of these two tasks, we can proceed with our topic modeling task. We will be using the `topicmodels` package to fit one of the most famous topic models, LDA, using an algorithm called **Gibbs sampling**. The process of fitting a topic model onto our dataset is quite straightforward. It can simply be achieved by calling the LDA function of the package. The following code will generate the topic models for both phases of our data. First, we will analyze the results that we get out of our initial models and then we will discuss what the tuning process may look like if the reader is looking for a more involved reiteration of the process:

```
burnin <- 4000
iter <- 200
thin <- 500
seed <-list(2003,5,63,100001,765)
nstart <- 5
best <- TRUE

#Number of topics
k <- 5
```

```
#Run LDA using Gibbs sampling
ldaOut <-LDA(dtm_trump_phase1,k, method="Gibbs",
             control=list(nstart=nstart, seed = seed, best=best,
burnin = burnin, iter = iter))
```

To develop our model, we set some parameters (mostly defaults from the vignette of the package) and then call the LDA function with the method set as "Gibbs". This selects the particular model-fitting procedure from the set of algorithms that can be used to perform the task. Another important parameter, and also a limitation of LDA, is the number of topics value. It is unlikely that you will be able to know how many types of topics there are in the corpus, so this value is often selected by the practitioners on the basis of domain-knowledge-based intuition. Once we get the initial results, we can go ahead and try different values of this parameter to get better topics.

Analysis of topics

The output of the preceding function will include the probability of each topic for every document in the corpus and the terms associated with each of the topics, among other things. Now comes the tricky part, which makes topic modeling useful but slightly tough to use. Before we come to that, let's see what the top 10 terms associated with each of the topics are for both our phases. The following code will generate those terms:

```
ldaOut.terms <- as.matrix(terms(ldaOut,10))
ldaOut.terms
```

The output of the code is given in the following image:

	Topic 1	Topic 2	Topic 3	Topic 4	Topic 5
[1,]	"like"	"trump"	"women"	"polit"	"american"
[2,]	"trump"	"republican"	"year"	"will"	"muslim"
[3,]	"itâ"	"candid"	"time"	"vote"	"right"
[4,]	"say"	"clinton"	"one"	"govern"	"black"
[5,]	"peopl"	"parti"	"work"	"chang"	"peopl"
[6,]	"just"	"presid"	"life"	"one"	"war"
[7,]	"can"	"campaign"	"men"	"right"	"america"
[8,]	"thing"	"will"	"new"	"leav"	"attack"
[9,]	"get"	"democrat"	"home"	"labour"	"immigr"
[10,]	"know"	"polit"	"itâ"	"world"	"white"

Topics in phase 1

The output will not give us very identifiable topics by itself. It will help us with the terms that can be associated with the topics, and then the user can make a call and label the topic accordingly. For example, it is tough to label **Topic 1** here, but we can see common themes in the other topics. **Topic 5** probably deals with Mr. Trump's major promotion theme. **Topic 2** can be termed Mr. Trump's comparison to the opponent. **Topic 3** is again tough to classify, but **Topic 4** can be attributed to Mr. Trump's appeal to the voters. This is a very subjective task and hence, although the procedure is very powerful, it is far from a magic wand.

Let us complete this discussion by taking a look at the topics from phase 2. The following image gives the similar terms output for the second phase of articles:

```
        Topic 1    Topic 2    Topic 3       Topic 4   Topic 5
 [1,]  "polit"    "year"     "trump"       "women"   "can"
 [2,]  "peopl"    "new"      "clinton"     "itA"     "peopl"
 [3,]  "will"     "one"      "elect"       "even"    "one"
 [4,]  "right"    "also"     "republican"  "just"    "think"
 [5,]  "brexit"   "last"     "campaign"    "trump"   "like"
 [6,]  "now"      "will"     "american"    "said"    "get"
 [7,]  "parti"    "system"   "presid"      "like"    "week"
 [8,]  "left"     "report"   "trumpA"      "say"     "good"
 [9,]  "countri"  "call"     "donald"      "donA"    "just"
[10,]  "econom"   "tax"      "vote"        "right"   "time"
```

Topics in phase 2

The topics in the second phase seem a little more defined. We still have some similar topics to the first phase but the biggest difference is the terms for Topic 1. We clearly see that this topic deals with some policy-related questions. Also gone is the topic from phase 1 that dealt with some controversial topics (refer to *Topic 5* in the earlier image). The story it paints is an interesting one. Post the confirmation of his candidacy, the opinion writers shifted to focus on the policies of Mr. Trump, whereas earlier the focus was not so much on those issues. This capability of topic modeling is what makes it a powerful tool for analyzing a large corpus of textual data.

The results of our primitive experiments are quite interesting. The reader can go back and tinker with the process to arrive at better/different results. There are broadly two ways in which we can achieve a little more refinement of the results:

- Based on the terms we observe in the topics, we can find words that are not very helpful. For example, words such as *year* can be safely removed from the corpus. This may give us better structured topics.

- Another way to modify the process is to fine tune the algorithm aspects. This is an area that usually requires a very good understanding of the algorithm. But we can also achieve a better set of results by tinkering with the parameter space of the algorithm. You can refer to the document for the `topicmodels` package for experimenting with those parameters (`https://cran.r-project.org/web/packages/topicmodels/topicmodels.pdf`).

As with our other modeling-related tasks, we will not go into the detailed process, but will give the reader a gentle introduction that can serve as a starting point for the future endeavors of the users.

Summarizing news articles

We have been dealing with a lot of data relevant to news articles in this chapter. So far, we have looked at solving problems such as analyzing the sentiments and emotions conveyed by various articles, and how to extract key topics and concepts from news articles. Another key use case or problem that is relevant in the world of news and journalism is the ability to summarize news articles. You are already aware that we are living in the age of digital revolution, and have moved on from a PC-first culture to a mobile-first culture, which is still rapidly evolving over time. Everyone is busy with their own lives and their work, but they will always have their smartphones, watches, and tablets with them on the go. Accessing the most relevant news as quickly as possible is definitely what customers look for when using their mobile devices or even their PCs. While news headlines do serve this purpose to some extent, the real challenge involves summarizing the core content of news articles and providing a bite-sized-summary format, which can be read easily and quickly even if people are on the go.

Thus, we can formulate the scope of this problem into a classical text-mining problem that encompasses the area of text summarization. There are various techniques that can be used to solve this problem. Typically, text summarization is in the form of extracting key phrases from sentences in a document, using topic models to extract key concepts or topics from documents, or summarizing an entire document into the gist of it, which retains the core essence of the document; this is also known as document summarization. You can consider any news article to be a fully-fledged text document, and hence we will be focusing on document summarization in this section.

Document summarization

Document summarization involves extracting key sentences from the document and forming an executive summary without using any manual human inputs to the process; hence, this is also often known as automated document summarization. Typically, there are two main approaches to automated document summarization and they are described as follows:

- **Extraction-based summarization**: This involves using statistical or mathematical techniques, including using concepts such as SVD matrices, graph-based approaches such as PageRank, and so on, to extract key sentences from the document and generate a document summary. Since no new content is created and the summary is extracted from the original document's sentences, these techniques are called extraction-based techniques.

- **Abstraction-based summarization**: These techniques involve using more complicated approaches such as natural language generation, language semantics, and representations such that the machine is able to create the summary on its own, just like a human writer would do in real life.

We will be focusing on an extraction-based summarization approach here, named LexRank, to summarize news articles.

Understanding LexRank

To summarize news articles, we will use the `lexRankr` package, which internally uses the LexRank algorithm. This algorithm is an implementation obtained from the paper *LexRank: Graph-based Lexical Centrality as Salience in Text Summarization* by *Güneş Erkan* and *Dragomir R. Radev*. LexRank is described by its authors as a stochastic graph-based technique for computing the relative importance of text-based units in **natural language processing (NLP)**.

By considering a text document to be composed of a group of sentences, the core method of LexRank involves computing sentence rank or importance based on the concept of Eigenvector centrality in a graph of connected sentences. This graph of connected sentences is basically a pairwise intra-sentence cosine similarity adjacency matrix. This similarity matrix is a measure between each pair of sentences in the document using a modified **inverse document frequency (IDF)** cosine similarity function. The graph is constructed from this matrix using the notion of significant similarities, where low-valued, pair-wise, similarity-based links are eliminated using a defined threshold, and we can build an undirected graph such that the nodes of the graph are the sentences of a document and only sentences with a significant similarity value are connected to each other by edges.

Thus, once we construct this graph, we can easily get the degree centrality of any node (sentence) by looking at the number of edges that node consists of in the graph. Sentences can then be ranked based on this degree centrality measure by using the raw value or an algorithm such as PageRank. To understand the algorithm in more detail, feel free to visit the following link, http://www.cs.cmu.edu/afs/cs/ project/jair/pub/volume22/erkan04a-html/erkan04a.html, which talks about the original paper on the LexRank algorithm.

Summarizing articles with lexRankr

As we mentioned before, there is an R package called lexRankr, which has an R implementation of the previously described LexRank algorithm. This package is also hosted on GitHub, which is owned and maintained by *Adam Spannbauer*, and is accessible at https://github.com/AdamSpannbauer/lexRankr. You can install it from GitHub or directly from CRAN using install.packages("lexRankr"), which should now make the lexRankr package available to use in your R environment.

We will summarize a couple of news articles from The Guardian in this section. We will be focusing more on the summarization aspect, rather than data extraction and parsing since that has already been covered in the previous sections. To start with, load the required package into your environment using the following code:

```
library(lexRankr)
```

Now, we will load a complete news article from The Guardian, which talks about a certain housing crisis in England. The article is available for you to see at https://www.theguardian.com/society/2017/apr/20/over-200000-homes-in-england-still-lying-empty-despite-housing-shortages, and its headline tells us *Housing crisis: more than 200,000 homes in England lie empty*. We have extracted the text content of this article and stored it in a file named Article-housing_crisis.txt, which is available along with the code files for this chapter. In the following code snippet, we will load this news article into R:

```
# read in the news article content
article_file <- 'Article-housing_crisis.txt'
article <- readChar(article_file, file.info(article_file)$size)
```

Now that we have our news article content in the article variable, we can view it, if needed, using the following code:

```
# view the news article content
View(article)
```

The preceding command will show you the contents of the article, a section of which is depicted in the following snapshot:

"More than 200,000 homes in England with a total value of Â£43bn were empty for at least six months during 2016 despite the desperate shortage of properties to rent and buy. \r\nAccording to official figures, Birmingham was the worst affected city outside London with 4,397 empty homes worth an estimated Â£956m, followed by Bradford and Liverpool.\r\nThe wealthy borough of Kensington and Chelsea was the worst performer in London as super-rich owners rejected renting them out or selling up in favour of leaving their properties lying idle.\r\nThe royal borough had 1,399 empty homes worth Â£664m, compared with second-placed Croydon, which had 1,216 empty homes worth Â£577m.\r\nAcross London

Article to summarize

If you compare this text with the article mentioned in the preceding URL for the news article, you will see the same content being displayed here in the raw format, including encodings, newlines, and more. Our next step involves extracting complete lines or sentences from the preceding text document. The typical pattern observed here is that we have newline and carriage-return characters, which we can remove, and usually lines are separated by a period (.) or a period followed by an end quote (.''), followed by one or more spaces. Using these patterns, we can extract out the lines using the following snippet:

```
lines <- trimws(unlist(strsplit(gsub("[\r\n]", " ", article), '(([.]
+)|([.]" +))')))

# view total lines extracted
> cat('Total lines: ', length(lines))
Total lines:  18
```

Thus, you can see that we have successfully split our text article into 18 lines or sentences. We can now extract the core or influential sentences using the LexRank algorithm. The lexRank function helps us to do so. An important point to remember here is that this function has multiple parameters, which enable us to customize the summarization algorithm. While you can always see the documentation on this function to get more details, we will be mainly using the following parameters of this function in our analysis:

- threshold: This is the minimum similarity value a sentence pair must have to be represented in the graph.

- `n`: This is the top ranked `n` number of sentences that will be returned as the extractive summary.

- `returnTies`: If `TRUE`, this returns more than the top n sentences if some of them have the same score or rank; if `FALSE`, then it's limited to `<= n`.

- `usePageRank`: This uses the PageRank algorithm for ranking the sentences if this is set to `TRUE`.

- `damping`: This is the damping factor used in the PageRank algorithm.

- `continuous`: This parameter uses continuous LexRank if set to `TRUE`, where it ignores the threshold and uses a weighted graph representation for the sentences. If set to `FALSE`, the threshold is used.

- `sentencesAsDocs`: This is either set to `TRUE` or `FALSE`, indicating whether or not to treat sentences as documents when computing the tf-idf similarity scores.

- `removePunc`: If `TRUE`, punctuation will be removed as a part of pre-processing.

- `removeNum`: If `TRUE`, numbers will be removed as a part of pre-processing.

- `toLower`: If `TRUE`, the sentences will be changed to lowercase as a part of pre-processing.

- `stemWords`: If `TRUE`, a snowball stemmer is applied to stem words as a part of pre-processing.

- `rmStopWords`: If `TRUE`, stopwords are removed before stemming as a part of pre-processing.

- `Verbose`: If `TRUE`, progress messages are displayed in the console when the algorithm runs.

You can see that there is a vast number of parameters that can be used to control and customize this algorithm, and we do not need to pre-process or normalize our text document since the algorithm has specific parameters to do the necessary pre-processing before applying the algorithm to extract the summary. The following code snippet helps us extract influential sentences from the text document. We set `n=5` to extract the top five most influential sentences to create our summary:

```
# extract influential sentences
> influential_sentences <- lexRank(text=lines, threshold=0.1,
+                          n=5, usePageRank=TRUE, damping=0.85,
+                          continuous=FALSE, sentencesAsDocs=TRUE, +
removePunc=TRUE, removeNum=TRUE,
+                          toLower=TRUE, stemWords=TRUE,
+                          rmStopWords=TRUE, Verbose=TRUE,
```

```
+                                    returnTies=TRUE)

Parsing text into sentences and tokens...DONE
Calculating pairwise sentence similarities...DONE
Applying LexRank...DONE
Formatting Output...DONE

# view the influential sentences
> View(influential_sentences)
```

This gives us the following DataFrame, which depicts the influential sentences, their position in the original article, and their score, based on which they were ranked:

	docId	sentenceId	sentence	value
1	13	13_1	Property investment firm Property Partner, which collate...	0.12858215
2	3	3_1	The wealthy borough of Kensington and Chelsea was th...	0.10947000
3	10	10_1	While Birmingham recorded a 13% jump in empty prope...	0.10889354
4	7	7_1	Councils and the government have worked to cut the n...	0.08571688
5	17	17_1	Property Partner said a large drop in the number of emp...	0.08490843

Influential sentences

We will now create our article summary from the preceding sentences by using the previous `docId` field to get the line numbers in our original article, sort them to retain their precedence in the original article, and join them together to get the extractive summary. The following snippet helps us achieve this:

```
# create text summary
summary <- paste(lines[sort(influential_sentences$docId)], collapse=".
")

# display summary
> cat(summary)
```

The wealthy borough of Kensington and Chelsea was the worst performer in London as the super-rich owners rejected renting their properties out or selling up, in favor of leaving their properties lying idle. Councils and the government have worked to cut the number of empty homes, primarily by reducing tax incentives that encouraged owners to leave properties unused. While Birmingham recorded a 13% jump in empty properties in the last year and Liverpool suffered a 5% rise to 3,449,

Manchester registered the greatest fall over a decade, dropping 88% to 1,365. Property investment firm Property Partner, which collated the report from the latest Department for Communities & Local Government figures, says that Kensington and Chelsea stood out from most London boroughs, which have recorded a fall in the number of empty homes over the last 10 years. Property Partner says that there has been a large drop in the number of empty homes across England from 2006 stalled in 2015.

Thus, we get our much-needed summary talking about the housing crisis in England where many houses are lying empty despite there being a shortage of housing. The previous summary gives you a clear idea of what the original news article is actually trying to convey, and you can go back and read the complete original article, and compare it with our previously generate summary to contrast and compare.

The beauty of this technique is that it is not restricted to the news articles of a specific category or even just news articles for that matter! Let's now try to use what we have learned so far and summarize another article from The Guardian from the Sports section.

The article is available at `https://www.theguardian.com/sport/2017/apr/04/chris-woakes-indian-premier-league-kolkata-knight-riders` and is headlined *"Chris Woakes: 'The IPL is a one-off opportunity I can't turn down.'"* This article is available in the `Article-chris_woakes.txt` file and talks about the English cricketer Chris Woakes, who is going to feature in the 2017 Indian Premier League for the Kolkata Knight Riders. The following code snippet helps us to create a summary out of the previously mentioned article:

```
# apply lexrank algorithm
article_file <- 'Article-chris_woakes.txt'
article <- readChar(article_file, file.info(article_file)$size)
lines <- trimws(unlist(strsplit(gsub("[\r\n]", " ", article), '(([.]
+)|([.]" +))')))
influential_sentences <- lexRank(text=lines, threshold=0.1,
                                 n=5, usePageRank=TRUE,
                                 damping=0.85, continuous=FALSE,
                                 sentencesAsDocs=TRUE,
                                 removePunc=TRUE,
                                 removeNum=TRUE, toLower=TRUE,
                                 stemWords=TRUE, rmStopWords=TRUE,
                                 Verbose=TRUE, returnTies=TRUE)


Parsing text into sentences and tokens...DONE
```

```
Calculating pairwise sentence similarities...DONE
Applying LexRank...DONE
Formatting Output...DONE

# create summary
summary <- paste(lines[sort(influential_sentences$docId)], collapse=".
")

# display summary
> cat(summary)
```

It does feel strange going away this time of year but at the same time I see it as a chance to improve myself as a cricketer and put Warwickshire on the map, says *Woakes*, whose side open up against the Gujarat Lions in Rajkot. *Death bowling is an area of my game that has improved dramatically, I think, but to be considered a world-class death bowler you have to do it against the best players in the IPL in high-pressure situations.* It was a high-pressure situation at the death in January that was probably responsible for his IPL payday—the proceeds from which, he jokes, will go toward paying off debts from his recent wedding—when India needed 16 from the final over of the third one-dayer in Kolkata. Birmingham-born and having been a part of the furniture at Edgbaston for more than a decade, which included being roped into groundstaff duties during the 2005 Ashes, there is little doubt which team he would want to turn out for. He says *It's a tricky one because I've played for Warwickshire my whole career so to think of playing for someone else doesn't seem right. If there's a Birmingham team, and I hope there is, I'd want to be in it.*

Thus, the preceding summary gives you an idea about Chris Woakes' thoughts before joining the IPL in 2017, and, indeed, he has made a good start in this year's tournament so far! The closing thoughts from this section are that there is a whole suite of text summarization techniques out there for you to explore; this should give you a head start on understanding the value behind this problem and a standard approach toward solving this problem. Feel free to experiment with the `lexRank` function and try it out on other news articles!

Challenges to news data analysis

The analysis of news data was probably one of the most challenging tasks in this book. We will try to give the reader a summary of the toughest problems that we encountered in the process of developing this chapter:

- **Lack of API sources**: News data providers are not always very API friendly. We were lucky to have a prestigious source such as The Guardian, which believes in open access to its data and goes to great lengths to ensure that. But, apart from a couple of big names such as The New York Times and The Guardian, we won't find a lot of data providers going down the API route.

- **Web scraping**: Web scraping HTML data for text is quite a complex process. Once again, we were lucky that the HTML structure for our data sources was quite simple. A more involved structure would have meant a larger and more elaborate process of data scraping. (We encourage the reader to take a look at the HTML structure for any New York Times article to realize the complexity that is involved in web scraping.) Another major problematic aspect of web scraping is the frequently changing landscape of most websites. This means that the painstakingly developed parsing structure can break any time the designers try to tinker with their web page.

- **Subjectivity of text analysis**: This challenging aspect of text analysis was witnessed in the use case of topic modeling. Based on the view point of the practitioner, the same output can be interpreted in a variety of ways. This creates a tough-to-solve problem, as it can cause some serious issues if the practitioner is not a neutral analyst. It is very easy to get biased in the case of textual data mining.

These were the major challenges that we encountered during the journey of this chapter. A lot of minor issues were also solved along the way, but those can be easily solved by making logical decisions and by creative Google searches.

Summary

News data is a very important data source as it gives us a collective glimpse of the major themes in our day-to-day lives. We have witnessed how it can be a difficult process to collect news data and do some text mining on it. We have understood the basic concepts of web scraping, which is required in most data collections from the public domain. We have learned about the various problems we can have with textual data and how to work around them. An important point to mention about this chapter is the importance of maintaining an unbiased point of view while analyzing text data. Otherwise, it is very easy for text data mining to denigrate into a bad case of selection bias. Text data analysis is very diverse, a rapidly developing area of research, and tough to contain in one chapter. We encourage our readers to explore different text mining tools and find out what different use cases they can build on the datasets that we collected; this will certainly make for an interesting exercise.

Index

O

Open Authentication (OAuth) 50

P

package topicmodels
  reference link 353
PageRank
  reference link 130
parts of speech (POS) 10
Parts of Speech (POS) 68

Q

Question and Answer (Q&A) platforms 255

R

Read-Evaluate-Print-Loop (REPL) 15
recommendation engine
  about 174
  issues, framing 174
  restaurant recommender, building 175-180
repository activity
  analyzing 206
  commit frequency distribution,
      analyzing 208-210
  daily commit frequency, analyzing 210
  trending repositories, retrieving 215-218
  weekly code modification history,
      analyzing 213-215
  weekly commit frequency,
      analyzing 206, 207
  weekly commit frequency comparison,
      analyzing 211-213
repository metrics
  analyzing 223-225
  relationship, analyzing between stargazer
      and fork counts 229-231
  relationship, analyzing between stargazer
      and repository counts 228, 229
  relationship, analyzing between total forks
      and repository count 232, 233
  relationship, analyzing between total forks
      and repository health 232, 233
  repository metric correlations,
      analyzing 226, 227

repository metric distributions,
    visualizing 225, 226
repository trends
  analyzing 218
  repository metrics, analyzing 223-225
  trending repositories analyzing, created
      over time 219, 220
  trending repositories analyzing, updated
      over time 221, 222
Rfacebook 94
rgithub package
  reference link 200
R package
  environment, setting up 196, 197
  reference link 196
R programming language
  about 13, 38
  environment setup 14-16
  help in 38
  packages, managing 39
R programming language 3.3.1
  URL, for downloading 15
RStudio
  reference link 15

S

sentimental rankings
  about 180
  final rankings 187-189
  textual data 182
  tips data, analysis 183
  tips data, extracting 180, 181
sentiment analysis 68
  about 66
  features 68, 69
  in R programming language 69-78
  key concepts 67
  N-grams 69
  opinion summarization 68
  Parts of Speech (POS) 68
  sentiment polarity 67
  subjectivity 67
sentiment trend analysis
  about 331
  basic descriptive statistics 333-335
  data, obtaining 332

ing Source UK Ltd.
eynes UK
0619030518
UK00004B/262/P